New Testament
Textual Criticism
for the 21st Century

New Testament Textual Criticism for the 21st Century

A PRACTICAL GUIDE

Charles L. Quarles

HENDRICKSON PUBLISHERS

New Testament Textual Criticism for the 21st Century: A Practical Guide

© 2025 by Charles L. Quarles

Hendrickson Publishers
3 Centennial Drive
Peabody, Massachusetts 01960
www.hendricksonpublishers.com

ISBN 978-1-4964-7627-2

Printed in the United States of America

First Printing — March 2025

Cover design by Karol Bailey. Abstract geometric cover background © iStock.com/shuoshu.

Library of Congress Control Number: 2024946100

TABLE OF CONTENTS

Expanded Table of Contents   vii

List of Illustrations   xiii

Acknowledgments   xv

Select Abbreviations   xvii

PART ONE: AN INTRODUCTION TO TEXTUAL CRITICISM

Chapter 1   The Need for New Testament Textual Criticism   3

Chapter 2   The Sources of Evidence for New Testament Textual Criticism   7

Chapter 3   Approaches to New Testament Textual Criticism   24

Chapter 4   The Tools for New Testament Textual Criticism   35

PART TWO: THE METHOD OF REASONED ECLECTICISM

Chapter 5   Preliminary Considerations   47

Chapter 6   Evaluation of External Evidence   49

Chapter 7   Evaluation of Internal Evidence   72

PART THREE: THE PRACTICE OF REASONED ECLECTICISM

Example A   Matthew 16:2b–3   103

Example B   John 1:18   113

Example C   Colossians 1:12   128

Appendix I   A Guide to Assessing Variant Readings   137

Appendix II   Early Church Fathers   139

Appendix III   Problems with the Text-Type Approach   147

Appendix IV   Thoroughgoing Eclecticism   155

Glossary   163

Bibliography   167

Index of Biblical References   179

Expanded Table of Contents

List of Illustrations   xiii

Acknowledgments   xv

Select Abbreviations   xvii

PART ONE: AN INTRODUCTION TO TEXTUAL CRITICISM

Chapter 1	The Need for New Testament Textual Criticism	3
Chapter 2	The Sources of Evidence for New Testament Textual Criticism	7
2.1	Papyri	8
2.2	Majuscules	11
2.3	Minuscules	17
2.4	Lectionaries	20
2.5	Early Versions	21
2.6	Early Church Fathers	22
Chapter 3	Approaches to New Testament Textual Criticism	24
3.1	Majority Text Approach	24
3.2	Reasoned Eclecticism	32
Chapter 4	The Tools for New Testament Textual Criticism	35
4.1	Nestle-Aland *Novum Testamentum Graece*	35
4.2	United Bible Societies' *Greek New Testament*	37
4.3	Editio Critica Maior	39
4.4	Institute for New Testament Textual Research Website	40
4.5	Center for the Study of New Testament Manuscripts Website	40
4.6	The International Greek New Testament Project	41
4.7	The Center for New Testament Textual Studies NT Critical Apparatus	41
4.8	Websites Devoted to Important Manuscripts and Major Text-Critical Issues	42
4.9	Conclusion	43

PART TWO: THE METHOD OF REASONED ECLECTICISM

Chapter 5	**Preliminary Considerations**	**47**
5.1	Identify the Variant Readings	47
5.2	Analyze the Nature of the Differences Between the Variants	48
5.3	Reflect on the Implications for the Text's Meaning	48
Chapter 6	**Evaluation of External Evidence**	**49**
6.1	CRITERION 1: Prefer readings that can be shown to be early	50
6.1.1	ADDITIONAL CONSIDERATION 1: Reevaluate the date assigned to readings found in early witnesses from various regions	56
6.1.2	ADDITIONAL CONSIDERATION 2: Reevaluate the date assigned to readings shared by early witnesses that are not closely related to each other	60
6.2	CRITERION 2: Prefer readings in witnesses that are known to be reliable and accurate	63
6.3	CRITERION 3: Prefer readings found in multiple early witnesses	68
6.4	Summarizing the External Evidence	70
Chapter 7	**Evaluation of Internal Evidence**	**72**
7.1	Transcriptional Evidence	72
7.1.1	Methods for Discovering the Tendencies of Ancient Scribes	74
	Anecdotal Method	74
	Singular Reading Method	74
	Close-Copy Method	75
7.1.2	Common Errors of Ancient Scribes	78
	Unintentional Changes	79
	Intentional Changes	84
	▪ Does the reading seem to be an attempt to clarify the meaning?	85
	▪ Does the reading seem to be an attempt to improve the style or grammar?	86
	▪ Does the reading seem to be an attempt at harmonization?	87
	▪ Does the reading seem to be a conflation of other variants?	89
	▪ Which reading seems initially difficult but makes better sense after further study?	89
	▪ Which reading best explains the origin of the other readings?	90

7.2		Intrinsic Evidence	93
	7.2.1	Which Reading Is Most Consistent with the Author's Grammar, Style, and Vocabulary?	93
	7.2.2	Which Reading Best Fits the Immediate Context?	94
	7.2.3	Which Reading Best Fits with the Author's Theology?	94
7.3		Exploring Other Potentially Relevant Evidence	95
7.4		Weighing the Evidence	97

PART THREE: THE PRACTICE OF REASONED ECLECTICISM

Example A		Matthew 16:2b–3	103
A.1		Preliminary Considerations	103
	A.1.1	Identify the Variant Readings	103
	A.1.2	Analyze the Nature of the Differences Between the Variants	103
	A.1.3	Reflect on the Implications for the Text's Meaning	104
A.2		External Evidence	104
	A.2.1	CRITERION 1: Prefer readings that can be shown to be early	104
		ADDITIONAL CONSIDERATION 1: *Reevaluate the date assigned to readings found in early witnesses from various regions*	105
		ADDITIONAL CONSIDERATION 2: *Reevaluate the date assigned to readings shared by early witnesses that are not closely related to each other*	106
	A.2.2	CRITERION 2: Prefer readings in witnesses that are known to be reliable and accurate	106
	A.2.3	CRITERION 3: Prefer readings found in multiple early witnesses	108
	A.2.4	Summarizing the External Evidence	108
A.3		Internal Evidence	108
	A.3.1	TRANSCRIPTIONAL EVIDENCE: Prefer the reading *least* likely to have resulted from common scribal changes	108
		Which reading did NOT *likely result from common errors related to sight, hearing, or memory?*	108
		Which reading did NOT *likely result from the scribe's effort to correct a perceived error, clarify the meaning, improve the style or grammar, harmonize to a parallel or the context, or conflate variants?*	109
		Which reading initially seems difficult but makes better sense after further study?	109
		Which reading best explains the origin of other readings?	110

A.3.2   INTRINSIC EVIDENCE: Prefer the reading that the author was *most* likely to have written   110

Which reading is most consistent with the author's grammar, style, and vocabulary?   110

Which reading best fits the immediate context?   111

Which reading best fits with the author's theology?   111

A.4   Exploring Other Potentially Relevant Evidence   111

A.5   Weighing the Evidence   112

Example B   John 1:18   113

B.1   Preliminary Considerations   113

B.1.1   Identify the Variant Readings   113

B.1.2   Analyze the Nature of the Differences Between the Variants   113

B.1.3   Reflect on the Implications for the Text's Meaning   114

B.2   External Evidence   114

B.2.1   CRITERION 1: Prefer readings that can be shown to be early.   114

ADDITIONAL CONSIDERATION 1: Reevaluate the date assigned to readings found in early witnesses from various regions   115

ADDITIONAL CONSIDERATION 2: Reevaluate the date assigned to readings shared by early witnesses that are not closely related to each other   117

B.2.2   CRITERION 2: Prefer readings in witnesses known to be reliable and accurate   119

B.2.3   CRITERION 3: Prefer readings found in multiple early witnesses   121

B.2.4   Summarizing the External Evidence   121

B.3   Internal Evidence   122

B.3.1   TRANSCRIPTIONAL EVIDENCE: Prefer the reading *least* likely to have resulted from common scribal changes   122

Which reading did NOT likely result from common errors related to sight, hearing, or memory?   122

Which reading did NOT likely result from the scribe's effort to correct a perceived error, clarify the meaning, improve the style or grammar, harmonize to a parallel or the context, or conflate variants?   122

Which reading initially seems difficult but makes better sense after further study?   122

Which reading best explains the origin of other readings?   123

B.3.2   INTRINSIC EVIDENCE: Prefer the reading that the author was *most* likely to have written   123

B.4.   Exploring Other Potentially Relevant Evidence   126

B.5.   Weighing the Evidence   126

Example C   Colossians 1:12   **128**

   C.1   Preliminary Considerations   128

           C.1.1   Identify the Variant Readings   128

           C.1.2   Analyze the Nature of the Differences Between the Variants   128

           C.1.3   Reflect on the Implications for the Text's Meaning   128

   C.2   External Evidence   129

           C.2.1   CRITERION 1: Prefer readings that can be shown to be early   129

                  ADDITIONAL CONSIDERATION 1: Reevaluate the date
                    assigned to readings found in early witnesses from
                    various regions   130

                  ADDITIONAL CONSIDERATION 2: Reevaluate the date
                    assigned to readings shared by early witnesses that are
                    not closely related to each other   130

           C.2.2   CRITERION 2: Prefer readings in witnesses that are known to
                be reliable and accurate   131

           C.2.3   CRITERION 3: Prefer readings found in multiple early witnesses 131

           C.2.4   Summarizing the External Evidence   132

   C.3   Internal Evidence   132

           C.3.1   TRANSCRIPTIONAL EVIDENCE: Prefer the reading *least* likely
                to have resulted from common scribal changes   132

                  Which reading did NOT likely result from common errors
                    related to sight, hearing, or memory?   132

                  Which reading did NOT likely result from the scribe's
                    effort to correct a perceived error, clarify the meaning,
                      improve the style or grammar, harmonize to a parallel
                      or the context, or conflate variants?   132

                  Which reading initially seems difficult but makes better
                      sense after further study?   133

                  Which reading best explains the origin of other readings?   134

           C.3.2   INTRINSIC EVIDENCE: Prefer the reading that the author was
                most likely to have written   135

                  Which reading is most consistent with the author's
                      grammar, style, and vocabulary?   135

                  Which reading best fits the immediate context?   136

                  Which reading best fits the author's theology?   136

   C.4   Exploring Other Potentially Relevant Evidence   136

   C.5   Weighing the Evidence   136

Appendix I   A Guide to Assessing Variant Readings   **137**

Appendix II   Early Church Fathers   **139**

Appendix III   **Problems with the Text-Type Approach**   **147**

Appendix IV   **Thoroughgoing Eclecticism**   **155**

Glossary   163

Bibliography   167

Index of Biblical References   179

LIST OF ILLUSTRATIONS

FIGURES

Figure 2.1	Examples of Majuscule Script	12
Figure 2.2	Examples of Minuscule Script	17
Figure 6.1	Witnesses to Acts Most Closely Related to the Initial Text	67
Figure 7.1	Examples of Potential Genealogies of Variants	91
Figure 7.2	Proposed Stemma of Variants in Luke 4:44	92
Figure A.1	Witnesses to Mark Most Closely Related to the Initial Text	107
Figure B.1	Witnesses to Mark Most Closely Related to Vaticanus (03)	118
Figure B.2	Witnesses to Mark Most Closely Related to the Initial Text	120
Figure C.1	Local Stemma of Variants in Col 1:12	135

TABLES

Chapter 4	**The Tools for New Testament Text Criticism**	
Table 4.1	Comparison of the Apparatuses for John 1:18	38
Chapter 6	**Evaluation of External Evidence**	
Table 6.1	Age of Witnesses Supporting Each Reading	53
Table 6.2	Early Greek Manuscripts	54
Table 6.3	Early Church Fathers	54
Table 6.4	Geographical Distribution of Readings in the Early Church Fathers and Versions	59
Table 6.5	Texts Most Closely Related to 05 in the Synoptic Gospels	62
Table 6.6	Preferred Witnesses in Matt 18:15	66
Table 6.7	Witnesses Closest to the Initial Text in the Synoptic Gospels	68
Table 6.8	Early Witnesses to Matt 18:15	70
Table 6.9	Summary of the External Evidence for Matt 18:15	70

Example A   **Matthew 16:2b–3**

Table A.1   Manuscripts of the Greek New Testament   104
Table A.2   Early Church Fathers   104
Table A.3   Geographical Distribution   105
Table A.4   Percentages of Agreement between Witnesses to the
             Longer Reading (Mark)   106
Table A.5   Percentages of Agreement between Witnesses to the
             Longer Reading (Parallel Pericopes)   106
Table A.6   Category I and II Witnesses   107
Table A.7   Evaluation of the External Evidence   108

Example B   **John 1:18**

Table B.1   Manuscripts of the Greek New Testament   115
Table B.2   Early Church Fathers   115
Table B.3   Early Geographical Distribution   116
Table B.4   Category I and II Witnesses   120
Table B.5   External Evidence   121

Example C   **Colossians 1:12**

Table C.1   Manuscripts of the Greek New Testament   129
Table C.2   Early Church Fathers   129
Table C.3   Geographical Distribution   130
Table C.4   Category I and II Witnesses   131
Table C.5   External Evidence   132

Acknowledgments

I would like to express my thanks to several people who have contributed to this book in a variety of ways. Students in my 2022 Doctor of Philosophy New Testament Textual Criticism seminar and 2023 graduate-level New Testament Textual Criticism class offered helpful feedback on an early draft of the book. Three scholars, Christian Askeland, Greg Paulson, and Pat Sanders, kindly read the first draft and offered helpful comments and corrections. My research assistants Seth Ellington, Tyler Craft, and Eli Stanley gathered data for Appendix II. My administrative assistant Anthony Ingram worked to secure permissions for the manuscript images used to illustrate majuscule and minuscule scripts and extrapolated the bibliography entries from the footnotes. He and research assistant Abigail Prejean worked together to produce the Scripture index. The keen editorial gifts of Jonathan Kline and Phil Frank of Hendrickson have significantly improved the book. Dr. Kline recognized the importance of this project from our very first discussion. In every interaction he has been unusually kind and encouraging. I am especially grateful for the careful work of Dr. Jason Driesbach, whose editorial feedback was truly invaluable.

Select Abbreviations

Byz	the variant reading contained in the majority of Byzantine manuscripts
CBGM	Coherence-Based Genealogical Method
CNTTS	Center for New Testament Textual Studies
CSNTM	Center for the Study of New Testament Manuscripts
ECM	Editio Critica Maior
IGNTP	International Greek New Testament Project
INTF	Institut für Neutestamentliche Textforschung (Institute for New Testament Textual Research)
LDAB	Leuven Database of Ancient Books
MS(S)	manuscript(s)
MT	Majority Text
NA	Nestle-Aland edition of the Greek New Testament
NETS	New English Translation of the Septuagint
NT	New Testament
NTVMR	New Testament Virtual Manuscript Room
OT	Old Testament
SBLGNT	Greek New Testament: Society of Biblical Literature edition
UBS	United Bible Societies editions of the Greek New Testament

Part One

———

AN INTRODUCTION TO TEXTUAL CRITICISM

1

THE NEED FOR NEW TESTAMENT TEXTUAL CRITICISM

In the study of literature, the term "criticism" refers to "the scientific investigation of literary documents (such as the Bible) in regard to such matters as origin, text, composition, or history."[1] *Textual* criticism refers to the scientific investigation that seeks to determine and restore the original text of a document or collection of documents by removing the errors introduced into it as it was copied and recopied. All ancient texts were corrupted as scribes made mistakes in the process of hand-copying the text century after century. Thus, all ancient texts need restoration. Scholars in classical studies must work to restore the original texts of works like Homer's *Iliad*. New Testament scholars must also compare the different readings in ancient manuscripts of the NT and seek to identify the original text of the NT. Textual criticism is "scientific" since it seeks to understand a phenomenon by following a systematic method based on evidence. Many consider modern textual criticism to be one of the most scientific disciplines in the realm of biblical studies because researchers utilize high-tech tools such as high-resolution photography and multispectral imaging and methods such as archaeology, paleography, and statistics.

Textual criticism is necessary because scribes sometimes changed the text unintentionally or, more rarely, intentionally as they copied it. The first Bible to be printed using the printing press was a Latin Bible printed by Johannes Gutenberg between 1452 and 1456. Prior to the mid-15th century, scribes hand-copied the NT. These scribes had different levels of proficiency, skill, and education. However, they all shared something in common. They were human, and, as ordinary human beings, they all made mistakes. Human scribes are copyists, not copy machines. No scribe was able to perfectly replicate the text of the manuscripts they attempted to copy. Some scribes were better than most and some were truly outstanding. None of them were perfect.

Twenty-first-century scholars are not the first to recognize that ancient scribes made errors. Ancient readers of the Greek NT sometimes pointed out the different and even contradictory readings that appeared in the copies of the NT available to them. In his *Commentary*

---

1. *Merriam-Webster's Collegiate Dictionary*, 11th ed., s.v. "criticism."

on Matthew in the early 3rd century, Origen complained: "But it is clear that the differences between the copies have become numerous, either from the shoddy work of copyists, or from the wicked recklessness of some either in neglecting to correct what is written, or even in adding or removing things based on their own opinions when they do correct."[2]

The ancient scribes humbly acknowledged their weaknesses and deficiencies in notes written in the margins of the copies they produced. C. Wendel gathered many of the self-deprecating epithets of the monastic scribes.[3] The scribes described themselves using such terms as χθαμαλός (lowly), ἀνάξιος (worthless), ἀνάξιος τοῦ ζῆν (unworthy to live), ἀνάξιος παρὰ πάντας (undeserving above all), ἀδόκιμος (reprobate), εὐτελής (worthless), εὐτελέστατος (most worthless), ὕστατος (most inferior), ἐλάχιστος (least), ἀχρεῖος (useless), δύσχρηστος (no good), and ἰδιώτης (unskilled amateur).[4] They assessed their skills and abilities using expressions such as ἀφυής (untalented), φρενόλειπτος (brainless), ἀφρονέστατος (most foolish), ἀσύνετος (without understanding), ἀβέλτερος (stupid), ἀμαθέστατος (most ignorant or unskilled), σκαιότατος πάντων ἀνθρώπων (most unskilled of all people), χωρικός (country bumpkin), and ἀγροικικός (parochial—in the negative sense of being small-minded and unsophisticated).[5] These self-assessments show that the scribes did not believe that even their best efforts were sufficient to copy the NT perfectly.

Scribes recognized that their predecessors had the same weaknesses with which they struggled. Ancient copyists sometimes complained about the poor quality of the work of the scribes who copied or influenced their exemplar.[6] The medieval monastic scribe Neilos, for example, complains of the poor eyesight of another scribe that introduced an error in the text: "The error of Theodore the squinter."[7] A late scribe who sought to correct the text of Codex Vaticanus (03) vented his frustration with one of his predecessors in a note in the left-hand margin beside the text of Heb 1:3: "Terribly ignorant and unskilled scribe, leave the old reading alone! Do not change it!"

Scribes often corrected errors that they spotted in the manuscripts that they used. The oldest complete manuscript of the Greek NT is Codex Sinaiticus (01). Scribes corrected this manuscript more thoroughly than any other. Some of the corrections were made very early before the manuscript left the scriptorium. Many others were made by later generations of scribes who used the codex up through the 12th century. The manuscript has an average of about thirty corrections per page for a total of nearly 23,000 corrections![8] The

---

2. *The Commentary of Origen on the Gospel of St Matthew*, 2 vols., trans. Ronald E. Heine (Oxford: Oxford University Press, 2018), 15.14.

3. C. Wendel, "Die ΤΑΠΕΙΝΟΤΗΣ des griechischen Schreibermönches," *Byzantinische Zeitschrift* 43 (1950): 259–66.

4. Wendel, Die ΤΑΠΕΙΝΟΤΗΣ des griechischen Schreibermönches," 260.

5. Wendel, Die ΤΑΠΕΙΝΟΤΗΣ des griechischen Schreibermönches," 261.

6. An "exemplar" is the manuscript that the scribe follows in making his own copy.

7. A. C. Myshrall, "An Introduction to Lectionary 299," in *Codex Zacynthius: Catena, Palimpsest, Lectionary,* ed. H. A. G. Houghton and D. C. Parker, TS 3.21 (Piscataway, NJ: Gorgias, 2020), 197–99.

8. D. C. Parker, *Codex Sinaiticus: The Story of the World's Oldest Bible* (Peabody, MA: Hendrickson, 2010), 3, 89. This estimate includes the corrections in both the OT and the NT and corrections of all kinds, including spelling corrections and reinking fading letters.

many corrections show that later generations of scribes respected and continued to use the ancient codex. Yet, they also show that the scribes recognized even the ancient copies were not perfect. Scribes worked to identify and correct errors in hopes of restoring the original text of the NT.

Modern-day textual critics continue this aspect of the work of ancient scribes. Although textual critics are not *copyists*, they are *correctors*. They compare the texts of the NT that appear in the ancient manuscripts. When these texts are different, they analyze these different readings (called variants) and attempt to identify and restore the text of the original.

The modern practice of textual criticism involves far more than the work of restoring the original text.[9] Yet the primary goal of the discipline continues to be the restoration of the original text. This is true whether we are referring to the textual criticism of the NT or the textual criticism of the Greek classics. Paul Maas, a textual critic working mainly in classical literature, wrote: "The business of textual criticism is to produce a text as close as possible to the original."[10] New Testament textual critics such as B. F. Westcott and F. J. A. Hort, Kirsopp Lake, Samuel P. Tregelles, F. H. A. Scrivener, Bruce Metzger, J. Harold Greenlee, Philip Comfort, and many others agree that the restoration of the original text is the fundamental task of the discipline.[11] As Constantin Tischendorf famously wrote in a letter to his fiancée, textual criticism is a "sacred task, the struggle to regain the original form of the New Testament."[12]

Textual critics today often specify that the goal of textual criticism is the "initial text" (German: *Ausgangstext*), the archetype of the texts preserved in the extant Greek manuscripts and early translations. Gerd Mink, who coined the term "initial text," defined it as "the reconstructed form of text from which the manuscript transmission started."[13] Scholars

---

9. For example, textual criticism often provides helpful insights into the history of interpretation.

10. Paul Maas, *Textual Criticism*, trans. Barbara Flower (Oxford: Clarendon, 1958), 1.

11. See B. F. Westcott and F. J. A. Hort, *Introduction to the New Testament in the Original Greek with Notes on Selected Readings* (New York: Harper & Brothers, 1882; repr., Peabody, MA: Hendrickson, 1988), 3; Samuel P. Tregelles, *An Account of the Printed Text of the Greek New Testament: With Remarks on Its Revision upon Critical Principles* (London: Samuel Bagster & Sons, 1854; repr., London: Forgotten Books, 2017), 174; F. H. A. Scrivener, *A Plain Introduction to the Criticism of the New Testament*, ed. Edward Miller, 4th ed., 2 vols. (1894), 1:5; Kirsopp Lake, *The Text of the New Testament*, 6th ed., Oxford Church Text Books (London: Billing and Sons, 1959), 1; Bruce M. Metzger and Bart D. Ehrman, *The Text of the New Testament: Its Transmission, Corruption, and Restoration*, 4th ed. (New York: Oxford University Press, 2005), xv; J. Harold Greenlee, *Introduction to New Testament Textual Criticism* (Grand Rapids: Eerdmans, 1964), 11; and Philip Comfort, *Encountering the Manuscripts: An Introduction to New Testament Paleography & Textual Criticism* (Nashville: Broadman & Holman, 2005), 289. The expression "most nearly conforming to the original" was used by Metzger in his preface to the 1st edition of *The Text of the New Testament: Its Transmission, Corruption, and Restoration*. The recent 4th edition clarifies that the "original text" referred to the "'final published' edition that served as the basis for all later copies" (273–74).

12. As quoted in Metzger and Ehrman, *Text of the New Testament*, 172.

13. Gerd Mink, "Contamination, Coherence, and Coincidence in Textual Transmission: The Coherence-Based Genealogical Method (CBGM) as a Complement and Corrective to Existing

acknowledge that this initial text probably differs at some points from the "authorial text," the final draft of each of the twenty-seven NT books that the author approved for publication. Holger Strutwolf has suggested that this initial text is in most cases a very early text that may be traced to as early as the middle of the 2nd century.[14] Obviously, some changes may have entered the tradition in the decades between the final draft of each NT book and the reconstructed initial text. For example, the reconstructed initial text of the Gospel of Mark ends with Mark 16:8. Many scholars argue that the original Gospel of Mark must have continued with an account of Jesus' resurrection and post-resurrection appearances. Since they reject alternative endings to the Gospel in the manuscript tradition, they conclude that the original ending of Mark must have been lost in the decades between the completion of the final draft of Mark and the initial text.[15] However, Holger Strutwolf correctly observed that "as long as we have no evidence that suggests a radical break in the textual transmission between the author's text and the initial text of our tradition, the best hypothesis concerning the original text still remains the reconstructed archetype to which our manuscript tradition and the evidence of early translations and the citations point."[16] He encouraged scholars to continue to pursue the goal of restoring the authorial text by noting that "the reconstruction of the original text of the New Testament is of vital theological and historical interest: we want to know what Paul really wrote to the Romans and what was the original form of the Gospel of Luke. The quest for the original text does not as such involve contradictions and logical impossibilities."[17]

Approaches," in *The Textual History of the Greek New Testament: Changing Views in Contemporary Research*, ed. Klaus Wachtel and Michael W. Holmes (Atlanta: Society of Biblical Literature, 2011), 143.

14. Holger Strutwolf, "Original Text and Textual History," in Wachtel and Holmes, *Textual History of the Greek New Testament*, 41.

15. See, for example, J. K. Elliott, "The Last Twelve Verses of Mark: Original or Not?," in *Perspectives on the Ending of Mark: Four Views*, ed. David Alan Black (Nashville: B&H Academic, 2008), 80–102. For a brief introduction to this textual issue, see Charles L. Quarles and L. Scott Kellum, *40 Questions about the Text and Canon of the New Testament* (Grand Rapids: Kregel Academic, 2023), 163–74.

16. Strutwolf, "Original Text and Textual History," 41.

17. Strutwolf, "Original Text and Textual History," 41.

2

THE SOURCES OF EVIDENCE FOR NEW TESTAMENT TEXTUAL CRITICISM

An abundance of resources for reconstructing the initial text of the NT is available today. Roughly five thousand six hundred manuscripts of the NT remain in existence. These manuscripts are variously categorized for citation in textual apparatuses based on the writing material used by the scribe, the script employed in the copy, and the content of the copy. In addition to these manuscripts, portions of the NT are preserved on ostraca (broken pieces of pottery) and amulets, though these are largely ignored by textual critics.[1] Lectionaries, versions, and quotations in the church fathers also provide valuable evidence and will be discussed later in this chapter.

The following sections will introduce readers to several important manuscripts of the Greek NT. Readers may access information about the many other important manuscripts in the standard critical editions of the Greek NT ("Appendix I.A. Codices Graeci" in the NA[28],[2] and section III.3, "The Greek Text Manuscripts" in the Introduction to UBS[5], 9*–29*). They will find more information about an even greater number of manuscripts in the *Kurzgefasste Liste Online*.[3]

---

1. Ernst von Dobschütz expanded Caspar René Gregory's official registry of NT manuscripts by adding talismans and ostraca. However, Kurt Aland later deleted these two types of witnesses when he published that official registry of known NT manuscripts (*Kurzgefasste Liste der griechischen Handschriften des Neues Testaments* [Berlin: de Gruyter, 1963]). Brice C. Jones has recently argued that this material may be important for textual criticism and valuable for the social studies of early Christianity and should be restored to the *Liste*. See Jones, *New Testament Texts of Greek Amulets from Late Antiquity*, LNTS 554 (New York: Bloomsbury T&T Clark, 2016). The amulets and ostraca now appear in the *Liste* in its current online format. These artifacts are named with the prefix T and their ID begins with 5.

2. Pages 792–814.

3. https://ntvmr.uni-muenster.de/liste. The *Kurzgefasste Liste Online* is intended to be the current edition of the *Liste* (see n. 1, above) going forward. The second print edition is Kurt Aland et al., *Kurzgefasste Liste der griechischen Handschriften des Neues Testaments*, 2nd ed. (Berlin: de Gruyter, 1994; repr., 2011).

2.1. Papyri

The papyri are manuscripts written on papyrus. Papyrus is a type of reed that grew bountifully in the marshes of the Nile Delta in Egypt. The plant reaches heights of about fifteen feet and has a triangular, jointless stem that can grow to a diameter of approximately two and a half inches. Egyptian workers peeled the tough rind from the stem, then peeled the pith into long thin strips. They placed the strips side-by-side on a board, then placed another layer of strips on top of the first perpendicular to them. When the stack was moistened and placed under pressure, the plant's natural juice served as a glue that bonded the layers together. The sheet was dried, trimmed, and smoothed with pumice. Papyrus sheets were used for a wide variety of purposes. Beginning around 3000 BC, sheets of papyrus were used as writing material. When long rolls of papyrus were used in scrolls, scribes usually wrote on just one side, the side with the strips running horizontally. However, when the sheets were bound together in a codex, scribes wrote on both sides.[4]

The papyrus sheets were similar to thick paper. Although the very ancient papyrus documents that have survived to the present day are brittle and fragile, in its original condition, papyrus was strong, flexible, and durable. Harry Gamble notes that it "was by far the prevalent writing material during the Hellenistic and early Roman imperial periods."[5] Adam Bülow-Jacobsen demonstrated that, at least when it comes to texts in Greek and Latin, "the overwhelming majority of ancient texts are written on this material."[6]

A modern apparatus normally refers to papyrus manuscripts using a Gothic "p" followed by a superscript Arabic number, e.g., $\mathfrak{P}^{46}$. By far, most of the surviving papyrus manuscripts of the NT (whose provenance is known) were recovered in Egypt, where the arid environment prevented their decay. However, a few have been found in Israel, and others may eventually be found in other parts of the Mediterranean world.[7]

At the time of writing, the official registry (*Liste*) of NT Greek manuscripts maintained by the Institute for New Testament Textual Research in Münster (Institut für Neutestamentliche Textforschung) lists 141 papyri. However, the *Liste* indicates that six of these have been removed from the registry; five of these were determined to be portions or duplicates

---

4. Information about the manufacture of ancient papyrus is derived from a description in Pliny (*Nat.* 13.74–82), examination of ancient papyri, and modern experiments attempting to replicate features of ancient papyri. For a more detailed overview of the process of making papyrus, see Adam Bülow-Jacobsen, "Writing Materials in the Ancient World," in *The Oxford Handbook of Papyrology*, ed. Roger S. Bagnall (Oxford: Oxford University Press, 2009), 3–29, esp. 3–10.

5. Harry Y. Gamble, *Books and Readers in the Early Church: A History of Early Christian Texts* (New Haven: Yale University Press, 1995), 45.

6. Bülow-Jacobsen, "Writing Materials in the Ancient World," 3–4.

7. Papyrus manuscripts of various Greek and Latin texts have been found in several sites such as Dura, the Middle Euphrates, Nessana, Nahal Hever, Petra, Khirbet Mird, Aï Khanoum, Bostra (modern Bosra), Jericho, and Herculaneum. See David Sider, "The Special Case of Herculaneum," in Bagnall, *Oxford Handbook of Papyrology*, 303–19; and Jean Gascou, "The Papyrology of the Near East," in Bagnall, *Oxford Handbook of Papyrology*, 473–94.

of other papyri already listed.[8] So far, scholars have identified papyri containing portions of every NT book except 2 Timothy.[9]

Some scholars view the papyrus manuscripts as the most important witnesses for reconstructing the original text of the NT. This estimation of their value is based primarily on the early date of some of the papyri. The papyrus manuscripts range in date from as early as the 2nd century (e.g., $\mathfrak{P}^{52}$) to as late as the 8th century (e.g., $\mathfrak{P}^{42}$).[10] However, the value of the papyri for restoring the NT text is mitigated by three factors.

First, some scholars have argued that the very early dates assigned to some of the manuscripts are too precise and that the methods used to establish these dates are too subjective.[11] Some of the papyri are probably not as old as was previously thought.

Second, most of the papyri are very fragmentary.[12] If we relied only on the papyrus manuscripts that predate the great majuscule texts from the 4th century, we would be able to reconstruct only a small portion of some NT books. For example, three papyrus manuscripts of Mark exist that potentially predate Vaticanus and Sinaiticus: $\mathfrak{P}^{45}$, $\mathfrak{P}^{88}$, and $\mathfrak{P}^{137}$. These manuscripts contain the following portions of Mark.

$\mathfrak{P}^{45}$ Mark 4:36–40; 5:15–26, 38–43; 6:1–3, 16–25, 36–50; 7:3–15, 25–37; 8:1, 10–26, 34–38; 9:1–9, 18–31; 11:27–33; 12:1, 5–8, 13–19, 24–28

$\mathfrak{P}^{88}$ Mark 2:1–26

$\mathfrak{P}^{137}$ Mark 1:7–9, 16–18

Even if we assume that these manuscripts contain the entirety of each verse listed (though they often contain only a portion of a given verse), these early witnesses can only be said to contain 179 of the total 666 verses in Mark. In other words, the early papyri by themselves would enable us to reconstruct only about 26.88 percent of this Gospel. Excluding $\mathfrak{P}^{88}$, which is dated to the 4th century and may be no earlier than Sinaiticus and Vaticanus, reduces coverage of Mark's Gospel to a mere 22.97 percent.

Similarly, three papyrus manuscripts containing portions of James may predate the great majuscules of the 4th century: $\mathfrak{P}^{20}$, $\mathfrak{P}^{23}$; and possibly $\mathfrak{P}^{100}$. These papyri contain Jas

---

8. The sixth one, $\mathfrak{P}^{99}$, was dropped from the list since it is not a manuscript of Paul's letters but a Greek-Latin glossary with short extracts from the Pauline corpus drawn from an early Christian work. See Eleanor Dickey, "A Re-examination of New Testament Papyrus P99 (Vetus Latina AN glo Paul)," *NTS* 65 (2019): 103–21.

9. In 2013, Eldon Jay Epp ("The Papyrus Manuscripts of the New Testament," in *The Text of the New Testament in Contemporary Research: Essays on the Status Quaestionis*, ed. Bart D. Ehrman and Michael W. Holmes, 2nd ed., NTTSD 42 [Boston: Brill, 2013], 4) stated that the only NT writings not represented among the papyri were 1–2 Tim. However, this changed with the discovery of $\mathfrak{P}^{133}$, which contains 1 Tim 3:13–4:8.

10. The dates used for the various manuscripts described in this chapter are those assigned in the *Liste*.

11. Brent Nongbri, *God's Library: The Archaeology of the Earliest Christian Manuscripts* (New Haven: Yale University Press, 2018), 47–82.

12. For an excellent discussion of the fragmentary nature of the papyri, see Epp, "Papyrus Manuscripts of the New Testament," 4.

1:10–12, 15–18; 2:19–26; 3:1–9, 13–18; 4:1–4, 9–17; 5:1. The three fragments cover only about 40.74 percent of this NT book. If we exclude $\mathfrak{P}^{100}$ (which may be dated to the 4th c.), the two remaining fragments preserve only about 22.22 percent of the book.

Third, the discovery of early papyrus manuscripts has generally confirmed the text already reconstructed by a comparison of the great majuscules. A careful comparison of critical editions of the Greek NT before and after the discovery of papyri that potentially date to the 2nd century showed that these earliest witnesses did not prompt editors to revise the Greek text.[13]

Nearly half of our NT papyri come from the ancient trash heap in Oxyrhynchus (modern *el-Bahnasa*), Egypt.[14] Bernard P. Grenfell and Arthur S. Hunt found their first papyrus there in 1897. Among the Oxyrhynchus papyri are some of the oldest extant fragments of several NT books. Fragments of three books may date to the 2nd century: Matthew ($\mathfrak{P}^{104}$), Mark ($\mathfrak{P}^{137}$), and John ($\mathfrak{P}^{90}$). Fragments of eleven books may date to the 3rd century: Matthew ($\mathfrak{P}^1$, $\mathfrak{P}^{70}$, $\mathfrak{P}^{77}$, $\mathfrak{P}^{101}$, $\mathfrak{P}^{103}$), Luke ($\mathfrak{P}^{69}$, $\mathfrak{P}^{111}$, $\mathfrak{P}^{138}$, $\mathfrak{P}^{141}$), John ($\mathfrak{P}^5$, $\mathfrak{P}^{22}$, $\mathfrak{P}^{28}$, $\mathfrak{P}^{39}$, $\mathfrak{P}^{106}$, $\mathfrak{P}^{107}$, $\mathfrak{P}^{108}$, $\mathfrak{P}^{109}$, $\mathfrak{P}^{119}$, $\mathfrak{P}^{121}$), Acts ($\mathfrak{P}^{29}$), Romans ($\mathfrak{P}^{27}$, $\mathfrak{P}^{113}$), 1 Corinthians ($\mathfrak{P}^{15}$), 1 Thessalonians ($\mathfrak{P}^{30}$), 2 Thessalonians ($\mathfrak{P}^{30}$), Hebrews ($\mathfrak{P}^{13}$, $\mathfrak{P}^{114}$), James ($\mathfrak{P}^{20}$, $\mathfrak{P}^{23}$), and 1 John ($\mathfrak{P}^9$).

The Oxyrhynchus papyri rank first in number of NT books covered. Furthermore, unlike most other papyrus manuscripts of NT books, the location of their discovery is known (though the location of discovery is not necessarily the provenance of the manuscripts, i.e., the place where they were copied). Nevertheless, two other collections are of similar importance.

The Chester Beatty papyri include three early and extensive papyrus manuscripts of the NT.[15] These manuscripts are much more extensive than the tiny scraps from Oxyrhynchus. $\mathfrak{P}^{45}$ (3rd c.) consists of thirty-one leaves (of an estimated original 110) containing portions of the four Gospels and Acts. $\mathfrak{P}^{46}$ (early 3rd c.) consists of eighty-six leaves (of an original 104) with portions of most of Paul's letters and Hebrews. The only books from the Pauline corpus not included in the surviving leaves are 2 Thessalonians, Philemon, 1–2 Timothy, and Titus. Most scholars believe that 2 Thessalonians and Philemon were contained in the leaves now lost, and some scholars argue that the Pastoral Letters could have been included as well. $\mathfrak{P}^{47}$ (late 3rd c.) consists of ten fragments (of an estimated original thirty-two) with portions of Rev 9–17.[16]

---

13. Elijah Hixson, "Does It Matter If Our New Testament Manuscripts Are Early?" (paper presented at the Annual Meeting of the Evangelical Theological Society, Denver, CO, November 16, 2022), 1–8.

14. As of June 24, 2024, fifty-eight of the 135 New Testament papyri came from the Oxyrhynchus dig.

15. In addition to these NT manuscripts, the collection includes at least nine manuscripts containing portions of books of the OT, the Apocrypha, Pseudepigrapha, and early Christian works. See Nongbri, *God's Library*, 116–56, esp. 118.

16. The definitive study is Peter Malik, *P.Beatty III ($\mathfrak{P}$47): The Codex, Its Scribe, and Its Text*, NTTSD 52 (Boston: Brill, 2017).

The Bodmer papyri include three early and extensive papyrus manuscripts of portions of the Greek NT.[17] 𝔓[66] (early 3rd c.) consists of seventy-five leaves (of an original seventy-eight) with large portions of John. 𝔓[72] (3rd or 4th c.) consists of eighteen leaves covering all of 1–2 Peter and Jude. 𝔓[75] (early 3rd c.) consists of fifty leaves (of an original sixty-four) with large portions of Luke and John. Scholars still debate the provenance of these papyri. James Robinson conducted the most extensive investigation of the provenance of the Bodmer collection and concluded that the papyri came from a monastic library in Dishna, about twenty miles down the Nile River from Nag Hammadi.[18] However, scholars have not yet reached a consensus regarding the provenance or social setting of these manuscripts. Many still favor Panopolis, modern-day Akhmim.[19]

The papyri are important representatives of the early stage in the transmission of the NT text. Eldon Epp is correct that the papyri "are viewed by many scholars as critical in seeking to solve some of the intractable problems of the New Testament text."[20] However, the presence of a reading in one of the early papyri does not necessarily indicate that this reading represents the original text. The early papyri contain scribal errors, too, and these early manuscripts sometimes disagree with one another. A textual critic must also depend on other categories of evidence to accomplish the task of reconstructing the text of the NT.

2.2. Majuscules

Majuscule manuscripts are identified on the basis of the script that the scribe employed, the writing material used, and the arrangement of the NT text within the manuscript.[21] First, majuscules are written in majuscule script. This distinguishes them from minuscules, which are written in a different script. In majuscule script, most of the characters resemble capital letters. Majuscule script is bilinear, meaning that each character is written between two imaginary parallel lines so that each character is approximately the same height, with few characters extending above the top imaginary line or below the bottom imaginary line.

The script of the majuscules of the Bible resembles this font:[22]

---

17. The total collection also includes two later manuscripts of NT books, as well as manuscripts of OT books and non-biblical literature. See Nongbri, *God's Library*, 157–215. 𝔓[74] is a 7th-century manuscript of Acts and the General Epistles. 𝔓[73] is a 7th-century fragment containing Matt 25:43 and 26:2–3.

18. James M. Robinson, *The Story of the Bodmer Papyri: From the First Monastery's Library in Upper Egypt to Geneva and Dublin* (Eugene, OR: Cascade Books, 2011).

19. See the discussion in Nongbri, *God's Library*, 159–215.

20. Epp, "Papyrus Manuscripts of the New Testament," 2.

21. Previous generations of scholars often referred to these texts as "uncials." However, scholars currently prefer the term "majuscule" and reserve the term "uncial" for Latin texts.

22. The font is 0512 Dioskurides. The Swiss calligrapher Klaus-Peter Schäffel developed the font to resemble manuscript Vienna, Österreichische Nationalbibliothek, Med. Gr. 1. The font is free and available online.

λ Β ΓΔ Є Ζ Η Θ Ι Κ Λ Μ Ν Ξ Ο Π Ρ С Τ Υ ϕ Χ ψ ω

Figure 2.1. Examples of Majuscule Script

Manuscript	Text Sample
𝔓46	[23]
Sinaiticus (01)	[24]

Second, majuscules are written on parchment, processed animal skins. This distinguishes them from the papyri, which also use majuscule script but are written on papyrus rather than parchment. Third, majuscules are "continuous text" manuscripts. They do not break up the text of NT books and assign these texts to various days of the year like lectionaries do. Majuscules present the text without significant disruption in the order in which the author penned it. Majuscule manuscripts are identified by a letter of the Hebrew, Latin, or Greek alphabet or by their Gregory-Aland number, an Arabic number prefixed with a zero. For example, the important majuscule Codex Sinaiticus is designated ℵ or 01.

The use of parchment for copies of Scripture may trace its origins to the late 3rd century: four majuscules (0220 0171 0189 0162) may be dated before the conversion of Constantine in AD 312.[25] Later, Constantine commissioned Eusebius to produce fifty copies of the Christian Scriptures to aid in the establishment of new churches in Constantinople where "a great mass of people [had] attached itself to the most holy Church." His instructions specified that the copies were to be written "on parchment."[26] In the late 4th century, church authorities ordered that the papyrus books in the Christian library in Caesarea be copied onto parchment to ensure their preservation since parchment was more durable than papyrus.[27] Although papyrus continued to be used for copying Scripture up through the 8th century, parchment increasingly became the preferred material.

Although around three hundred majuscule manuscripts are extant, four of these may be described as the "great majuscule codices."[28] These four are pandects ("books that contain everything"), single volumes that originally contained the text of the whole Bible in Greek. Although a few earlier manuscripts contained the Gospels and Acts or the Epistles

---

23. CBL BP II. CC BY – 4.0. Chester Beatty, Dublin.

24. The British Library, Add. 43725 200b.

25. David C. Parker, "The Majuscule Manuscripts of the New Testament," in Ehrman and Holmes, *Text of the New Testament in Contemporary Research*, 49–51.

26. Eusebius, *Vit. Const.* 4.36. This is the traditional interpretation of Eusebius's phrase ἐν διφθέραις. Cf. Gamble, *Books and Readers in the Early Church*, 158–59. However, Averil Cameron and Stuart G. Hall (*Eusebius: Life of Constantine* [Oxford: Clarendon, 1999], 166–67) suggest that Constantine was referring to "ornamental leather bindings."

27. Jerome, *Epist.* 34.1; *Vir. ill.* 113.

28. Westcott and Hort (*Introduction to the New Testament*, 74) referred to them as "the four great uncial Bibles." The term "uncial" is best reserved for Latin manuscripts.

of Paul in a single volume, most were small, compact books containing only a single NT document.[29] These four pandects mark "the high point in the technology of ancient Christian book production in terms of materials, construction, layout, inscription and scope."[30]

Codex Sinaiticus (‭א‬ or 01) is the only extant majuscule manuscript that still contains the entire NT.[31] The massive manuscript originally contained the Greek OT (including the Apocrypha), the Greek NT, plus the Epistle of Barnabas and the Shepherd of Hermas. The books of the NT were placed in this order: Gospels (Matthew, Mark, Luke, John), Paul's letters (with Hebrews placed between 2 Thessalonians and 1 Timothy), Acts, the General Epistles, and Revelation. Since the codex contains the Eusebian section and canon numbers, it must have been produced sometime after AD 300.[32] Based on an evaluation of the script, it was probably copied before AD 425.[33] The provenance of Sinaiticus is unknown; its name reflects only the location of its rediscovery in the 19th century. Scholars have suggested that it was produced in Caesarea,[34] Egypt,[35] or the West, perhaps in Rome.[36] The balance of evidence slightly favors a Caesarean provenance.[37]

Codex Alexandrinus (A or 02) is a 5th-century manuscript.[38] The manuscript originally contained the entire OT (including the Apocrypha), the epistle of Athanasius to Marcellinus on the Psalms, Eusebius's Hypothesis on the Psalms, the entire NT, plus 1 and 2 Clement and the Psalms of Solomon.[39] The manuscript still contains the complete NT except for these sections that were contained in leaves that are now missing:

---

29. Harry Gamble, "Codex Sinaiticus in Its Fourth Century Setting," in *Codex Sinaiticus: New Perspectives on the Ancient Biblical Manuscript*, ed. Scot McKendrick et al. (Peabody, MA: Hendrickson, 2015), 4.

30. Gamble, "Codex Sinaiticus in Its Fourth Century Setting," 5.

31. For high resolution images of Codex Sinaiticus, see https://codexsinaiticus.org/en/.

32. The Eusebian numbers marked various sections of the Gospels at a time before there were chapter or verse divisions. The canon numbers indicated if the section had a parallel in another Gospel(s) and, if so, which Gospel(s).

33. For a recent discussion of the date, see Brent Nongbri, "The Date of Codex Sinaiticus," *JTS* 73 (2022): 516–34.

34. H. J. Milne and T. C. Skeat, *Scribes and Correctors of the Codex Sinaiticus* (London: British Museum, 1938), 66–69; Klaus Wachtel, "The Corrected New Testament Text of Codex Sinaiticus," in McKendrick et al., *Codex Sinaiticus*, 97–98 (but see 105n3).

35. H. Lake and K. Lake, *Codex Sinaiticus Petropolitanus: New Testament, the Epistle of Barnabas and the Shepherd of Hermas* (Oxford: Clarendon, 1911), x–xv.

36. Westcott and Hort, *Introduction to the New Testament*, 264–67.

37. T. C. Skeat, "The Codex Sinaiticus, the Codex Vaticanus and Constantine," *JTS* 50 (1999): 583–625; J. K. Elliott, "T. C. Skeat on the Dating and Origin of Codex Vaticanus," in *New Testament Textual Criticism: The Application of Thoroughgoing Principles*, NovTSup 137 (Leiden: Brill, 2010), 65–78. Note that LDAB identifies "Kaisareia" as the provenance, though it marks it with a question mark to signal that the provenance is uncertain.

38. For high-resolution images of Codex Alexandrinus, see https://www.bl.uk/collection-items/codex-alexandrinus#.

39. For the complete list of contents, see https://searcharchives.bl.uk/primo_library/libweb/action/dlDisplay.do?docId=IAMS040-002353500&vid=IAMS_VU2&indx=1&dym=false&dscnt=1&onCampus=false&group=ALL&institution=BL&ct=search&vl(freeText0)=040-002353500&submit=search.

Matt 1:1–25:6; John 6:50–8:52; 2 Cor 4:13–12:6. The NT is arranged in the following order: Gospels (Matthew, Mark, Luke, John), Acts, General Epistles, Paul's letters (with Hebrews between 2 Thessalonians and 1 Timothy), and Revelation. Different exemplars were used for the major sections of the NT. The exemplar used for the Gospels was of poor quality compared to the rest of the NT. Alexandrinus is considered to be a reliable witness outside of the Gospels and one of the best witnesses to the book of Revelation.[40] The provenance of the codex is unknown. The name Alexandrinus refers to the patriarchal library where the manuscript was kept from the 11th century to the early 17th century, not to its provenance. Andrew Smith has revealed the weakness of the old argument that spelling habits in the manuscript favor an Egyptian provenance.[41]

Codex Vaticanus (B or 03) is a 4th-century manuscript.[42] It originally contained the entire OT (including the Apocrypha except 1–4 Maccabees and the Prayer of Manasseh) and the entire NT. The leaves containing the portion of the NT from Heb 9:14 to the end are now lost. The NT was arranged in this order: Gospels (Matthew, Mark, Luke, John), Acts, General Epistles, Paul's letters (with Hebrews after 2 Thessalonians). The remaining NT books, 1–2 Timothy, Philemon, and Revelation were almost certainly contained in the missing leaves. Since both Sinaiticus and Alexandrinus contained books from the Apostolic Fathers, Vaticanus may have as well. Although it has long resided at the Vatican Library in Rome, the provenance of Vaticanus is unknown. Suggestions have included the West, possibly Rome,[43] Alexandria,[44] or Caesarea.[45] Vaticanus and Sinaiticus were probably copied at the same scriptorium.[46] The Caesarean provenance seems most likely. This codex is generally considered to be the most important and most reliable manuscript of the Greek NT. It has been described as "by far the most significant of the uncials."[47]

Codex Ephraemi Rescriptus (C or 04) is a 5th-century manuscript.[48] The manuscript is a palimpsest, which means that the biblical text was erased so that the parchment could

---

40. Kurt Aland and Barbara Aland, *The Text of the New Testament: An Introduction to the Critical Editions and to the Theory and Practice of Modern Textual Criticism*, trans. Erroll F. Rhodes, 2nd ed. (Grand Rapids: Eerdmans, 1989), 108–9.

41. W. Andrew Smith, *A Study of the Gospels in Codex Alexandrinus: Codicology, Palaeography, and Scribal Hands*, NTTSD 48 (Boston: Brill, 2014), 192–246, esp. 242–43.

42. For high-resolution images of Codex Vaticanus, see https://digi.vatlib.it/view/MSS_Vat.gr.1209.

43. Westcott and Hort, *Introduction to the New Testament*, 264–67.

44. Stephen Pisano, "The Vaticanus graecus 1209: A Witness to the Text of the New Testament," in *Le manuscript B de la Bible (Vaticanus graecus 1209)*, ed. Patrick Andrist, Histoire du texte biblique 7 (Lausanne: Éditions du Zèbre, 2009), 77–97.

45. Skeat, "Codex Sinaiticus, the Codex Vaticanus and Constantine," 583–625; Elliott, "T. C. Skeat on the Dating and Origin of Codex Vaticanus," 65–78. Note that LDAB identifies "Kaisareia" as the provenance and, in this case, uses no question mark.

46. The great similarity in the colophon design at the end of Deuteronomy in B and the end of Mark in ℵ suggests this. See Plate 1 in Skeat, "Codex Sinaiticus, the Codex Vaticanus and Constantine."

47. Aland and Aland, *Text of the New Testament*, 109.

48. For high-resolution images of Codex Ephraemi Rescriptus, see https://gallica.bnf.fr/ark:/12148/btv1b8470433r/f1.item.r=.langEN.zoom.

be used by a scribe who wished to write or copy another text. In the 12th century, a scribe erased the majuscule text and used the sheets to write thirty-eight sermons and treatises of the 4th-century Syrian church father, St. Ephraem, in minuscule script. The undertext of the sixty-four surviving leaves of the manuscript contains the OT wisdom books and the NT (except for 2 Thessalonians and 2 John). Many believe that the manuscript originally contained the entire Bible. However, the script on the OT pages is significantly different from that used in the NT pages. Thus, the OT and NT sections are possibly from two different manuscripts.[49] In the 1830s, scholars used chemical agents to restore the erased text.[50] Tischendorf published the first full transcription of the NT text in this manuscript in 1843. Unfortunately, even as early as the late 1800s, Scrivener rightly complained that the chemical preparation "has defaced the vellum with stains of various colours, from green and blue to black and brown."[51] Now much of the manuscript is illegible. Two different scribes later corrected the text, a 6th-century corrector (probably in Palestine) and a 9th-century corrector (probably in Constantinople).[52]

In addition to these four great majuscules, three other early majuscules deserve mention, even in this brief treatment. Codex Bezae (D or 05) is a 5th-century manuscript of the four Gospels and Acts.[53] The manuscript presents the Greek text and a Latin translation in parallel columns, with the Greek on the left page and the Latin on the right page. The four Gospels are arranged in the "Western order," which places the two Gospels written by Jesus's apostles first: Matthew, John, Luke, Mark. Scrivener, who published an edition of the codex in 1864, wrote: "No known manuscript contains so many bold and extensive interpolations."[54] He added that these interpolations often had no support in any other witness or had support only in Old Latin manuscripts and the Curetonian Syriac version. Parker noted that the scribe who copied the manuscript "has been seen as a person with too much ink in his well" and added: "[T]he fact is that the longer I have studied it, the more I have become convinced that its many unique readings only very rarely deserve serious consideration if one is trying to establish the best available text."[55] On the other hand, many text critics argue that D remains important for the reconstruction of the original

---

49. D. C. Parker, *An Introduction to the New Testament Manuscripts and Their Texts* (Cambridge: Cambridge University Press, 2008), 73.

50. Although Metzger and Ehrman (*Text of the New Testament*, 69) claim that Tischendorf applied the chemical agents, earlier scholars disagreed. Scrivener says that this was done "at the instance of Fleck in 1834" (*Plain Introduction to the Criticism of the New Testament*, 1:121). Marvin R. Vincent (*A History of the Textual Criticism of the New Testament* [London: Macmillan, 1899], 16) indicates that the application of prussiate of potash was performed by Carl Hase in 1834–1835.

51. Scrivener, *Plain Introduction to the Criticism of the New Testament*, 1:121.

52. Metzger and Ehrman, *Text of the New Testament*, 70.

53. The manuscript appears to have originally contained at least some of the General Epistles as well. A fragment of 3 John 11–15 in Latin stands between the Gospels and Acts. D. C. Parker (*Codex Bezae: An Early Christian Manuscript and Its Text* [Cambridge: Cambridge University Press, 1992], 281) dates Bezae to "about the year 400."

54. Scrivener, *Plain Introduction to the Criticism of the New Testament*, 1:130.

55. Parker, *Codex Bezae*, 1.

text. When D agrees with other early Greek manuscripts such as B or ℵ, the agreement suggests that the shared reading is very ancient and arguably original.

The text of the manuscript has three characteristic features: the tendency to harmonize the Gospels, the tendency to add new material to the Gospels and Acts from other sources, and the intention to rewrite the text in a style more easily understandable to the anticipated readers.[56] The provenance of Bezae is unknown. After dismissing other suggested sites (e.g., Italy, Sardinia, Sicily, Gaul, North Africa, Egypt, Antioch, Jerusalem), Parker offers evidence supporting a provenance in ancient Berytus (modern Beirut).[57]

Codex Claromontanus (D[P], D[2], or 06) is a 6th-century manuscript of the letters of Paul, plus Hebrews. Unlike the early manuscripts that place Hebrews between 2 Thessalonians and 1 Timothy, this manuscript places Hebrews at the end of the Pauline corpus after Philemon. Like Codex Bezae, this codex is bilingual, with the Greek text on the left-hand page and Latin on the right-hand page. Its provenance is unknown. Most surmise that the text was copied in Southern Italy.

Codex Washingtonianus (W or 032) is a 4th- or 5th-century manuscript of the four Gospels in the "Western order," Matthew, John, Luke, and Mark. The text of the manuscript seems to have been copied from fragments of several different earlier manuscripts since different portions of the text belong to different families.[58] Washingtonianus is the only extant Greek manuscript containing an ending of Mark known as the Freer Logion, an ending that Jerome mentions could be found in some Greek manuscripts in his era. The manuscript was found in Egypt and was likely copied in Egypt as well. The first sixteen pages of John, containing John 1:1–5:11, are in a different hand and are generally dated to the 7th or 8th century but could be as early as the late 4th century.[59] This supplement differs from other portions of the manuscript in its textual character. Larry Hurtado noted that it "has some Alexandrian readings and some readings of the so-called 'Western' text-type."[60]

---

56. Parker, *Codex Bezae*, 279.

57. Parker, *Codex Bezae*, 261–78. For a very detailed discussion of the probable origin of the codex and the reasons for its distinct text, see Peter E. Lorenz, *A History of Codex Bezae's Text in the Gospel of Mark*, ANTF 53 (Berlin: de Gruyter, 2022).

58. Henry A. Sanders (*The New Testament Manuscripts in the Freer Collection* [New York: Macmillan, 1912], 4–133) first observed the block mixture in W (032). His observations were recently confirmed by Megan Leigh Burnett (*Codex Washingtonianus: An Analysis of the Textual Affiliations of the Freer Gospels Manuscript*, TS 3.27 [Piscataway, NJ: Gorgias, 2022]).

59. Metzger and Ehrman, *Text of the New Testament*, 80. However, Henry A. Sanders (*Facsimile of the Washington Manuscript of the Four Gospels in the Freer Collection* [Ann Arbor: University of Michigan Press, 1912], v) noted that the first sixteen pages of John in the manuscript seem to be *earlier* than the rest. He gave an extended explanation for this assessment in Sanders, *New Testament Manuscripts in the Freer Collection*, 135–37.

60. Larry W. Hurtado, "Introduction," in *The Freer Biblical Manuscripts: Fresh Studies of an American Treasure Trove*, ed. Larry W. Hurtado (Atlanta: Society of Biblical Literature, 2006), 7.

2.3. Minuscules

Minuscule manuscripts, like majuscules, are written on parchment, but they use a different script. Minuscule script has four important features. First, as its name implies, minuscule script is generally smaller and more compact than majuscule script, enabling the scribe to copy more text on less parchment. Second, the script is quadrilinear. Although the body of each character remains within two imaginary lines, many of the characters have long descenders that extend below the bottom line or long ascenders that extend above the top line. Third, minuscule script is characterized by the more frequent use of ligatures. Series of letters are connected to one another so that the scribe could copy the series in one fluid motion without lifting the pen. For this reason, minuscule script is sometimes called "cursive." Finally, minuscule script often makes extensive use of contractions and abbreviations. Many of the abbreviations would be difficult to decipher without the benefit of tools from the late nineteenth and early twentieth centuries.[61]

The script of minuscule manuscripts of the Bible resembles these fonts:[62]

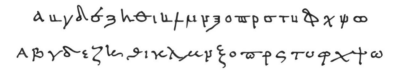

Figure 2.2. Examples of Minuscule Script

Manuscript	Text Sample
Mich. Ms. 18	[63]
MOTB.MS.000474.1-.2 folio 17r	[64]

61. Some of the more helpful tools are Carl Faulmann, *Das Buch der Schrift, enthaltend die Schriften und Alphabete aller Zeiten und aller Völker des gesammten Erdkreises; Zusammengestellt und erläutert* (Wein: K. K. Hof- und Staatsdruckerei, 1878); T. W. Allen, *Notes on Abbreviations in Greek Manuscripts* (Oxford: Clarendon, 1889); William Wallace, "An Index of Greek Ligatures and Contractions," *JHS* 43 (1923): 183–93. Especially helpful recent resources include the online resource developed by the Center for Research of Biblical Manuscripts and Inscriptions called the CRMBI Searchable Ligature Tool (https://airtable.com/appgrNuo12M56MZkN/shrjBIO9cbWMIZGFO /tbl3GfXLCvhcXclbN). The most comprehensive resource will be the forthcoming *A Lexicon of Abbreviations and Ligatures in Greek Minuscule Hands: ca. 8th Century to ca. 1600* produced by the University of London.
62. Klaus-Peter Schäffel developed both fonts. The first resembles the script of a 9th-century minuscule and the second resembles an undated manuscript. The fonts are free and available online.
63. Mich. Ms. 18 (12th century Gospel). University of Michigan Library (Special Collections Research Center).
64. MOTB.MS.000474.1-.2 folio 17r (the "Ussher" Gospels; 12th century). Courtesy Museum of the Bible Collection. All rights reserved. ©Museum of the Bible, 2024.

Although cursive had long been used for everyday documents, scribes probably began to use minuscule script to copy Scripture by the 8th century at the latest. The *Liste* contains thirteen minuscules that possibly date to the 9th century. The proliferation of minuscules in that century implies that the use of minuscule script to copy Scripture has still earlier origins. The first dated minuscule of the NT is minuscule 461, which was dated by its scribe to the year 835. The shift to minuscule script significantly reduced the amount of time and material required to produce a copy of the NT. Although majuscule script continued to be used for several more centuries, by the 10th century, minuscules significantly outnumbered majuscules. The vast majority of the Greek manuscripts of the NT now extant were copied in minuscule script. Metzger noted that "The minuscule manuscripts of the New Testament outnumber the majuscule manuscripts by more than ten to one."[65]

Although the early majuscules have significant differences that make it difficult to classify them into various families, the minuscules exhibit greater similarity. Manuscripts from the second millennium are usually remarkably similar and contain a standardized form of text known as the Koine or Byzantine text. Byzantine text advocates argue that this text, contained in the vast majority of late manuscripts, is generally the original text. Many of the readings of the Koine text existed early. Gordon Fee found that John Chrysostom's Greek text "had a text probably 75 percent along the way toward that resultant text-type."[66] More recent studies have tended to confirm Fee's findings.[67] Strands of Byzantine tradition can be found in some 6th- and even 5th-century majuscules (e.g., A Q N O Σ Φ).[68]

Nevertheless, if the Byzantine text were the original text, one would expect this form of the text to be preserved in the majority of early manuscripts and not merely the majority of late manuscripts. However, this form of the text does not become the majority until after the 9th century. Even Photius, the Patriarch of Constantinople (858–867, 877–886), did not normally cite the Koine form of the text.[69] The historical evidence suggests that the standardization of this particular form of the text is associated with the shift to minuscule script, a process known as μεταχαρακτηρισμός. Based on statements made by Jerome about a recension of the Greek text by Lucian, scholars once attributed the origin of the

---

65. Metzger and Ehrman, *Text of the New Testament*, 21.

66. Gordon D. Fee, "The Text of John and Mark in the Writings of Chrysostom," *NTS* 26 (1980): 525–47, here 547.

67. Barbara Aland and Klaus Wachtel, "The Greek Minuscules of the New Testament," in Ehrman and Holmes, *Text of the New Testament in Contemporary Research*, 71n8.

68. These manuscripts may be located in the *Liste* using their Gregory-Aland numbers, which are 02, 026, 022, 023, 042, and 043, respectively. Appendix I in the NA[28] contains tables listing the majuscules by their traditional symbols and identifying their matching Gregory-Aland numbers.

69. See the three-part essay, J. N. Birdsall, "The Text of the Gospels in Photius," *JTS* 7 (1956): 42–55, 190–98; 9 (1958): 278–91.

Byzantine text-type to Lucian's editorial activity.[70] But even scholars like Barbara Aland, who once affirmed this theory, have since abandoned it.[71]

Although most of the minuscule manuscripts preserve the Byzantine text-type, some manuscripts so closely resemble one another as to constitute a distinct family within the larger text-type. The most important of these families are Family 1 and Family 13. In the UBS and NA editions, families are designated with an italic "f" followed by a superscript number.

Family 1 was identified in 1902 by Kirsopp Lake. It includes minuscules 1, 118, 131, 209, and 1582, which range in date from the 10th to the 14th centuries. Despite the name of this group, 1582 is the leading member. This text was copied by the monk Ephraim and has a text similar to the one used by Origen.[72] Its text of Mark is similar to the 9th-century Codex Koridethi (Θ).

Family 13 was identified in 1868 by William Ferrar. Although Ferrar only noted the close relationship between four medieval manuscripts (13, 69, 124, and 346), later studies identified other members of the family including 230, 543, 788, 826, 983, 1689, and 1709. One of the distinctives of this family is its placement of the story about the adulterous woman (John 7:53–8:11) after Luke 21:38. A recent study identified 788 as the member of the group closest to the archetype.[73]

Of the thousands of minuscule manuscripts available today, two deserve special mention. Minuscule 33 is widely known as the "queen of the cursives" since the 9th-century codex largely preserves a very early and reliable text of the Gospels and General Epistles. Its text of Paul and Acts contains some Byzantine readings.

Minuscule 1739 is a 10th-century manuscript that originally contained all of the NT except Revelation, although now only Acts, Paul's letters, and the General Epistles survive.[74] A colophon identifies the scribe who copied the manuscript as Ephraim. The manuscript has marginal notes from several early Greek church fathers: Irenaeus, Clement, Origen,

---

70. Jerome's statement appears in *Patrologia Latina* 29, col. 527. For an example of a recent scholar who affirms the theory of Lucian's recension, see Comfort, *Encountering the Manuscripts*, 275 and 278. Comfort cites F. F. Bruce in support, but Bruce characterized his statement as merely a "guess" that he "hazarded." For arguments against the theory, see H. C. Brennecke, "Lucian von Antiochien," *TRE* 21 (Berlin: de Gruyter, 1991), 478.

71. See Aland and Wachtel, "Greek Minuscules," 71n7.

72. Amy S. Anderson, *The Textual Tradition of the Gospels: Family 1 in Matthew*, NTTS 32 (Boston: Brill, 2004). Several scholars have shown that the family consists of more manuscripts than those identified by Lake. See Alison Sarah Welsby, *A Textual Study of Family 1 in the Gospel of John*, ANTF 45 (New York: de Gruyter, 2013); and Amy S. Anderson, "Family 1 in Mark: Preliminary Results," in *Early Readers, Scholars, and Editors of the New Testament: Papers from the Eighth Birmingham Colloquium on the Textual Criticism of the New Testament*, ed. H. A. G. Houghton, TS 3.11 (Piscataway, NJ: Gorgias, 2014), 119–61.

73. Didier Lafleur, *La Famille 13 dans l'évangile de Marc*, NTTSD 41 (Leiden: Brill, 2013). See also Jac D. Perrin, *Family 13 in St. John's Gospel: A Computer Assisted Phylogenetic Analysis*, NTTSD 58 (Leiden: Brill, 2019).

74. Kirsopp Lake and Silva New, *Six Collations of New Testament Manuscripts*, HTS 17 (Cambridge: Harvard University Press, 1932), 142.

Eusebius, and Basil. The ancestor of 1739 was copied sometime after Basil's death in 379. However, that ancestor must have been relatively early since a note on Jas 2:13 refers to a manuscript written by Eusebius of Caesarea "with his own hand." A mutilated note on Gal 5:15 refers to a manuscript written in prison, possibly the manuscript written by Pamphilus mentioned in the colophon in Codex Sinaiticus (01). A note also indicates that the "very ancient codex" from which the exemplar of 1739 was copied contained Origen's text. This was confirmed by the early scribe's comparison of the codex to Origen's commentary. The scribe who compiled the exemplar drew his text of Romans from quotations in Origen's commentary, though he continued to consult his ancient codex. These features suggest that the ancestor of 1739 may have been produced in Caesarea. Günther Zuntz pointed out that although the text of Romans in 1739 essentially preserves Origen's text, the rest of the text in 1739 was from a manuscript as old as, or even older than, Origen's text.[75]

Zuntz demonstrated that 1739 preserved "rare, ancient readings" that proved it was "a faithful representative of its archetype and therewith of the παλαιόν which served as its model."[76] In particular, Zuntz noted important agreements of 1739 with $\mathfrak{P}^{46}$ and B (03). An example was 1739's omission of the phrase ἐν Ἐφέσῳ in Eph 1:1. Of the minuscules known to Zuntz, only 1739 supported the omission and stood in agreement with $\mathfrak{P}^{46}$, ℵ, B, Origen, Basil, and Marcion.[77] This manuscript demonstrates that a late manuscript may preserve very early readings. Thus, the minuscules cannot be ignored simply due to their age.

2.4. Lectionaries

Lectionaries are NT texts in which the text is segmented, portions are rearranged, and each portion is assigned for reading on specific days of the year. A complete lectionary contains two distinct sets of assigned readings. A *synaxarion* assigns Scripture readings according to the days of the church year, which begins at Easter (a moveable holiday). A *menologion* assigns Scripture readings beginning on September 1, the first day of the year in the civil calendar of the Byzantine Empire. A *menologion* celebrates the great feast days and honors the apostles, the family of Jesus, and many respected saints. In addition to the assigned readings from the NT, a *menologion* also includes accounts of the lives and martyrdom of the saints, as well as selections from other ancient texts, such as the Protevangelium of James.[78] About half of the extant manuscripts of the Greek NT are lectionaries. Although the *Liste* currently enumerates lectionaries up to 2,571, dozens of these were accidentally listed multiple times, and in some cases fragments were errone-

---

75. Günther Zuntz, *The Text of the Epistles: A Disquisition upon the Corpus Paulinum* (British Academy, 1953; repr., Eugene, OR: Wipf & Stock, 2007), 81.

76. Zuntz, *Text of the Epistles*, 81.

77. Minuscule 6 (13th c.) and the correction in 424 also support the omission.

78. Parker, *Introduction to the New Testament Manuscripts*, 56–57. One of the most helpful introductions to lectionaries is still Scrivener, *Plain Introduction to the Criticism of the New Testament*, 1:74–77, 80–89.

ously combined with others, so the actual number is around 2,437.[79] Unfortunately, the lectionaries have not been adequately studied, and no critical edition of the lectionaries has been published.[80] Although scholars sometimes dismiss their importance for the reconstruction of the original text,[81] Carroll Osburn wrote more cautiously: "While it is evident that lectionaries have much to contribute to the later NT MS tradition, much remains to be done in clarifying the value of lectionaries for understanding better the earlier forms of the textual tradition."[82]

2.5. Early Versions

Beginning in the 2nd and 3rd centuries, Christians began translating the Greek NT into Syriac, Latin, and Coptic. Since scholars can sometimes infer the readings in the Greek text that serve as the basis for the translation, in some cases these early versions provide helpful information about the early text of the NT that supplements what can be known from Greek manuscripts alone. Although the provenance of most of our early Greek manuscripts is unknown, the provenance of the early versions is sometimes obvious. Thus, the early versions can assist in determining the geographical distribution of a reading in the manner discussed in Part Two.

Attempting to reconstruct the Greek text used in these translations is challenging. The early versions will usually show if a phrase or even a word was present in the Greek text used for the translation, but they may not reveal some of the important grammatical details of the underlying Greek text. The grammar of the languages of the early versions is sometimes different enough from Greek grammar that we cannot confidently reconstruct the Greek text behind the translation.[83] Furthermore, ancient translators (like modern translators) had different approaches to translation. Most did not attempt a strict word-for-word translation. The translations often made explicit what was merely implicit in the Greek text and thus interpreted the meaning (correctly or incorrectly) of the Greek text for their readers.[84] They often paraphrased rather than seeking to compose a literal translation. Agreement between a version and a manuscript may result from a Greek copyist who felt the freedom to clarify the text and a translator independently interpreting the text in a

---

79. As of June 2024. Duplicates and recombined portions are identified by red font in the online *Liste*.

80. A critical edition of the lectionaries has been proposed and is currently under development. See Gregory S. Paulson, "A Proposal for a Critical Edition of the Greek New Testament Lectionary," in *Liturgy and the Living Text of the New Testament: Papers from the Tenth Birmingham Colloquium on the Textual Criticism of the New Testament*, ed. H. A. G. Houghton, TS 3.16 (Piscataway, NJ: Gorgias, 2018), 121–50.

81. See, for example, Aland and Aland, *Text of the New Testament*, 169.

82. Carroll Osburn, "The Greek Lectionaries of the New Testament," in Ehrman and Holmes, *Text of the New Testament in Contemporary Research*, 109.

83. For examples, see Metzger and Ehrman, *Text of the New Testament*, 95.

84. For an introduction to several categories of explication, see Christian Askeland, *John's Gospel: The Coptic Translations of Its Greek Text*, ANTF 44 (Boston: de Gruyter, 2012), 9–10.

similar way rather than sharing the same Greek source.[85] Thus, versions should be cited as witnesses to a reading in the Greek text with caution.

The UBS[5] and NA[28] cite evidence from the early versions in instances where the underlying Greek text can be reconstructed with a high degree of probability. Both editions place evidence from the early versions immediately after Greek manuscripts and before references to the church fathers in the apparatus. The NA[28] appropriately emphasizes the Latin, Syriac, and Coptic versions since these "were unquestionably made directly from the Greek and at an early period."[86] The UBS[5] also includes evidence from the Armenian, Georgian, Ethiopic, and Old Church Slavonic versions. The editors of the NA[28] state: "The versions still enjoy an important role in critical decisions because they represent Greek witnesses of an early period. But their value for scholarship today in comparison with earlier generations has been modified by the great number of Greek manuscripts on papyrus and parchment discovered in the twentieth century."[87]

2.6. Early Church Fathers

Early Christians often quoted the NT in their sermons, commentaries, and theological treatises. These early quotations are helpful evidence for reconstructing the original text. Although the provenance of most of our early Greek manuscripts is unknown, we can often pinpoint where and when a church father wrote. This helps in determining the geographical distribution of a particular reading at a specific time. The apparatuses of modern critical editions cite a church father in support of a particular reading "only if they can be considered reliable witnesses to the text of the manuscripts quoted."[88]

To use the church fathers to date and localize particular readings, scholars must make sure that the father is quoting a text as he read it rather than from memory, and that the father intended to give a verbatim quotation rather than a paraphrase. Since the writings of the church fathers have gone through the same lengthy process of hand-copying as the NT text, scholars must use a reliable critical edition of these works to make sure that a later copyist did not conform a father's quotations to the form of the text current in the copyist's own time. Unfortunately, good critical editions of the works of the church fathers do not always exist.

The church fathers are especially helpful on those occasions when they explicitly discuss textual variants that appear in the manuscripts available to them.[89] The readings that the fathers describe as contained in many or most of the ancient manuscripts may be pre-

---

85. See Askeland, *John's Gospel*, 44; Parker, *Codex Bezae*, 258.

86. NA[28], 67*.

87. NA[28], 68*. For detailed introductions to the important versions of the New Testament, see Ehrman and Holmes, *Text of the New Testament in Contemporary Research*, 115–350.

88. NA[28], 78*.

89. For a helpful exploration of discussions of textual variants by the early church fathers, see Amy M. Donaldson, "Explicit References to New Testament Variant Readings among Greek and Latin Church Fathers," 2 vols. (PhD diss., Graduate School of the University of Notre Dame, 2009).

served in only a few of the manuscripts extant today. This is a helpful reminder that only a tiny fraction of the manuscripts from the earliest centuries of the church have survived and that today's majority reading may once have been a minority reading.[90]

Both the NA[28] and the UBS[5] cite church fathers in their apparatuses. However, the UBS[5] does so far more frequently and extensively. Both list patristic evidence after the versional evidence in the apparatus.

---

90. For helpful introductions to the use of the church fathers in textual criticism, see Ehrman and Holmes, *Text of the New Testament in Contemporary Research*, 351–427.

3

Approaches to New Testament Textual Criticism

Scholars have used several different approaches to textual criticism. Among the most important are the Majority Text approach and reasoned eclecticism. Interestingly, those who utilize these different approaches still agree on the wording of the vast majority of the NT. Although the Majority Text approach and reasoned eclecticism are fundamentally different, the text of Acts reconstructed by reasoned eclectics and the text of Acts established in the Majority Text approach agree on 91.52 percent of variant units! Similarly, the texts of Mark established by the two different methods agree on 88.71 percent of variant units.

Nevertheless, the method that one chooses to apply will lead to different conclusions about the remaining 10 percent or so of the NT text. The choice of method does have significant ramifications. This section will briefly introduce these two major methods of NT textual criticism and explain their strengths and weaknesses.

3.1. Majority Text Approach

Some scholars believe that the original text is to be found in the consensus of the surviving manuscripts. This is often described as the Majority Text (MT) approach because in this approach, the reading supported by the majority of the Greek manuscripts is ordinarily the accepted reading.[1] Since the vast majority of extant Greek manuscripts belong to the Byzantine textform, the MT approach is sometimes called the Byzantine Priority approach.

The origins of the MT approach may be traced to the writings of John Burgon. Burgon was alarmed by the departures of the Westcott and Hort edition of the Greek NT from the "Traditional Text."[2] By "Traditional Text," Burgon did not mean the Textus Receptus. Instead, he meant "the text founded upon the vast majority of authorities," which differed

---

1. The use of MT as an abbreviation for "Majority Text" in NT textual studies should not be confused with the convention in OT textual criticism that uses MT for "Masoretic Text."

2. John Burgon, *The Revision Revised* (London: John Murray, 1883). The Westcott and Hort edition was published in 1881 under the title *The New Testament in the Original Greek*. The edition largely following readings in the two oldest majuscules, Vaticanus and Sinaiticus.

from the Textus Receptus at some 150 places in the Gospel of Matthew alone.[3] Burgon appealed to two theological principles to defend the Traditional Text. First, he argued that God's providence ensured the preservation of the Holy Scriptures.[4] Second, he argued that ecclesiastical authority, the same authority of the church that established the NT canon, had protected and approved the Traditional Text so that late manuscripts were guaranteed to preserve the reading of the original with very little modification.[5]

Burgon's method relied on "seven notes of truth," which are antiquity, number, variety, respectability, continuity, context, and reasonableness.[6] Many of these categories are similar to the criteria used by other scholars. However, Burgon approached several of these categories very differently. For example, although "antiquity" was the first note of truth Burgon listed, he objected to methods that first sought the original reading in the oldest Greek manuscripts (as Westcott and Hort had often done in their edition). He insisted on a method that relied on "the whole body of documents" or "the entire mass of ancient witnesses" rather than a mere "fragment of Antiquity arbitrarily broken off."[7] He argued that the major majuscules like Vaticanus and Sinaiticus had survived only because they were "refuse copies" that "were anciently recognized as untrustworthy documents."[8] He also rejected the old maxim that witnesses are to be weighed, not merely counted. He objected that "'number' is the most ordinary ingredient of weight."[9] He concluded:

> When therefore the great bulk of the witnesses,—in the proportion suppose of a hundred or even fifty to one,—yield unfaltering testimony to a certain reading; and the remaining little handful of authorities, while advocating a different reading, are yet observed to be unable to agree among themselves as to what that different reading shall precisely be,—then that other reading concerning which all that discrepancy of detail is observed to exist, may be regarded as certainly false.[10]

Nearly a century later, Zane Hodges and Arthur Farstad revived Burgon's theories and approach and published *The Greek New Testament according to the Majority Text*.[11] The authors plainly stated the rationale for the approach: "Any reading overwhelmingly

---

3. John Burgon and Edward Miller, *The Traditional Text of the Holy Gospels Vindicated and Established* (London: George Bell and Sons, 1896), 5, 13, 15.

4. Burgon and Miller, *The Traditional Text*, 11–12.

5. Burgon and Miller, *The Traditional Text*, 13–14.

6. Burgon and Miller, *The Traditional Text*, 40–67.

7. Burgon and Miller, *The Traditional Text*, 31.

8. Burgon and Miller, *The Traditional Text*, 36. Burgon later acknowledged (p. 41), however, that as a general rule "a single early Uncial possesses more authority than a single later Uncial or Cursive" but added that "a still earlier Version or Quotation by a Father must be placed before the reading of the early Uncial." The use of the adjective "single" in reference to later manuscripts is very important. In Burgon's method, the authority of multiple cursive (late) manuscripts overrode preference for a single majuscule (early) manuscript.

9. Burgon and Miller, *The Traditional Text*, 43.

10. Burgon and Miller, *The Traditional Text*, 47.

11. Zane C. Hodges and Arthur Farstad, *The Greek New Testament according to the Majority Text* (Nashville: Thomas Nelson, 1982).

attested by the manuscript tradition is more likely to be original than its rivals."[12] The editors argued that the early manuscripts (Sinaiticus, Vaticanus, and early papyri) are strictly from Egypt, the only place with the climate favorable to the preservation of such ancient manuscripts. These manuscripts merely preserve a "local text," a text known and respected almost exclusively in Egypt. However, the witnesses to the MT were from all over the world and must "represent a long and widespread chain of manuscript tradition."[13] The wide distribution of this type of text showed that the later manuscripts "are descended from nonextant ancestral documents of the highest antiquity."[14]

The zenith of the MT approach was the 1991 publication of *The New Testament in the Original Greek: Byzantine Textform* by William Pierpont and Maurice Robinson.[15] Robinson has emerged as "the most articulate, prolific, and able defender of the MT position."[16] Like Burgon, Pierpont and Robinson appeal to the doctrine of preservation to support their approach: "[T]his revelation has been kept pure in all ages by the singular care and providence of God."[17] However, they argue more extensively that statistical probability ensured that the text of the consensus of manuscripts would preserve the original text:

> From a transmissional standpoint, a single Textform would be expected to predominate among the vast majority of manuscripts in the absence of radical and well-documented upheavals in the manuscript tradition. This 'normal' state of transmission assumes that the aggregate consentient testimony of the extant manuscript base is more likely to reflect its archetypal source (in this case the canonical autographs) than any single manuscript, small group of manuscripts, or isolated versional or patristic readings that failed to achieve widespread diversity or transmissional continuity.[18]

---

12. Hodges and Farstad, *Majority Text*, ix.

13. Hodges and Farstad, *Majority Text*, ix.

14. Hodges and Farstad, *Majority Text*, x. A second premise of the method is "Final decisions about readings ought to be made on the basis of a reconstruction of their history in the manuscript tradition" (xii). This required developing a genealogy of manuscripts for each NT book. However, the editors supplied a primitive genealogy only for John 7:53–8:11 and the book of Revelation, and they admitted that stemmatic work for most of the NT "is not yet feasible" (xiii).

15. The original publication was Maurice A. Robinson, William G. Pierpont, and William McBrayer, eds., *The New Testament in the Original Greek: According to the Byzantine/Majority Textform* (Atlanta, GA: Original Word, 1991). The most recent edition is Maurice A. Robinson and William G. Pierpont, *The New Testament in the Original Greek: Byzantine Textform 2018* (Nuremberg: VTR Publications, 2018). This edition lacks the detailed defense of Byzantine priority that appeared in pre-2016 editions since it is now available in Maurice A. Robinson, "The Case for Byzantine Priority," *TC* 6 (2001).

16. Daniel B. Wallace, "The Majority Text Theory: History, Methods, and Critique," in Ehrman and Holmes, *Text of the New Testament in Contemporary Research*, 711–44, here 722n46.

17. Maurice A. Robinson and William G. Pierpont, *The New Testament in the Original Greek: Byzantine Textform 2005* (Southborough, MA: Chilton Book Publishing, 2005), xxi. These "Concluding Observations" were omitted from the preface in the 2018 edition.

18. Robinson and Pierpont, *Byzantine Textform 2005*, v. Westcott and Hort affirmed the "theoretical presupposition" that "a majority of extant documents is more likely to represent a majority of

Despite the claims of these volumes to preserve the MT or the "consensus text,"[19] the true MT for the entire NT is not currently known. These editions are heavily dependent on the extensive apparatus in the two-volume Greek NT by Hermann Freiherr von Soden published in 1913 and other sources.[20] However, neither von Soden nor any scholar since has completely collated every known Greek manuscript of every NT book in order to identify the consensus text. The editions of the MT are based on selected groups of Byzantine manuscripts, not on a comparison of all extant manuscripts.[21] Gregory Paulson highlighted the problem:

> The major flaw of the reconstructed text of 𝔐 [the Majority Text in the NA[26–27] editions], HF [Hodges and Farstad], and RP [Robinson and Pierpoint] is dependency on von Soden: his MS collations are not complete and his MS groups are not based on systematic analysis. The solution to discovering the Byzantine text, its representatives, and its groups is to have full collations of all MSS and a way to manage the large amount of data, which is the practice of the ECM [*Editio Critica Maior*]. From full collations and consistent, scientific principles, it is possible to redefine von Soden's groups and provide an accurate apparatus that can display the textual history of the Byzantine text.[22]

Robinson and Pierpont argue that the primary basis for identifying the original text in their method is "non-quantitative":

> Although the far greater numerical quantity of Byzantine manuscripts (approaching 80%) exists among the documents of the twelfth and later centuries, the readings of

---

ancestral documents at each stage of transmission" (*Introduction to the New Testament*, 45). However, they argued that "the smallest tangible evidence of other kinds" outweighs this presumption and that the presumption "falls to the ground" when one considers the impossibility of determining how many copies were made of each individual ancestor or how many of the copies made were preserved to be copied in a future age.

19. Although the original title used the term "Majority Textform," in later editions (e.g., *The New Testament in the Original Greek: Byzantine Textform 2005*, i–xxiii) Robinson and Pierpont abandon the term and prefer to use the terms "consensus text" (4x), "dominant text," "dominant consensus text," "Koine Greek archetype," "Byzantine Consensus Text," "mutual consensus text," "general consensus text," "basic consensus text," "consensus-based text," and the "preserved Greek transmissional consensus."

20. Hermann Freiherr von Soden, *Die Schriften des Neues Testaments in ihrer ältesten erreichbaren Textgestalt hergestellt auf Grund ihrer Textgeschichte*, I. Teil, *Untersuchungen* (Berlin: A. Glaue, 1902–1913); II. Teil, *Text mit Apparat* (Göttingen: Vandenhoeck & Ruprecht, 1913).

21. This is also true of the Majority Text used for comparison in the Coherence-Based Genealogical Method (CBGM). Although the online tools use the label "MT," the readings of this text were not selected by majority consensus but taken from a few dozen witnesses deemed to represent "nearly pure Byzantine manuscripts." See Aland et al., eds., *Catholic Letters*, vol. 4 of *Novum Testamentum Graece: Editio Critica Maior* (Stuttgart: Deutsche Bibelgesellschaft, 2013), 2:15–17. The Editio Critica Maior (ECM) used fifty-two witnesses for 1 John and thirty-eight for 2–3 John in identifying the Byzantine text (Byz).

22. Gregory S. Paulson, "An Investigation of the Byzantine Text of the Johannine Epistles," *RevExp* 114 (2017): 589.

the Byzantine Textform almost always are fully established from the earlier Byzantine lines of transmission that extend through the eleventh century. The documents of the twelfth and later centuries generally are irrelevant to the establishment of primary Byzantine readings, and at best serve only a confirmatory purpose.[23]

However, Robinson and Pierpont later state "A consensus-based text – derived from the entire body of extant Greek witnesses – is fully compatible with the concept of a benevolent overarching providence that has maintained the autographs in their basic integrity by means of normal transmission." Thus, this text is not yet a true "consensus text" based on an evaluation of the entire body of evidence, however massive that body of evidence. Current editions must be viewed as mere approximations of the consensus text.

Although the Byzantine text is important and its readings should be carefully considered when making text-critical decisions, most scholars are not convinced that it provides the only key to reconstructing the original text. First and most importantly, there is no evidence supporting the existence of the Byzantine textform in the earliest manuscripts, the earliest versions, or the church fathers of the first three centuries.[24] Wallace posed a reasonable question: If the Byzantine text preserves the original text, "would we not expect to see at least some early papyri (let alone a majority of them) with a distinctively Byzantine text form?"[25] Although a few isolated Byzantine readings appear in the papyri, none of the early papyri have a consistent pattern of Byzantine readings.

Harry Sturz located 150 distinctively Byzantine readings in the early Egyptian papyri.[26] Space will not permit a detailed discussion of each of these. Other scholars have pointed out that the vast majority of the Byzantine readings are the types of variants that scribes commonly introduced, so these could be examples of coincidental agreements in readings rather than an indication of dependence on an early Byzantine exemplar.[27] Hurtado's critique is on point: "[C]ertainly some Byzantine readings are attested in the early papyri. But is this proof of the early existence of the Byzantine text-type, or is it only an indication that some of the scribal tendencies reflected in the Byzantine MSS had early beginnings?"[28]

---

23. Robinson and Pierpont, *Byzantine Textform 2005*, xiv.

24. The first known source to cite a text very similar to the later Byzantine text was the Arian rhetorician Asterius the Sophist (d. after 341). The first church father to consistently cite a text similar to the later Byzantine text was John Chrysostom, bishop of Antioch and later of Constantinople. Gordon D. Fee ("The Use of Greek Patristic Citations in New Testament Textual Criticism: The State of the Question," in *Studies in the Theory and Method of New Testament Textual Criticism*, ed., Eldon J. Epp and Gordon D. Fee, SD 45 [Grand Rapids: Eerdmans, 1993], 358–59) suggests that the text cited by Chrysostom was "about seventy-five percent along the way to the text that would eventually dominate in the Greek church—probably very much under the influence of Chrysostom himself."

25. Wallace, "Majority Text Theory," 731.

26. Harry A. Sturz, *The Byzantine Text-Type and New Testament Textual Criticism* (Nashville: Thomas Nelson, 1984), 145–59.

27. See Wallace, "Majority Text Theory," 718–19n35; and Michael W. Holmes, review of *The Byzantine Text-Type and New Testament Textual Criticism*, by Harry A. Sturz, *TrinJ* 6 (1985): 225–28.

28. Larry W. Hurtado, review of *The Byzantine Text-Type and New Testament Textual Criticism*, by Harry A. Sturz, *CBQ* 48 (1986): 150.

In the Gospel of Mark, Sturz finds eighteen Byzantine readings in $\mathfrak{P}^{45}$. However, the data produced in the creation of the ECM of Mark reveals that $\mathfrak{P}^{45}$ agrees with the MT in 80.59 percent of variant units, with Vaticanus (03) in 81.45 percent, and with Sinaiticus in 79.36 percent. Vaticanus agrees with the MT in Mark in 84.43 percent of variant units. Thus, $\mathfrak{P}^{45}$ agrees with the MT significantly less often than Vaticanus does! Yet no textual critic views Vaticanus as a witness to the Byzantine text.

In Acts, all of the Byzantine readings found by Sturz, except one, are from $\mathfrak{P}^{45}$. In Acts, $\mathfrak{P}^{45}$ agrees with the MT in 83.73 percent of variant units, with Vaticanus in 86.53 percent, and with Sinaiticus in 85.21 percent. Yet, Vaticanus agrees with the MT in 87.47 percent of the variant units in Acts. So, once again, Vaticanus is more similar to the MT than $\mathfrak{P}^{45}$ is!

In the Catholic Letters, the only papyrus that agrees with the MT more frequently than with Vaticanus is $\mathfrak{P}^{23}$. $\mathfrak{P}^{23}$ agrees with the MT in 97.87 percent of the variant units and with Vaticanus in 95.92 percent. However, $\mathfrak{P}^{23}$ is a small fragment consisting of only Jas 1:10–12, 15–16, a portion of James with only forty-nine variant units. $\mathfrak{P}^{23}$ agrees with the MT in all but one variant unit and with Vaticanus in all but two. The portion of James in $\mathfrak{P}^{23}$ happens to be a section with remarkable agreement between Vaticanus and the MT. The two disagreements between $\mathfrak{P}^{23}$ and Vaticanus involve Vaticanus's accidental omission of αὐτοῦ (due to haplography) after προσώπου in Jas 1:11, and variant unit 40–60 in Jas 1:17 where $\mathfrak{P}^{23}$ also differs from the Byzantine textform.[29]

Admittedly, the complete lack of evidence for the existence of the Byzantine text in the first three centuries does not constitute proof that the Byzantine text did not yet exist. After all, absence of evidence is not evidence of absence. Yet, this lack of evidence for the existence of the Byzantine text in the early period does place a greater burden of proof on MT advocates. Unless Byzantine priorists can offer persuasive explanations for the complete disappearance of early Byzantine manuscripts, the position seems untenable. So far, no satisfactory explanation for this disappearance has been offered.

Some proponents of the theory argue that no early Byzantine manuscripts are extant because all the papyri and early majuscules that survived were from Egypt where the climate was conducive to their preservation. They further argue that "the Egyptian text" (the text found in Vaticanus, Sinaiticus, and their close relatives) was a text whose "existence in early times outside of Egypt is unproved."[30] However, evidence for the existence of the Egyptian text outside of Egypt in the early period is strong. Zuntz demonstrated the archetype of MS 1739 was a very ancient text of Paul's letters that was "as old as, or even older than" Origen.[31] Based on the evidence of two scribal notes, this old manuscript probably

---

29. This variant unit could have been divided into two units. $\mathfrak{P}^{23}$ has the singular reading παραλλαγης while both Codex B and the MT have παραλλαγη. However, $\mathfrak{P}^{23}$ agrees with B on the reading αποσκιασματος where the Byzantine textform correctly has αποσκιασμα. If this had been considered two variant units rather than merely one, $\mathfrak{P}^{23}$ would have equal levels of agreement with both MT and B. Furthermore, if the variant units were divided in this way, B would be judged to have as much agreement with the MT as $\mathfrak{P}^{23}$ does.

30. Hodges and Farstad, *Majority Text,* ix.

31. Zuntz, *Text of the Epistles,* 81.

came from the library of Pamphilus in Caesarea.[32] The text of the old manuscript closely resembles the text of Vaticanus and $\mathfrak{P}^{46}$. A good case can be made that both Vaticanus and Sinaiticus were copied at Caesarea and, if so, this suggests that the so-called Egyptian text could be found in Caesarea prior to the 4th century (assuming that the exemplars from which each was copied were several decades older).[33] Majuscule 015 is a 6th-century manuscript of Paul's letters. A scribal note at the end of Titus states that the text was corrected from a copy in the library of Caesarea that was written in the hand of Pamphilus and must have predated Pamphilus's martyrdom in February of 309. Thus, several manuscripts suggest that the "Egyptian text" was in Caesarea during the 3rd century. Even if the existence of the "Egyptian text" outside of Egypt in the first three centuries could not be proved, the fact remains that the existence of the Byzantine text *anywhere* in the first three or four centuries is unproven. Although most of the early papyri were indeed found in Egypt, a wide variety of different texts has been found there. However, the Byzantine text is strikingly absent.

Some MT advocates argue that two great copying revolutions resulted in the loss and destruction of the exemplars from which the early minuscule manuscripts were copied. These revolutions were the shift from papyrus to parchment in the early 4th century and the shift from majuscule to minuscule script in the 9th century. Majority Text theorists claim that the exemplars that had been copied using the new material or script were destroyed: "Once copied, the uncial exemplars were apparently disassembled and utilized for scrap and secular purposes, or washed and scraped and reused for palimpsest works both sacred and secular."[34] However, the disclaimer "apparently" in this statement is very important. The statement is based on a hypothesis of the textual scholar Kirsopp Lake.[35] So far, scholars have not found a single reference to the practice of destroying or erasing majuscules after minuscule copies were produced in any of the ancient literary descriptions of the work of the scribes. In fact, solid evidence counters this claim since we have approximately twenty-three *Abschriften*, manuscripts with an identified *and extant* exemplar. These include four majuscules that are copies of known majuscules, three minuscules that are copies of known majuscules, and sixteen minuscules that are copies of known minuscules.[36] Especially important is minuscule 2110, a 10th-century copy of a 9th-century majuscule. This copy was produced during the second great copying revolution, but the exemplar was still preserved. We must not assume that the practice

---

32. Lake and New, *Six Collations of New Testament Manuscripts*, 144–45.

33. See the discussion of these two manuscripts under 2.2 Majuscules, above.

34. Robinson and Pierpont, *Byzantine Textform 2005*, 561.

35. Lake attempted to explain (1) why few manuscripts dating to before the 10th c. survived in the monastic collections, (2) why no known exemplars of the Byzantine manuscripts were extant, and (3) why so few sibling manuscripts exist. Although Lake's hypothesis is a satisfactory explanation of observations 1 and 2, it fails to explain 3. D. A. Carson (*The King James Debate: A Plea for Realism* [Grand Rapids: Baker Academic, 1978], 47n5) rightly calls Lake's view "a hypothesis built on silence."

36. Alan Taylor Farnes, *Simply Come Copying: Direct Copies as Test Cases in the Quest for Scribal Habits*, WUNT 2.481 (Tübingen: Mohr Siebeck, 2019), 24–29.

of the scribes was "out with the old, in with the new." The great copying revolutions do not provide an adequate explanation for the absence of any evidence for the Byzantine textform in the early period.

Wallace summarized the evidence well:

> The combined testimony of the external evidence—virtually the only evidence that the MT defenders consider—is that the Byzantine text apparently did not exist in the first three centuries. The Greek MSS, the versions, and the Church Fathers provide a threefold cord not easily broken. Although isolated Byzantine readings have been located, the Byzantine text has not.[37]

Wallace noted: "As far as the *extant* MSS reveal, the Byzantine text did not become a majority until the ninth century (although *historically* it probably became a majority several centuries earlier)."[38] Strong evidence indicates that the late manuscripts that constitute the vast majority of our NT witnesses do not preserve the majority readings from the early period. Explicit statements in the early church fathers confirm this claim. For example, no extant minuscule text of the Gospel of Mark ends at Mark 16:8.[39] However, in the early 4th century Eusebius observed that "more or less all the copies" of Mark known to him lacked the longer ending—the ending that would later dominate the minuscule text.[40] In Eusebius's day, the longer ending found in the vast majority of the manuscripts extant today was found in only a small minority of manuscripts. Eusebius was familiar with the holdings of the Christian library in Jerusalem and supervised the even more important Christian library in Caesarea.[41] He was probably as familiar with the various readings of manuscripts circulating in his time as anyone. A century later, Jerome confirmed Eusebius's statement.[42] In this extreme case, the MT in the early centuries appears to have had a major difference from the unanimous testimony of the minuscules!

For these reasons (and others),[43] few scholars believe that the MT approach is the best path to the restoration of the original text of the NT. Most scholars are convinced that another approach, called "reasoned eclecticism," is the most sensible approach to deciding the reading of the original text when different readings appear in the manuscripts.

---

37. Wallace, "Majority Text Theory," 733.

38. Wallace, "Majority Text Theory," 727 [emphasis original].

39. H. A. G. Houghton ("Unfinished Business: The Ending of Mark in Two Catena Manuscripts," *NTS* 69 [2023]: 42) demonstrated that minuscule 305 is not a witness to the short ending and concluded: "In sum, there are no known Greek minuscule manuscripts which only preserve the Short Ending of Mark."

40. Eusebius, *Quaestiones ad Marinum* 1.1.

41. For a helpful discussion of these two major early Christian libraries and Eusebius's access to them, see Gamble, *Books and Readers in the Early Church*, 154–61.

42. Jerome, *Epist.* 120. Jerome claims that "almost all the Greek codices lack it [the ending of Mark containing what is now known as Mark 16:9–11 quoted in Hedibia's letter]."

43. For other problems with the Majority Text view, see Quarles and Kellum, *40 Questions about the Text and Canon*, 129–36; and Wallace, "Majority Text Theory," 725–38.

3.2. Reasoned Eclecticism

Most NT scholars (and textual critics of the NT) use an approach called "reasoned eclecticism." The word "eclecticism" is derived from the Greek verb ἐκλέγομαι, which means "to select." This name is appropriate because the method does not presume to find the original reading in one manuscript or group of manuscripts. Instead, it recognizes that the reading must be selected from different texts in different manuscripts. The adjective "reasoned" distinguishes this method from "thoroughgoing eclecticism."[44] The major contemporary proponent of this approach, J. Keith Elliott,[45] explains that "Thoroughgoing text critics prefer to edit a text by solving textual variation with an appeal primarily to purely internal considerations."[46] These "internal considerations" refer to the evidence in the individual readings themselves. Elliott explained:

> When confronted by textual variants in the Greek New Testament, the thoroughgoing critic asks the following questions: Which reading best accounts for the rise of the other variants? Which reading is the likeliest to have suffered change at the hands of early copyists? Which reading is in keeping with the style and thought of the author and makes best sense in the context? These considerations, rather than concerns about the weight, provenance, and the alleged authority of the manuscripts supporting the variant, are the important ones.[47]

Reasoned eclecticism carefully examines internal evidence, too. However, it also examines and sometimes even prioritizes "external evidence." "External evidence" refers to the clues to the original reading found outside of that particular reading. Reasoned eclectics recognize that the age of a manuscript is generally a helpful indicator of the number of copies that stand between the manuscript and the original. They recognize that the fewer generations of copies between the original and an extant manuscript, the greater the probability that it preserves original readings. Reasoned eclectics recognize that some manuscripts more faithfully preserve the original text than others do. They reason that if a manuscript proves to be more reliable than others again and again, it should be given preference in the most difficult variant units when other evidence seems equally balanced.

Reasoned eclecticism is committed to examining and carefully considering all the evidence and every potential clue to the original reading. It is not a mechanical method in which a simple step-by-step procedure is assumed to always identify the original reading. It recognizes that because variant units are different, the solutions to them will vary. Evidence

---

44. This method has also been called rational criticism, radical criticism, rigorous criticism, or consistent criticism.

45. Elliott (*New Testament Textual Criticism*, 1–2) named C. H. Turner, A. C. Clark, A. E. Housman, and George Kilpatrick as pioneers of the approach. In his more recent essay ("Thoroughgoing Eclecticism in New Testament Textual Criticism," in Ehrman and Holmes, *Text of the New Testament in Contemporary Research*, 745–70; see 748, 751), Elliott lists J. M. Ross, J. O'Callaghan, Charles Landon, Eberhard Güting, Heinrich Greeven, and several commentators as examples of recent scholars who generally employ thoroughgoing eclecticism.

46. Elliott, "Thoroughgoing Eclecticism," 745.

47. Elliott, "Thoroughgoing Eclecticism," 748.

that may not matter much in some cases may be the most important piece of evidence in others. The goal of reasoned eclecticism is to leave no stone unturned, to examine every piece of evidence, recognizing that what initially seems to be irrelevant may be the very detail that leads to identifying the original text.

Imagine a criminal investigator who seeks to solve a case by exclusively examining the evidence at the crime scene. Fingerprints, DNA samples, and fibers from an article of clothing reveal a lot. They may reveal who recently visited the scene. But more than mere presence at the crime scene will be necessary to reconstruct the events that took place there and to identify who was responsible for the crime. Evidence found only at the scene is usually not enough to build a convincing case. The investigator must also examine other kinds of evidence. Interviews of close associates of the victim may reveal who had a motive to commit the crime. Interviews of potential suspects and investigations into their alibis may show who had the opportunity to commit the crime. Searches of the potential suspects' homes and vehicles may reveal who had the means to commit the crime. The investigator who wants to discover the truth must examine all the evidence, evidence at the crime scene *and* evidence found *outside* of the crime scene.

In a similar way, a scholar who wants to identify the original readings of the Greek NT must be committed to examining all the evidence. This includes the internal evidence that is the focus of the thoroughgoing eclectic. Yet, it includes external evidence as well.

In the examination of external evidence, a reasoned eclectic follows principles such as these:

- Prefer a reading that can be shown to be early.
- Prefer readings in witnesses that are known to be reliable and accurate.
- Prefer readings found in multiple early witnesses.

Reasoned eclectics often divide internal evidence into two subcategories: *transcriptional* evidence and *intrinsic* evidence. Transcriptional evidence refers to the practices and common mistakes of ancient scribes. The evaluation of transcriptional evidence seeks to answer the question: "What changes were the scribes most likely to make?" The original reading will probably be the one that is least likely to contain changes introduced by a scribe. In the evaluation of transcriptional evidence, reasoned eclectics apply principles such as these:

- Prefer the reading that best explains the origin of the other readings.
- Prefer readings that did not likely result from one of the common scribal mistakes.
- Prefer readings that do not appear to be an attempt to clarify the meaning for later generations of readers.
- Prefer readings that do not seem to be an attempt to improve the style or grammar.
- Prefer readings that do not seem to be an attempt to harmonize the passage to its context or a parallel passage in another book.
- Prefer readings that seem initially difficult but make better sense after further study.

Intrinsic evidence relates to what the original author was most likely to have written. Especially when an extensive writing sample exists (like the Gospel of Matthew, Luke-Acts, or the letters of Paul), we can develop a good profile of the author's normal way of expressing himself. This profile helps the researcher identify the reading that has the hallmarks, the literary thumbprint, of the NT writer. In the evaluation of intrinsic evidence, reasoned eclectics follow such principles as:

- Prefer the reading that is most consistent with the author's grammar, style, and vocabulary.
- Prefer the reading that best fits the immediate context.
- Prefer the reading that best fits with the author's theology.

Part Two will briefly explain the more recent history of the various principles of reasoned eclecticism. Some of these principles have been followed for over a millennium and were applied even by the early church fathers as they sought to reconstruct the original text. Part Two will explain the rationale behind each principle and give an example of its application. First, we must introduce several of the tools that are indispensable for text-critical work.

4

THE TOOLS FOR NEW TESTAMENT TEXTUAL CRITICISM

Having the right tools is often critical to doing a job well. A mechanic who owns only an adjustable wrench will not work nearly as effectively as one who has a shop full of precision tools engineered for specific tasks. In some cases, the poorly equipped mechanic may damage the very engine that he is seeking to repair simply because he does not have the tools needed for the job.[1]

Modern textual critics have a significant advantage over previous generations of textual scholars because of the amazing tools that are now available. These tools enable textual scholars to work more efficiently and will usually produce more accurate results. We will now introduce some of the most indispensable tools for cutting-edge text-critical work.

4.1. Nestle-Aland *Novum Testamentum Graece*

Eberhard Nestle published the first edition of his *Novum Testamentum Graece* in 1898. In comparison to the recent editions of this text, Nestle's original approach was simple. The text was a consensus of the three respected scholarly editions by Tischendorf, Westcott and Hort, and Weymouth (soon replaced by Weiss). When those editions differed, Nestle adopted the text agreed upon by two of these editions and placed the minority reading in the apparatus. Beginning with the 13th edition (1927), Nestle's son Erwin added a critical apparatus that identified the readings from Greek manuscripts, early versions, and quotations in the early church fathers. Early editions based the apparatus solely on information derived from earlier critical editions. However, in the mid-1950s Kurt Aland began systematically checking the primary sources to correct errors in the apparatus.

Starting with the 26th edition (1979), the editors abandoned the approach of printing a consensus of other critical editions. Instead, the editorial committee began making its own text-critical decisions based on the principles of reasoned eclecticism. The

---

1. Parts of this chapter are based on Quarles and Kellum, *40 Questions about the Text and Canon*, 149–61. Used with permission.

committee wished to take advantage of the 20th-century discoveries of early papyri and other manuscripts.

The 28th edition (2012) presents the same text as the 26th and 27th editions except in the Catholic Letters. The editors adopted the text established in the Editio Critica Maior (ECM) of the Catholic Letters (see section 4.3, below). This text was reconstructed using a new approach called the Coherence-Based Genealogical Method (CBGM). This method uses computer tools to manage copious, detailed information on the relationships between texts of the NT on all shared variant units in order to construct an accurate and detailed genealogy of these texts.[2] The editors of the NA[28] revised the entire apparatus to make it more accurate and user-friendly.

The apparatus of the NA[28] treats more variant units than any of the other current single-volume editions. The apparatus identifies the readings of all consistently cited witnesses (listed on 63*–67*) unless the witness has a lacuna or the reading is unclear at that point.[3] This edition does not attempt to list all significant witnesses or all known variants since this is not feasible in a single-volume hand edition. That huge task is reserved for the multivolume ECM.[4] The purpose of the Nestle-Aland critical edition is primarily to provide the user with "the basis for studying the text and evaluating the most important variants."[5] Important variants have a positive apparatus (giving evidence supporting the reading in the text) and a negative apparatus (identifying other variant readings and their support). In contrast, for cases where the editors are confident that they have restored the initial text but think that variant readings may be helpful for interpreting the text or understanding its history, the edition gives only a negative apparatus. This shorter treatment serves to keep the size of the edition manageable.

The apparatus normally cites the evidence of the earliest versions that were made directly from the Greek text (the Latin, Syriac, and Coptic versions). Other versions are cited only when these offer especially important support for a particular reading. The apparatus mentions quotations of the text in the church fathers prior to the 8th century if it appears that the father intended to quote the text precisely and if the quotation appears to have been accurately preserved in the available manuscripts.

The apparatus is more difficult to use than those in some other editions. The user must become familiar with a list of critical signs, carefully watch for the symbols that separate variant units and those that separate variants (| and ¦ respectively), and learn about a dozen abbreviations (mostly Latin). The fonts used in the apparatus are smaller than those used for the main text and may be challenging to read. Fortunately, the NA[28] is available in a large-print edition that is preferable when portability is not a concern.

---

2. For a brief introduction to the CBGM, see Quarles and Kellum, *40 Questions about the Text and Canon*, 183–87. For a more detailed introduction, see Tommy Wasserman and Peter J. Gurry, *A New Approach to Textual Criticism: An Introduction to the Coherence-Based Genealogical Method* (Atlanta: Society of Biblical Literature, 2017).

3. NA[28], 48*.

4. So far, five volumes have appeared: the Gospel of Mark, Parallel Pericopes, the Catholic Letters, Acts, and Revelation.

5. NA[28], 55*.

4.2. United Bible Societies' *Greek New Testament*

The United Bible Societies first published an edition of the Greek New Testament in 1966. The primary purpose of the edition was to provide Bible translators around the world with a reliable basis for their translation work. Beginning with the 3rd edition, the text has been essentially identical to the text printed in the then-current NA edition (UBS[3]=NA[26]; UBS[4]=NA[27]; UBS[5]=NA[28]). The readings selected for the UBS[5] base text are identical to those printed in the NA[28]. The Greek texts of the two editions are distinguished only by occasional differences in punctuation and capitalization.

The purpose of the edition is "to enable its readers to read, understand, and translate the New Testament in its original language in as competent and skilled a manner as possible."[6] This edition treats significantly fewer variant units than the NA[28]. However, this reduction enables the edition to present more evidence in a clearer format for the treated variant units than was possible in the NA[28]. The apparatus gives the evidence of all papyri extant for a given passage and all majuscules except those belonging to the Byzantine text-type. Byzantine manuscripts as a group are identified with the abbreviation *Byz* rather than identifying them individually (though important Byzantine witnesses like K [018] L [020] P [025] in Paul are sometimes listed in brackets as well). Minuscules that frequently have readings distinct from the Byzantine text-type are listed in the apparatus.[7] The apparatus presents the evidence in this order: (1) papyri, (2) majuscules, (3) minuscules, and (4) lectionaries.

The UBS[5] lists evidence for the preferred reading first (which is a more intuitive ordering than in the NA[28]). It also includes more evidence from ancient versions. The NA[28] focuses on the earliest versions (Latin, Syriac, Coptic), but the UBS[5] also frequently cites Armenian, Georgian, Ethiopic, and Old Church Slavonic versions. The UBS[5] also offers "as complete a survey as possible of the Fathers through the mid-5th century, because the citations of these authors are of the greatest importance for reconstructing the original text of the New Testament."[8] If one of the selected important English, French, Spanish, and German translations preferred a variant reading to the one selected in the UBS[5], the apparatus identifies those translations. The UBS[5] also includes a discourse segmentation apparatus, a feature that can be helpful to both translators and exegetes.

The UBS[5] uses a helpful grading system by which the editors express their degree of confidence in the variant selected for the text. The editors explain that an {A} designation "indicates that the text is certain," a {B} "indicates that the text is almost certain," a {C}

---

6. UBS[5], 1*.

7. The UBS[5] selected texts for inclusion in the apparatus using the classifications in Aland and Aland, *Text of the New Testament*, 317–37. The apparatus lists all minuscules from Categories I and II (manuscripts of special quality with a text resembling that of the earliest majuscules), ten minuscules from Category III (manuscripts with a distinctive character and some Byzantine influence) for each major part of the New Testament (Gospels, Acts, Paul, and Revelation). No minuscules belong to Category IV (manuscripts characterized by paraphrase and resembling D). Minuscules from Category V (Byzantine manuscripts) are identified by the abbreviation *Byz*.

8. UBS[5], 37*.

"indicates that the Committee had difficulty in deciding which variant to place in the text," and finally the designation {D}, "which occurs only rarely, indicates that the Committee had great difficulty in arriving at a decision."[9]

The diamond (♦) signifies the highest level of uncertainty and indicates that the Committee was unable to make a decision based on the evidence presently available. Double brackets (⟦ ⟧) wrap around lengthier readings that are generally viewed as later additions to the original text, though these texts are retained due to their importance in church history.

The table below compares the apparatus of the NA[28] with the treatment of the variant unit in John 1:18 in the UBS[5] apparatus. The material highlighted in the table appears in one apparatus but not the other.

Table 4.1. Comparison of the Apparatuses for John 1:18

NA[28]	18 ⸆ ο μονογενης θεος $\mathfrak{P}^{75}$ $\aleph^1$ 33; Cl[pt] Cl[exThd pt] Or[pt] ¦ ο μονογενης υιος A C[3] K Γ Δ Θ Ψ $f^{1.13}$ 565. 579. 700. 892. 1241. 1424 𝔐 lat sy[c.h]; Cl[pt] Cl[exThd pt] ¦ ει μη ο μονογενης υιος W[s] it; Ir[lat pt] (+ θεου Ir[lat pt]) ¦ txt $\mathfrak{P}^{66}$ $\aleph^*$ B C[*] L sy[p.hmg]; Or[pt] Did	
UBS[5]	{B} μονογενὴς θεός $\mathfrak{P}^{66}$ $\aleph^*$ B C[*] L syr[p, hmg] geo[2] Origen[gr 2/4] Didymus Cyril[1/4] // ὁ μονογενὴς θεός $\mathfrak{P}^{75}$ $\aleph^2$ 33 cop[bo] Clement[2/3] Clement[from Theodotus 1/2] Origen[gr 2/4] Eusebius[3/7] Basil[1/2] Gregory-Nyssa Epiphanius Serapion[1/2] Cyril[2/4] // ὁ μονογενὴς υἱός A C[3] W[supp] Δ Θ Ψ 0141 f^1 f^{13} 28 157 180 205 565 579 597 700 892 1006 1010 1071 1241 1243 1292 1342 1424 1505 Byz [E F G H] Lect it[a, aur, b, c, e, f, ff2, l] vg syr[c, h, pal] arm eth geo[1] slav Irenaeus[lat 1/3] Clement[from Theodotus 1/2] Clement[1/3] Hippolytus Origen[lat 1/2] Letter of Hymenaeus Alexander Eustathius Eusebius[4/7] Serapion[1/2] Athanasius Basil[1/2] Gregory-Nazianzus Chrysostom Theodore Cyril[1/4] Proclus Theodoret John-Damascus; Tertullian Hegemonius Victorinus-Rome Ambrosiaster Hilary[5/7] Ps-Priscillian Ambrose[10/11] Faustinus Gregory-Elvira Phoebadius Jerome Augustine Varimadum REB BJ // μονογενὴς υἱὸς θεοῦ it[q] Irenaeus[lat 1/3]; Ambrose[1/11 vid] // ὁ μονογενὴς vg[ms] Ps-Vigilius[1/2]

Obviously, the UBS[5] provides significantly more information regarding the readings of the minuscules, ancient versions, and church fathers. Again, the UBS[5] had to reduce the number of variant units that it treats to create space for this more extensive information. This variant unit in John 1:18 is the thirteenth unit in the Gospel of John to be treated in the NA[28], but only the fifth variant unit to be treated in the UBS[5].

A complementary volume titled *A Textual Commentary on the Greek New Testament* briefly explains the decisions made by the committee of the UBS[5]. The current edition of the *Textual Commentary* is based on the UBS[4]. The *Textual Commentary* discusses every variant unit treated in the apparatus of the UBS[4] plus several hundred additional variant units. The volume seeks to "set forth the reasons that led the Committee, or a majority of the members of the Committee, to adopt certain variant readings for inclusion in the text

---

9. UBS[5], 8*–9*.

and to relegate certain other readings to the apparatus."[10] When possible, the comments are based on the notes from the Committee's discussions. When one of the Committee members strongly objected to a decision made by the Committee, his explanation for his dissenting opinion is appended to the discussion and the objector is identified by his initials. The *Textual Commentary* contains a helpful Introduction that details the Committee's view of the history of the transmission of the NT text and explains their general approach to making text-critical decisions. The Introduction identifies the criteria that the Committee used to evaluate the various categories of evidence that are especially important in reasoned eclecticism.

4.3. Editio Critica Maior

The goal of the ECM is to provide "the full range of resources necessary for scholarly research in establishing the text and reconstructing the history of the New Testament text during its first thousand years."[11] The ECM volumes list more variant units and more witnesses in support of variant readings than any previously published editions. For example, the volume on Acts presents all the variants that appear in the 183 manuscripts selected for the edition. These manuscripts were selected based on the recognition that they either differed from the MT (by agreeing with it in less than 85 percent of 104 test passages) or almost completely agreed with the MT on these test passages. Other manuscripts were used to create some uniformity across the different volumes of the ECM.

The ECM includes evidence from the citations of the NT by the Greek church fathers (even when these have only been preserved in Latin translation) and from Tertullian since he used a Greek exemplar for his own Latin translation.[12] It also presents the evidence for variants from the four most significant early versions, the Latin, Coptic, Syriac, and Ethiopic. Occasionally, the apparatus cites evidence from the Armenian, Georgian, and Old Church Slavonic versions, but "only with restraint" since good critical editions of these versions are not available and their "origins and history are not sufficiently understood."[13] The ECM includes valuable supplementary studies that explain textual decisions, theories related to text-types, and other important topics.

Since most textual variations involve only a few manuscripts, the ECM often presents only a "negative apparatus" that lists witnesses that differ from the reading in the base text. A positive apparatus presenting evidence for the base text is supplied only when fifteen or more witnesses differ from the base text.

The main text of the ECM was established using reasoned eclecticism, facilitated by the Coherence-Based Genealogical Method mentioned earlier. At completion, the ECM

---

10. Bruce M. Metzger, *A Textual Commentary on the Greek New Testament*, 2nd ed. (Stuttgart: Deutsche Bibelgesellschaft, 1994), vii.

11. Holger Strutwolf et al., eds. *Acts of the Apostles*, vol. 3 of *Novum Testamentum Graecum: Editio Critica Maior* (Stuttgart: Deutsche Bibelgesellschaft, 2017), 1.1:18*.

12. ECM, 3.1.1:19*.

13. ECM, 3.1.1:23*.

will comprise six volumes:[14] I. Synoptic Gospels; II. Gospel of John; III. Acts; IV. Catholic Letters; V. Pauline Letters; and VI. John's Apocalypse. The order of the volumes is based on the order of the NT books in most Greek manuscripts.

4.4. Institute for New Testament Textual Research Website

The website of the Institute for New Testament Textual Research (Institut für Neutesta-mentliche Textforschung, hereafter, INTF)[15] provides online utilities that are immensely helpful for advanced text-critical research. At this site, users will find the most recent and reliable version of the *Kurzgefasste Liste Online*, the official registry of known NT manuscripts. The website also provides tools that enable users to see how closely related the important texts are for the NT books and corpora already treated in existing volumes of the ECM.[16] As we will see later, this is crucial for a proper evaluation of the external evidence for variant readings. The NTVMR (NT Virtual Manuscript Room) provides photographs and transcriptions of many of the important manuscripts in the *Liste*. Many of these photographs are high-resolution color images, though some are from black-and-white microfilm. The ability to zoom in on details and adjust brightness and contrast can sometimes give the user advantages over examining the manuscript directly. The NTVMR is constantly improving and adding new resources and features. The NTVMR provides tools needed to conveniently transcribe and index texts. The impressive Amsterdam Database of New Testament Conjectural Emendation gives researchers the ability to trace the history of conjectural emendations, the sources that suggested them, and the arguments given in their support.[17] Due to the willingness of the INTF to make their resources widely available, anyone with the necessary skills and an internet connection can engage in textual research and make important contributions to the field.

4.5. Center for the Study of New Testament Manuscripts Website

The Center for the Study of New Testament Manuscripts[18] uses the most recent technology to produce high-resolution, full-color images of Greek NT manuscripts. It uses developing technologies such as multispectral imaging to read ancient manuscripts and create complete transcriptions. The Center also produces images of important but often hard-to-access resources that are important for the study of the history of NT textual criticism

---

14. Each of these volumes is, in fact, a multivolume work. For example, the "volume" on Acts consists of four large volumes.

15. http://uni-muenster.de/INTF/en/datenbanken/index.html.

16. These tools are associated with the links to "Genealogical Queries" and "Manuscript Clusters."

17. Jan Krans et al., eds., *The Amsterdam Database of New Testament Conjectural Emendation* (https://ntvmr.uni-muenster.de/nt-conjectures). A conjectural emendation is a proposed reading of the Greek NT that is not supported by any Greek manuscript. However, the database also includes readings that merely adjust punctuation, accents, or word division (rather than emending the majuscule text written in *scriptio continua*) and readings supported by later manuscript discoveries.

18. https://www.csntm.org.

such as the editions of the Greek NT by Erasmus, Robertus Stephanus, Theodore Beza, John Mill, Samuel Tregelles, and Hermann Freiherr von Soden.

4.6. The International Greek New Testament Project

The International Greek New Testament Project (IGNTP) is an international committee of textual scholars who contribute in various ways to the production of critical editions of the books of the NT. The project has produced a two-volume critical edition of the Gospel according to Luke with an extensive apparatus of the variant readings found in Greek manuscripts, early versions, and the early church fathers. Members of the committee are currently working on the editions of the Gospel according to John and the Epistles of Paul that will appear in the Editio Critica Maior series. The project has published the evidence for the twenty-three papyri and the oldest parchment manuscripts of John in Greek in Brill's New Testament Tools, Studies and Documents series. However, transcriptions of the papyri, majuscules, minuscules, and Old Latin and Coptic texts of John are freely available on the IGNTP website. Transcriptions of Greek and Latin manuscripts of Paul's letters are also available online at several different sites, and the IGNTP website has links to each of these. The website contains a helpful list of recently completed and ongoing master's and doctoral research in the field of NT textual criticism with the goal of preventing unnecessary duplication in research. The site also posts helpful bibliographies on several topics and links to audio and video recordings related to the discipline.

4.7. The Center for New Testament Textual Studies
NT Critical Apparatus

The Center for New Testament Textual Studies (CNTTS), at New Orleans Baptist Theological Seminary, has developed an extensive digital critical apparatus.[19] This apparatus is largely derived from fresh transcriptions and collations by researchers at the CNTTS. The procedure is a careful one in which two different researchers independently transcribe each manuscript and the two transcriptions are compared. When they differ, the transcriptions are reconciled by reexamining images of the manuscripts. When possible, the transcriptions are compared to other existing transcriptions for final verification. The most recent update of the apparatus includes data from 126 papyri, 47 majuscules, 165 minuscules, 12 Latin witnesses in the Gospels, 2 families of manuscripts (*f*1 *f*13), and 3 printed editions. Thus, this apparatus is currently the most detailed critical apparatus available for the entire NT.[20]

In addition to listing variant readings and the witnesses that support them, the apparatus classifies different types of variants and indicates whether a particular variant is

---

19. The project home page can be viewed at http://www.nobts.edu/cntts/general-overview.html.

20. Only volumes on individual New Testament books or sections of the New Testament in series like the Editio Critica Maior and the International Greek New Testament Project have more extensive apparatuses.

or is not helpful for tracing relationships to other texts. It also identifies the variant as an addition, omission, replacement, transposition, or a nonsense reading. It also notes features of the text such as homoeoteleuton (confusion due to similar endings of lines or words) or homoeoarcton (confusion due to similar beginnings of lines or words) that may have led to the variation. The platforms for the database (Accordance and Logos) enable users to perform helpful searches. With little effort, a researcher can locate all examples of nonsense readings, orthographical differences, or homoeoteleuton.

Users may open a window with important details about each witness in the apparatus by placing the cursor over the witness in the apparatus. This will save users the time that might otherwise be required to consult the *Liste* or the charts describing witnesses in the front matter or appendices of printed critical editions. The base text for the apparatus is the UBS[3], but this detracts little from the usefulness of the apparatus. This helpful tool is a significant improvement over older apparatuses, such as the 8th edition of Constantin Tischendorf's multivolume *Novum Testamentum Graece* or S. C. E. Legg's *Novum Testamentum Graece*.

4.8. Websites Devoted to Important Manuscripts and Major Text-Critical Issues

Researchers around the world are engaged in projects devoted to the study of specific manuscripts. Libraries holding several of the most important manuscripts, such as Codex Vaticanus, Codex Sinaiticus, Codex Bezae, and Codex Ephraemi Rescriptus, now make high-resolution photographs of these manuscripts available, sometimes with transcriptions, translations, up-to-date introductions, and other detailed studies.[21] The University of Cambridge Digital Library provides access to the multispectral images of Codex Zacynthius, which enable researchers to read the erased undertext of both the text of Luke and the commentary in the frame catena.[22] The library also provides transcriptions and English translations of both the biblical text and the commentary, as well as a "concordance" that helps researchers navigate the text of the manuscript since the pages were rearranged when the original text was scraped off and the new text was overlaid. A table is available that identifies the sources of the various marginal comments in the surviving pages of the codex.

Other websites are devoted to the study of specific text-critical issues. The MARK16 virtual research environment appears to be the first to focus exclusively on the textual issues of a single chapter of the Bible.[23] The materials on the site are primarily related to the various endings of the Gospel of Mark. This virtual research environment "allows scholars to explore the complexity of the textual tradition of the Markan manuscripts

---

21. For Vaticanus, see https://digi.vatlib.it/view/MSS_Vat.gr.1209. For Sinaiticus, see https://codexsinaiticus.org/en/project/. For Bezae, see https://cudl.lib.cam.ac.uk/view/MS-NN-00002-00041/1.

22. Readers may begin exploring the rich resources related to Codex Zacynthius at https://cudl.lib.cam.ac.uk/collections/codexzacynthius/1.

23. https://mark16.sib.swiss.

and to analyse the historical tensions between diverse, early Christian groups during the first and second century CE, specifically in Egypt."[24] The project has constructed a virtual "manuscript room" that provides high-quality images of the various endings of Mark in manuscripts in several ancient languages. It also provides interesting "eTalks," images of important critical editions, bibliographies, links to open access publications, and access to multimedia presentations related to the endings of Mark.

4.9. Conclusion

Those who want to make helpful contributions in the field of NT textual criticism have impressive resources at their disposal now that would have stirred the envy of 19th- and 20th-century scholars. First, updated and expanded critical editions are now available. Moreover, contemporary researchers no longer need to travel to libraries across the world to access important manuscripts, nor study those manuscripts in dimly lit rooms with only the aid of a magnifying glass. Those who wish to contribute to the task of restoring the original Greek NT have the most important resources at their fingertips if they merely have a computer and an internet connection. Many different institutions happily cooperate and freely share resources to advance our understanding of the NT text and its transmission.

---

24. Claire Clivaz, "SNSF MARK16," *Digital Humanities +*, 7 March 2020, https://claireclivaz. hypotheses.org/990.

Part Two

———

THE METHOD OF REASONED ECLECTICISM

We will now explain important principles of reasoned eclecticism and illustrate how these principles may be applied by offering practical examples. Not all the principles apply to every textual challenge. Thus, the examples will be drawn from texts that helpfully demonstrate the importance of the specific principle under discussion. In Part Three, however, we will demonstrate how all the applicable principles coalesce to help identify the original reading in a single variant unit.

5

PRELIMINARY CONSIDERATIONS

5.1. Identify the Variant Readings

Currently, most readers will begin their text-critical work by consulting either the UBS or the NA edition. As explained earlier, the NA edition contains more variant units, but the UBS edition often lists more supporting evidence for the variants that it treats. In general, students should identify variant readings using the NA edition. The purpose of the NA is to provide a resource for "studying the text and evaluating the most important variants."[1] They should also consult the UBS[5] to see if it treats the variant unit and provides more detailed information.

In the NA[28] the first sentence of Matt 18:15 reads:

Ἐὰν δὲ ἁμαρτήσῃ □[εἰς σὲ]` ὁ ἀδελφός σου, ὕπαγε ἔλεγξον αὐτὸν μεταξὺ σοῦ καὶ αὐτοῦ μόνου.

The brackets around εἰς σέ indicate a degree of doubt about the authenticity of the enclosed words and are intended to prompt users to evaluate the variant themselves. The siglum □ signifies that the text that follows is omitted in the cited witnesses. The siglum ` marks the end of the omitted text. In the apparatus at the bottom of the page, locate the verse number 15 (which is placed in bold and marked by a bold dot, i.e., •15) and you will find this:

□ ℵ B 0281 f^1 579 sa bo^{pt}; Or^{lem} ¦ *txt* D K L N W Γ Δ Θ 078 f^{13} 33. 565. 700. 892. 1241. 1424 𝔐 latt sy mae bo^{pt}

After the omission mark □, important witnesses supporting the omission are listed. These will follow the order: papyri (though no papyri are extant for this variant unit), majuscules, minuscule families, individual minuscules, early versions, and church fathers. The siglum ¦ marks a shift to another variant in the same variant unit. The italicized *txt* indicates that this section gives the evidence for the reading in the main text, which contains the prepositional phrase. The witnesses presented following the *txt* siglum include the prepositional phrase. If the verse had contained another variant unit, the bold solid line | would mark

---

1. NA[28], 55*.

the end of the evidence related to this specific variant unit. After that line, another variant unit in the same verse would be treated.

If we consult the apparatus of the UBS[5], we discover that the variant unit is slightly more complicated. The UBS[5] enlarges the scope of the variant unit to include the verb. Some witnesses use the form ἁμαρτήσῃ, but others use the form ἁμάρτῃ. Each of the different verb forms occurs in two different combinations, both with and without the prepositional phrase. Thus, in the UBS[5], the apparatus presents evidence for four different variants within this single variant unit. Each variant is separated by the double forward slash //. The apparatus lists the variants: (1) ἁμαρτήσῃ εἰς σέ, (2) ἁμάρτῃ εἰς σέ, (3) ἁμαρτήσῃ, and (4) ἁμάρτῃ.

5.2. Analyze the Nature of the Differences Between the Variants

Sometimes the analysis of variants is complex, such as when variants result from spelling differences, grammatical differences (such as differences in tense, mood, person, or number), or lexical differences. In this variant unit, the verbal variant offers some complexity, but another difference is simple—the presence or absence of the prepositional phrase εἰς σέ, which in this context means "against you."

5.3. Reflect on the Implications for the Text's Meaning

The difference in verb forms (variation between 1st and 2nd aorist) does not affect the meaning of the text. The presence or absence of the prepositional phrase, however, does affect the meaning of the statement. Without the phrase, Jesus is teaching how to respond to sin committed by another disciple regardless of whom the sin may have harmed. With the phrase, the topic is how a disciple is to respond to the sin another disciple commits against him personally. Here is the issue: Is the topic of Matt 18:15 addressing a personal grievance or addressing sin in the life of a fellow disciple regardless of whether the sin has personally affected the respondent?

After listing the variants, considering the nature of their differences, and reflecting on the implications of the variants for the meaning of the text, we proceed to an analysis of the external evidence supporting each variant.

6

EVALUATION OF EXTERNAL EVIDENCE

External evidence relates to the ancient witnesses that preserve the various readings. It focuses on the ancient Greek manuscripts, early versions, and quotations in the early church fathers. By contrast, internal evidence relates to evidence that emerges from the readings themselves. Analysis of external evidence asks questions such as:

- What is the earliest evidence for the reading?
- Do the early witnesses to the reading come from various regions?
- Does the reading appear among witnesses that are not closely related to each other?
- What is the general reliability of the earliest witnesses that support the reading?
- Do multiple early witnesses share the reading?

The practice of reasoned eclecticism normally begins with an examination and analysis of the external evidence. Kurt and Barbara Aland identified twelve "basic rules for textual criticism," and the third of these is this: "Criticism of the text must always begin from the evidence of the manuscript tradition and only afterward turn to a consideration of internal criteria."[1] Most scholars who practice reasoned eclecticism would probably agree, although we will soon see that some criteria for evaluating external evidence assume a prior examination of internal evidence. Tackling external evidence first does not imply that external evidence will necessarily carry greater weight in making final decisions about readings. In some cases, internal evidence may be the determining factor in text-critical decisions.[2]

---

1. Aland and Aland, *Text of the New Testament*, 280.
2. Some scholars will disagree with this statement. For example, Stanley E. Porter and Andrew W. Pitts (*Fundamentals of New Testament Textual Criticism* [Grand Rapids: Eerdmans, 2015], 101) state: "External evidence, most textual critics agree, should take priority in making text-critical judgments, because it is the most objective tangible evidence that we have for the textual history of the NT." They add that "[S]ubstantial external support (i.e., where a reading is supported by the old, high quality, geographically and genetically diverse witnesses . . .) should typically rule out even the most powerful internal considerations" (101). However, Metzger and Ehrman (*Text of the New Testament*, 314) state that when external evidence and internal evidence seem to conflict, "the decision of the textual critic will be made in accordance with a general philosophy of textual methodology." Their own

Scholars often warn of the dangers of reducing textual criticism to a mechanical process.[3] This reduction oversimplifies the analysis of the critical evidence and often yields unreliable results. Introductions to textual criticism especially risk this danger because scholars hope to make the discipline as simple and understandable as possible. Thus, students often learn to weigh the external evidence by simply identifying the date, text-type, and geographical distribution of witnesses supporting the different variants. Unfortunately, this may give the impression that the analysis of the evidence is simply a matter of checking off boxes: "Early witnesses? Check. Wide geographical distribution? Check. Multiple text-types? Check. We have identified the original reading!" But this is not the best approach. On the contrary, accurate analysis of the evidence requires the exercise of good critical thinking skills. It demands precise nuancing and careful qualification of the criteria for evaluating readings. Günther Zuntz, the author of a ground-breaking study of the text of Paul's letters, stated this bluntly:

> [Textual criticism] cannot be carried out mechanically. At every stage the critic has to use his brains. Were it different, we could put the critical slide-rule into the hands of any fool and leave it to him to settle the problems of the New Testament text.[4]

This introduction to reasoned eclecticism will guide readers in learning to exercise good critical thinking skills in their efforts to establish the text of the NT. It will also caution against common misunderstandings of the major principles of reasoned eclecticism. The goal is not to complicate the practice of reasoned eclecticism but to formulate reliable criteria that guide students to discover the original reading and avoid the common abuses of these criteria as they make early attempts at settling text-critical questions. We thus continue below with the variant unit in Matt 18:15 in view.

6.1. Criterion 1: Prefer readings that can be shown to be early

The researcher begins with the question, "How early did this reading exist according to the presently available evidence?" An emphasis on the importance of the testimony of the oldest manuscripts (and other early witnesses such as the church fathers and early versions) arose among 18th-century textual critics such as John Mill, Richard Bentley,

---

philosophy allows internal evidence to outweigh external evidence: "The possibility must always be kept open that the original reading has been preserved alone in any one group of manuscripts, even, in extremely rare instances, in the Koine or Byzantine text" (315). They do advise: "It is probably safest for the beginner to rely on the weight of external evidence rather than on what may be an imperfect knowledge of the author's usage" (314).

3. Note, for example, how frequently the Alands (*Text of the New Testament*, 281) warn against a mechanical approach in their twelve rules for textual criticism. Rules 6, 10, and 11 warn: "[No piece of external evidence] can be followed mechanically"; "This principle must not be taken too mechanically"; and "But here again the principle cannot be applied mechanically."

4. Zuntz, *Text of the Epistles*, 12. A slide-rule is a mechanical calculator widely used in mathematics prior to the advent of electronic calculators and computers.

Johann Albrecht Bengel, Johann Jakob Wettstein, and Johann Jakob Griesbach.[5] In 1742, Bengel expressed the principle thusly: "Most important of all, ancient witnesses [are to be preferred] to modern ones."[6]

The rationale behind this principle is simple. A direct copy of the original is probably more accurate than a copy of a copy of a copy of the original. Each new generation of copying introduces new copyist errors, which are added to the errors accumulated over the previous generations of copying. Scribes often corrected obvious errors that appeared in their exemplars. However, the corrector may not have restored the original reading by consulting another, more reliable manuscript. Instead, the "correction" may merely be what the corrector assumed the reading must have been. Generally, fewer generations of copies between a manuscript and the original increase the likelihood that the manuscript preserves original readings. Inversely, greater numbers of generations of copies between a manuscript and the original decrease the general reliability of the manuscript.[7] Ordinarily, an earlier manuscript has fewer generations of copies between it and the original than a later manuscript does. Thus, the readings found in earlier manuscripts are more likely to be original.

Samuel Tregelles pointed out that the only proof that a reading is ancient (and thus, potentially the original reading) is its appearance in an ancient document.[8] The most important ancient documents for establishing the precise words of the original text of the NT are actual manuscripts of the Greek NT rather than early versions or references to the text by the early church fathers.[9] Thus, researchers should be hesitant to adopt a reading that does not appear in an ancient manuscript of the Greek NT. Readings that do not appear in any Greek manuscript until the 9th century or later are unlikely to be the original reading in most cases.

Readers might assume, based on these principles, that textual critics should strictly follow the readings of the very earliest manuscripts. They are, however, surprised to find that reasoned eclectics often follow the readings of later manuscripts instead. They may wonder why I have chosen to phrase the principle as "Prefer a reading that can be shown to be early" rather than "Adopt the reading supported by the earliest manuscript."

The critical factor is not the number of *years* between the time that an author published his work and the time that a later manuscript was copied. What really matters is

---

5. Eldon Jay Epp, "Traditional 'Canons' of New Testament Textual Criticism: Their Value, Validity, and Viability—or Lack Thereof," in Wachtel and Holmes, *Textual History of the Greek New Testament*, 80–81, 93–94.

6. Johann Albrecht Bengel, *New Testament Word Studies*, trans. Charlton T. Lewis and Marvin R. Vincent, 2 vols. (Grand Rapids: Kregel, 1971), 1:xviii.

7. Westcott and Hort (*Introduction to the New Testament*, 5–6) observed, "[R]epeated transcription involves multiplication of error." They insisted that good evidence confirmed this principle: "The consequent presumption that a relatively late text is likely to be a relatively corrupt text is found true on the application of all available tests in an overwhelming proportion of the extant MSS in which ancient literature has been preserved."

8. Tregelles, *Account of the Printed Text of the Greek New Testament*, 175.

9. See the cautions expressed in sections 2.5 and 2.6 above.

the number of *copies* that stand between the manuscript and the original. The date of a manuscript does not *necessarily* indicate the number of copies that stand between it and the original. In most cases, we do not know how old an exemplar was at the time that it was copied. Copies were not always made from exemplars that were only a few decades old. If they were, a manuscript dating to the late 2nd or early 3rd century (like $\mathfrak{P}^{46}$) might be a third-generation copy. A manuscript from the mid-4th century (like ℵ) might be a sixth-generation copy and thus more likely to contain an error. A manuscript from the 10th century (like minuscule 1739) might be an eighteenth-generation copy and thus much more likely to contain an error. But this reconstructed scenario assumes far too much and, as we will see in a moment, is certainly wrong. It overlooks the fact that some copies were made from exemplars that were practically brand new, while other copies were made from exemplars that were centuries old.[10]

Some ancient manuscripts were carefully preserved and continued to be copied for centuries, even though they are now lost or destroyed.[11] Some late manuscripts are direct copies or second-generation descendants of these much earlier manuscripts. For example, 1739, a minuscule manuscript copied by a scribe named Ephraim in the 10th century, is the direct copy of a very good text produced in the early 5th century.[12] Notes in the manuscript show that the 5th-century copyist had relied on a manuscript of Romans that contained the text used by Origen in his commentary in the early 3rd century. The text for the rest of Paul's letters in 1739 was taken from a manuscript as old or even older than Origen's text.[13] Minuscule 1739 often agrees with the text of Paul in two much earlier manuscripts, $\mathfrak{P}^{46}$ and B. Although 1739 was copied much later than these earlier manuscripts, 1739 may be nearly as close to the original as $\mathfrak{P}^{46}$ in terms of generations of copies. However, although late manuscripts may preserve early readings, scholars generally reject readings that appear exclusively in late manuscripts. They assume that a large enough sample of texts from the first eight centuries exists to ensure that the original reading can almost always be found in at least one of the manuscripts from this early period.

Scholars may conveniently express this important principle of textual criticism by saying, "Prefer the reading attested by the oldest manuscripts."[14] However, researchers should remember that the real goal is to prefer copies closer to the original in the line of descent to those farther removed in this line. Late manuscripts can contain a very early text.

---

10. Westcott and Hort correctly cautioned, "The number of transcriptions, and consequent opportunities of corruption, cannot be accurately measured by difference of date, for at any date a transcript might be made either from a contemporary manuscript or from one written any number of centuries before" (*Introduction to the New Testament*, 5).

11. Craig A. Evans, "How Long Were Late Antique Books in Use? Possible Implications for New Testament Textual Criticism," *BBR* 25 (2015): 23–37.

12. Lake and New, *Six Collations of New Testament Manuscripts*, 142–45.

13. Zuntz, *Text of the Epistles*, 81.

14. David Alan Black, *New Testament Textual Criticism: A Concise Guide* (Grand Rapids: Baker, 1994), 34. Amy Anderson and Wendy Widder (*Textual Criticism of the Bible*, rev. ed., Lexham Methods Series [Bellingham, WA: Lexham, 2018], 156) similarly say, "Prefer the reading from the earliest manuscripts."

Epp noted that this principle has become one of the most important in the discipline of textual criticism: "Normally, this criterion, emphasizing the antiquity of witnesses, would be placed first because virtually the entire history of critical editions of the Greek New Testament, and the accompanying development of criteria for the priority of readings, is the story of how the relatively few ancient manuscripts triumphed over the exceedingly numerous later manuscripts."[15] He argued that this criterion is reasonable since those who have studied the history of the text have concluded that "ancient manuscripts have been less likely subject to conflation, conformity to ecclesiastical texts or traditions, and other scribal alterations."[16] However, Epp warned that the preference for the earliest witnesses is not always a dependable guide since "scribal alterations intrude from the earliest time."[17] Since our earliest manuscripts disagree with one another at various points, antiquity alone is not a guarantee of accuracy.

Furthermore, being fewer copies removed from the original would always ensure greater accuracy *if* all scribes were equally skilled. Of course, not all scribes were equally skilled. A manuscript that is eight generations removed from the original may be more accurate and reliable than one that is only four generations removed from the original if that eighth-generation manuscript belonged to a scribal tradition that exercised greater care and skill in copying manuscripts.

Assessments of the age of witnesses attesting to the various readings can be tabulated using a table like the one below.

Table 6.1. Age of Witnesses Supporting Each Reading

	2nd c.	3rd c.	4th c.	5th c.	6th c.	7th c.	8th c.	9th c.
Reading 1								
Reading 2								
Reading 3								

Using the apparatus of Matt 18:15 in the UBS[5], we will tabulate, by century, the witnesses for each reading. We will consider both Greek NT manuscripts from the 9th century and earlier and the testimony of the early church fathers from the mid-5th century and earlier (since these are the fathers listed in the apparatus of the UBS[5]). Due to some of the challenges related to using the church fathers to date readings, we will separate the data using two different tables.

---

15. Epp, "Traditional 'Canons,'" 97.
16. Epp, "Traditional 'Canons,'" 97.
17. Epp, "Traditional 'Canons,'" 97.

Table 6.2. Early Greek Manuscripts

	3rd c.	4th c.	5th c.	6th c.	7th c.	8th c.	9th c.
1. ἁμαρτήσῃ εἰς σέ			D	N O Σ 078		E L	F G H Δ Θ 28 565 892
2. ἁμάρτῃ εἰς σέ			W				33 (1424)[18]
3. ἁμαρτήσῃ		ℵ B					
4. ἁμάρτῃ							

Table 6.3. Early Church Fathers

	2nd c.	3rd c.	4th c.	5th c.
1. ἁμαρτήσῃ εἰς σέ			Basil[mss] Chrysostom[mss] Hilary Lucifer Pacian Chromatius	Jerome Augustine[6/7]
2. ἁμάρτῃ εἰς σέ			Basil[5/9] Didymus Chrysostom	Theodoret
3. ἁμαρτήσῃ				Cyril Augustine[1/7]
4. ἁμάρτῃ		Origen[lem]	Basil[4/9]	

As far as the manuscripts of the Greek NT are concerned, the witnesses supporting reading 3 are about a century earlier than the witnesses for readings 1 and 2.

If we add the references to Matt 18:15 in the early church fathers to the evidence from Greek manuscripts of the NT, we may initially conclude that all four readings existed in the 4th century. However, several considerations undermine this tentative conclusion. First, the writings from the individual fathers (like Basil and Chrysostom) support more than one reading.[19] This inconsistency could result from the church father consulting different manuscripts with different readings. In that case, the two readings are both important textual evidence. However, the inconsistency could result from the father quoting loosely from memory. Perhaps a later scribe who copied the father's work conformed the quotation to the reading of Matt 18:15 with which the scribe was most familiar, or conflated the reading with the wording of the parallel in Luke 17:3. In those cases, the reading that appears in the father's work does not help in tracing the earliest date for the reading.

Second, the dates assigned to the testimony of the fathers are questionable since the earliest manuscripts of a father's works are often centuries later than the date on which the

---

18. The UBS[5] places parentheses around 1424 since it generally supports reading 2 but is slightly different. This manuscript has the prepositional phrase εἰς σέ but spells the verb ἁμάρτει.

19. E.g., "Basil[4/9]" in the UBS[5] apparatus and row 4 of the table here indicates that this passage occurs nine times in Basil's writing, and in four of those occurrences he omits εἰς σέ.

father originally composed his work. For example, the text used in Origen's commentary could imply that reading 4 existed a century earlier than other readings. Not only does the lemma in the commentary lack the prepositional phrase, but Origen's extensive comments on the passage also make no reference to it. However, using Origen's commentary to date this reading is problematic since the oldest extant Greek manuscript of this portion of Origen's commentary dates to the 13th century.[20] Thus, placing the reference in Origen in the century in which Origen composed his commentary grants an advantage to the citations in the church fathers that strongly prejudice the dating of the readings. The dates assigned in the table of Early Greek Manuscripts reflect the probable dates on which the manuscripts were copied, *not* the date when the Gospel of Matthew was written. But the date assigned in the table of Early Church Fathers reflects the probable date Origen wrote his commentary on Matthew, *not* the date of the manuscript that preserves the commentary. If the table of Early Church Fathers used the same criterion for dating as the table of Early Greek Manuscripts, the reading in Origen would be dated an entire millennium later!

Third, the evidence from Origen is mitigated by the fact that no manuscript of the Greek NT up through the 9th century shares this reading. Ordinarily, scholars reject readings that are not attested in any Greek manuscripts from the 8th century or earlier. In this case, heavy dependence on the evidence from Origen would favor the least probable reading. These considerations show that the evidence from the Greek manuscripts of the NT should carry much more weight than the evidence from the church fathers for text-critical decisions.

With the dates of the witnesses before us, we may apply this first criterion and rank the readings by preference in descending order (from the most probable to the least probable). Our rankings are 3, 1, 2, 4. Given the absence of any early Greek manuscripts supporting reading 4 and the late date of the extant manuscripts of this portion of Origen's commentary, reading 4 deserves no further consideration as the original reading.

Before moving on to other criteria for the evaluation of external evidence, we must explore the question of the date of readings further. Although readings that appear in the earliest manuscripts are obviously early, other factors sometimes suggest that the readings in manuscripts centuries later are probably just as early. In addition to the dates of manuscripts, the effort to date readings should also examine the geographical distribution of the readings and the potential relationship between the texts that preserve these readings.

Some introductions to NT textual criticism suggest that researchers should prefer readings that have a wide geographical distribution or are preserved in multiple text-types (texts that are not closely related). However, this principle grossly exaggerates the value of geographical distribution and requires thorough revision. Parker strongly objects to this principle and correctly insists, "The geographical range of a reading may show its age or its popularity, but it will not demonstrate its superiority."[21] A reading with a wider

---

20. Codex Monacensis 191 in Munich. See Heine, trans., *Commentary of Origen on the Gospel of St Matthew*, 1:29.

21. D. C. Parker, *Textual Scholarship and the Making of the New Testament* (Oxford: Oxford University Press, 2012), 80.

geographical distribution is not necessarily more likely to be original than another reading. This does not mean that an examination of geographical distribution is pointless. Wide geographical distribution can indicate that a reading is significantly older than the witnesses that contain it.

Similarly, the appearance of a reading in texts that are distant relatives of approximately the same date can indicate that a reading is significantly older than the witnesses that contain it. These factors indicate the *antiquity* of the reading, without necessarily implying that the reading is *original*. Thus, rather than advising readers to "prefer the reading with the best geographic distribution" and "prefer the reading from the largest variety of text-types," we should view the wide geographic distribution of a reading and the presence of the reading in distant relatives as further evidence in establishing the antiquity of readings. In other words, the two criteria that we are about to treat are additional considerations that aid in the application of criterion 1: "Prefer readings that can be shown to be early."

6.1.1 ADDITIONAL CONSIDERATION 1: Reevaluate the date assigned to readings found in early witnesses from various regions

In 1713, Richard Bentley argued that, when manuscripts from all over the world share the same reading, this indicates that the reading is probably original. Bentley wrote:

> Tis a good providence and a great blessing, that so many manuscripts of the New Testament are still amongst us; some procured from Egypt, others from Asia, others found in the Western churches. For the very distances of places as well as number of the books demonstrate, that there could be no collusion, no altering nor interpolating one copy by another, nor all by any of them.[22]

Bentley observed that readings found in manuscripts produced at localities that were distant from each other were probably not the result of intentional changes.

Some scribal errors were so common that different scribes in different areas could conceivably make the same error independently of one another. This phenomenon is now referred to as "multiple emergence and coincidental agreement."[23] Wide geographical distribution does not make such errors less likely.

However, some variant readings are *not* the result of common scribal errors. Some variants have specific features that suggest that the manuscripts that share the reading must ultimately have derived it from the same source. In these cases, if manuscripts from the same period but from several distant locations share the same reading, then the text from

---

22. Richard Bentley, *Remarks upon a Late Discourse in Free Thinking: In a Letter to F. H. [Francis Hare], D. D.*, 8th ed. (Cambridge: W. Thurlbourn, 1743), 91–92 §32.

23. This nomenclature was suggested by Gerd Mink. The CBGM uses the assessment of pre-genealogical coherence to identify probable instances of multiple emergence of identical variants resulting in coincidental agreement. See Mink, "Contamination, Coherence, and Coincidence," 141–216, esp. 149, 175. For an introduction to this element of the CBGM, see Charles L. Quarles, "The Usefulness of Pre-genealogical Coherence for Detecting Multiple Emergence and Coincidental Agreement: Matthew 16:2b–3 as a Test Case," *NTS* 67 (2021): 424–46.

which they all ultimately derived that reading is probably significantly older than these manuscripts. These manuscripts are not likely copies of the same exemplar. The manuscripts are likely distant cousins rather than siblings. Thus, the shared reading can be traced several generations of copies earlier.[24] Porter and Pitts are correct that wide geographical distribution points to "an earlier common tradition."[25] Ehrman states the principle most clearly: "Any form of the text that is found in witnesses scattered over a wide geographical range, as opposed to one found in manuscripts located, e.g., in only one city or region, has a greater chance of being ancient."[26]

Although the wide geographical distribution suggests that the shared reading is significantly older than the manuscripts that preserve the reading, determining the early geographical distribution of a reading is, unfortunately, a very difficult task. The NT papyri originated almost exclusively in Egypt, and the more specific provenance of most of them is unknown. Scholars still debate the provenance of the early majuscules, and we may never know the critical details with any degree of certainty. Efforts to examine the geographical distribution of readings must resort to a study of the early versions and citations in the works of the early church fathers since their provenances are often known.[27] Yet, using the versions and fathers faces serious difficulties.[28] For example, although these versions and church fathers are often early, the extant manuscripts of these versions and fathers are usually significantly later. The fathers sometimes quoted texts from memory without consulting a manuscript or intentionally paraphrased the text. Early versions sometimes resorted to paraphrase as well. Other changes were necessitated by differences between Greek and the language of the version.

---

24. Unfortunately, the evidence is not sufficient to determine the precise number of generations (or years) earlier to which the reading may be traced. However, we may confidently assert that readings whose earliest contemporaneous witnesses have a wide geographical distribution probably predate readings whose earliest witnesses are from the same period but all come from the same region.

25. Porter and Pitts, *Fundamentals of New Testament Textual Criticism*, 105.

26. Ehrman, *Studies in the Textual Criticism of the New Testament*, NTTS 33 (Boston: Brill, 2006), 5. Unfortunately, the statement jumps from a discussion of the distribution of a "reading" to a discussion of the "form" of the text. The two terms are distinct in meaning. A "reading" refers to a single variant, but a "form" seems to refer to a text with a specific combination of readings spread over many variant units. I think that the author means to affirm that both a specific reading and a more extensive form that are widely distributed are likely to be ancient. A shared form consisting of a particular combination of many readings is probably more ancient than a single shared reading.

27. Epp, "Traditional 'Canons,'" 100. The editors of the NA[28] observed, "As the lives and works of the Church Fathers are fairly well defined both geographically and historically, their witness is highly significant for the history of the New Testament text and for the reconstruction of the initial form" (p. 78* in NA[28]). For some of the difficulties in attempting to use the works of the early church fathers in New Testament textual criticism, see Gordon D. Fee, "The Use of the Greek Fathers for New Testament Textual Criticism," rev. Roderic L. Mullen, in Ehrman and Holmes, *Text of the New Testament in Contemporary Research*, 351–73; and H. A. G. Houghton, "The Use of the Latin Fathers for New Testament Textual Criticism," in Ehrman and Holmes, *Text of the New Testament in Contemporary Research*, 375–405.

28. See the discussions in sections 2.5 and 2.6 above.

Metzger and Ehrman caution further: "One must be certain, however, that geographically remote witnesses are really independent of one another."[29] Travel between important Christian sites was more common and frequent than some modern scholars have assumed, and even geographically remote witnesses' dependence on a single source or closely related sources is possible. In summary, although the examination of the geographical distribution of readings is useful theoretically, it is often impractical and rarely affects the final decision regarding the original reading.

If a researcher seeks to examine the early geographical distribution of specific readings, he or she must be prepared to conduct a detailed study of the early church fathers and early versions. The study of the father must rely on the best critical editions of the father's work (assuming any exists), consider the consistency of multiple citations in the father's various works, calculate the probability that the father intended to quote directly from a written text of the NT, and factor in the age of the extant manuscripts of the father's work. Since no good critical editions of some works of the church fathers exist, the researcher should be prepared to conduct a text-critical analysis of the father's citation if variation among the extant manuscripts exists. In the case of an early version, one should consider the history of that version, the stability of the translation, differences between Greek grammar and the grammar of the language of the version, and the age of the extant manuscripts of the version.

The UBS[5] provides a more thorough treatment of NT quotations in the works of the early church fathers than other recent hand editions.[30] Unfortunately, although modern editions of the Greek NT like the UBS[5] and NA[28] give approximate dates for the death of the early church fathers, they do not consistently identify the locations in which they lived and produced their writings.[31]

Appendix II lists the known places of extended service for the church fathers to assist the reader in determining the geographical distribution of readings. It identifies the abbreviation used for the father in NA[28], the name of the father, locations in which the father composed his writings (noting important movements), a specific geographical label, and the estimated date of the father's death. Appendix II separates the Greek and Latin fathers since this is the approach of both the apparatus and the front matter of the UBS[5].

Researchers might want to display the geographical distribution of readings graphically by marking a photocopy of a map of the ancient Mediterranean world for each reading. Or, they may prefer to use a table to record these locations. The table below describes locations in terms of their relationship to a focal point near the center of the Mediterranean Sea.

---

29. Metzger and Ehrman, *Text of the New Testament*, 302.
30. The editors of the NA[28] treated quotations of the church fathers "rather selectively" (p. 78*).
31. See pp. 38*–43* in UBS[5] and pp. 80*–81* in NA[28].

- North (Greece, Asia Minor)
- Northeast (Syria)
- East (Palestine and Cyprus)
- Southeast (Egypt)
- Southwest (North Africa)
- Northwest (Iberian Peninsula, Gaul, Italy)
- Remote (outside of the Mediterranean world)

The UBS[5] apparatus includes church fathers from the mid-5th century and earlier. In the table below, church fathers and versions that belong to the mid-4th century or earlier are set in bold type since these may be especially important for understanding the geographical distribution of readings in the earliest period. Although the Ethiopic, Armenian, Georgian, and Old Church Slavonic versions are included in the table below, they are so late that they are of little value for establishing the antiquity of a reading; hence, they are set in strikethrough text. Researchers may want to include only the Old Latin, Vulgate, Coptic, and Syriac versions in the table since these are the earliest and most important for our purposes.

Table 6.4. Geographical Distribution of Readings in the Early Church Fathers and Versions

	North	Northeast	East	Southeast	Southwest	Northwest	Remote
ἁμαρτήσῃ εἰς σέ		Basil[mss];	Chrysostom[mss]	Coptic	Augustine[6/7]	**Hilary Lucifer** Pacian Chromatius Jerome Old Latin Vulgate	~~Armenian Ethiopic Georgian Slavonic~~
ἁμάρτῃ εἰς σέ		Basil[5/9]	Chrysostom Theodoret	Didymus			
ἁμαρτήσῃ				Cyril	Augustine[1/7]		~~Slavonic~~[mss]
ἁμαρτῃ		Basil[4/9]	**Origen**[lem]				

Reading 1 is supported by witnesses characterized by the widest geographical distribution in general. Reading 2, which also has the prepositional phrase, has the second-widest distribution. However, the fact that Basil, Chrysostom, and Augustine each support more than one reading undermines confidence in any conclusions drawn from geographical distribution. In this case (and this is often true), the examination of geographical distribution yields no useful results.

6.1.2 ADDITIONAL CONSIDERATION 2: Reevaluate the date assigned to readings shared by early witnesses that are not closely related to each other

Metzger and Ehrman suggest that an important feature of external evidence is "the genealogical relationship of texts and families of witnesses."[32] The readings that can be traced back to the earliest point in the genealogy of texts are likely original.

Textual scholars have often used the imperfect analogy of family relationships to illustrate textual relationships. All NT manuscripts belong to one large family tree. The many similar readings shared by all NT manuscripts show that all manuscripts are related to some degree. For this reason, we can recognize a particular manuscript as a *New Testament* manuscript as opposed to the manuscript of some other document. Some manuscripts have very similar readings (traits) because one is the exemplar (parent) and the other is a direct copy (child). Others have very similar readings because they are textual siblings, separate manuscripts both copied from the same exemplar (parent). Other manuscripts share the same readings because they are textual first, second, or third (etc.) cousins. Several generations of copies earlier, their family lines intersected. In other words, when manuscripts that are closely related share the same reading, this usually means that a recent ancestor of the two manuscripts contained that reading. When manuscripts that are more distantly related share the same reading, this may mean that the reading can be traced many generations earlier.[33]

Manuscripts that are closely related have a high percentage of agreement over many different variant units. Manuscripts that are not closely related often share the same readings too. The shared reading may be the result of one of three different causes. First, the shared reading may result from contamination. Contamination occurred when a scribe (or corrector) occasionally consulted and copied readings from a second (or third, etc.) manuscript in addition to his primary exemplar. Even if this other exemplar was closely related to the other, it would contain different readings at various points. This dependence on multiple exemplars resulted in the copy containing a mixture of different readings from different textual groups.[34]

Second, readings shared by distant relatives may be the result of multiple emergence and coincidental agreement. Multiple emergence occurs when two or more scribes independently make the same change and produce the same reading in their copies. These two copies now agree on this specific reading, but that agreement is purely coincidental. The agreement does not imply a relationship between the two manuscripts. Multiple

---

32. Metzger and Ehrman, *Text of the New Testament*, 302.

33. In applying this principle, the researcher will not be able to determine the precise number of generations of copies earlier to which the reading may be traced. The principle merely asserts that if a reading's earliest witnesses are roughly contemporaneous and are distant (rather than close) relatives, that reading may be presumed to be earlier than readings whose earliest witnesses are from the same period but are all close relatives.

34. For various kinds of mixture, see Michael W. Holmes, "Working with an Open Textual Tradition: Challenges in Theory and Practice," in Wachtel and Holmes, *Textual History of the Greek New Testament*, 68–69.

emergence is normally the result of common scribal errors. Knowledge of these common errors (part of the examination of internal evidence) helps to identify probable cases of multiple emergence.

Third, readings shared by distant relatives may be traced back to an ancestor many generations earlier whose readings have sometimes been preserved by both family lines. Such readings shared by distant relatives are probably much older than the manuscripts that preserve them. The readings probably belong to the period before the two family lines split.

Naturally, we must distinguish readings that are shared by distant relatives due to contamination from those shared by distant relatives due to a much earlier shared ancestor. This can be done by comparing the readings in manuscripts more closely related to these two witnesses. If close relatives do not share the reading that the manuscript has in common with the distant relative, the shared reading is probably the result of contamination. However, if close relatives of both witnesses share that reading, the agreement is probably the result of influence from a much earlier ancestor.

Based on these factors, Scrivener argued: "In weighing conflicting evidence we must assign the highest value not to those readings which are attested by the greatest number of witnesses, but to those which come to us from several remote and independent sources, and which bear the least likeness to each other in respect to genius and general character."[35] Scholars in the 19th and 20th centuries assigned texts to three or four major text-types: Alexandrian, Western, Caesarean, and Byzantine. These text-types were an attempt to simplify the comparison of manuscripts. Theories about the origin and relationship of these text-types served as an important guide in textual criticism. However, now that researchers can evaluate the relationships between individual texts in much greater detail with the assistance of computers, text critics have recognized that the old text-type approach is problematic and must be abandoned. Appendix III explains several of the major shortcomings of the text-type approach.

However, we can conduct an assessment of the relationship of the early witnesses that share a specific reading without resorting to the old text-type approach by using data compiled for the production of the Editio Critica Maior volumes. We will use the Manuscript Clusters tool on the INTF website to determine how closely related the different manuscripts are that support each reading for our example variant unit, Matt 18:15.[36] At the INTF website (uni-muenster.de/INTF/en/index.html), click "Databases," then "Manuscript Clusters" under "Links," then "Parallel Pericopes Mss. Clusters." In the Manuscript box, type the numerical designation of the first manuscript listed in the attestation for reading 1 (in this case, "05" for D, since we will work through the witnesses in the order in which they appear in the apparatus). Make sure that "Synoptic Gospels," "Simple Grouping," and "Show Further Relations" are selected. Click "GO!" The search will output the data shown in the table below. We will scan it looking for other witnesses to reading 1 and highlight those that we find. Then we will note the percentage of agreement between those witnesses.

---

35. Scrivener, *Plain Introduction to the Criticism of the New Testament*, 2:301.

36. The four variant readings are (1) ἁμαρτήσῃ εἰς σέ, (2) ἁμάρτῃ εἰς σέ, (3) ἁμαρτήσῃ, and (4) ἁμάρτῃ.

Table 6.5. Texts Most Closely Related to 05 in the Synoptic Gospels[37]

05, Simple Grouping, Showing Further Relations, Basis: PP Apparatus of Mt-Mk-Lk			
05 - MT 69.4%	11) 565 (70.3)	21) 2193 (70.0) - 209 (93.8)	31) 1328 (69.6) - 1334 (98.6)
1) A (72.4) - 019 (89.3)	12) 1582 (70.3) - 209 (94.6)	22) 031 (69.8)	32) 1340 (69.6)
2) 033 (71.7)	13) 1338 (70.2)	23) 35 (69.8)	33) 1341 (69.6)
3) 038 (71.6) - 044 (84.0)	14) 1421 (70.2) - 041 (94.4)	24) 1339 (69.8) - 1334 (99.1)	34) 07 (69.5)
4) 2737 (71.1)	15) 03 (70.1) - 01 (84.9)	25) 036 (69.7)	35) 030 (69.5)
5) 043 (71.0)	16) 892 (70.1) - 019 (88.0)	26) 174 (69.7)	36) 045 (69.5)
6) 372 (71.0)	17) 1110 (70.1)	27) 788 (69.7) - 826 (96.6)	37) 3 (69.5) - 1296 (99.1)
7) 011 (70.6)	18) 034 (70.0)	28) 2546 (69.7)	38) 1230 (69.5)
8) 22 (70.6)	19) 1 (70.0) - 209 (94.7)	29) 18 (69.6) - 1334 (99.0)	39) 2372 (69.5)
9) 1343 (70.4)	20) 700 (70.0)	30) 150 (69.6)	40) 233 (69.4)
10) 028 (70.3)			41) 1348 (69.4) - 1296 (93.9)

The results first highlight the rate of agreement between D (05) and the MT, namely, 69.4 percent. Notice that D is not closely related to even its nearest relatives (e.g., A and 033). Although D is more closely related to 892 than to the MT (thus 892 shows up on the list), it agrees with readings in 892 only 70.1 percent of the time. This agreement is only a fraction of a percentage point (0.7 percent) greater than D's rate of agreement with the MT. The data output shows the difference between the rate of agreement between D and 892 versus the rate of agreement between 892 and 892's own closest relative (88 percent agreement with the majuscule 019), an increase of nearly 18 percentage points. Thus, although 892 "made the list," this is only because D has *no* close relatives, so D and 892 are not close relatives at all.

This procedure should be completed for each of the witnesses. We will find that, of the witnesses to reading 1, L (019), Δ (037), and 892 are closely related. The rates of agreement for Δ and 892 with L are high, 85.1 percent and 88 percent respectively. These two texts are L's closest relatives except for the hypothetical initial text. However, D is not a close relative of any of the other early witnesses in the attestation for reading 1. Thus, reading 1 initially seems to satisfy the criterion of being one that we can show to be early in consideration of the fact that it appears in early witnesses that are not closely related. However, further consideration undermines that initial conclusion. The presence of a shared reading in two witnesses that are not closely related may imply that the reading predates those witnesses. However, this is most probable when the two witnesses are at least roughly contemporary. L (019) is dated three centuries later than D (05). Thus, the reading in L may have been influenced by D itself or by one of the descendants of D rather than an early ancestor of D. Our analysis does not support dating reading 1 significantly earlier than its earliest extant witness.

Of the witnesses to reading 2 (W [032], 33, 1424), none are closely related. However, since 33 and 1424 are relatively late witnesses, their agreement on this reading does not necessarily imply that the reading significantly predates W.

The only two early witnesses supporting reading 3 (א [01], B [03]) are closely related to each other. Thus, the criterion does not apply for reading 3. The presence of the read-

37. Used with permission of the Institute for New Testament Textual Research (INTF), University of Münster.

ing in two closely related witnesses does not support dating the reading any earlier than its earliest witness (B).

Remember that the ultimate purpose of this criterion is to trace the existence of a particular reading as early as possible. However, in this case, the criterion does not support dating any of the readings earlier than their earliest extant witness.

6.2. CRITERION 2: Prefer readings in witnesses that are known to be reliable and accurate

The two scholars who have arguably had the greatest influence on the modern practice of NT textual criticism are the 19th-century scholars Westcott and Hort. They famously argued: "KNOWLEDGE OF DOCUMENTS SHOULD PRECEDE FINAL JUDGMENT UPON READINGS."[38] Westcott and Hort argued that some text-critical questions can be decided based on internal evidence alone. The text critic can then identify the manuscripts that most frequently preserve the original readings that were identified based on the internal evidence. The researcher may reasonably assume that the manuscripts that are most accurate in these clear cases are probably the most accurate elsewhere as well.[39]

Scholars have discovered the kinds of errors that scribes were most prone to make, and sometimes this knowledge alone is sufficient to identify the original reading confidently. Scholars also have advanced tools for studying the typical grammar, style, vocabulary, and theological convictions of the various NT authors. These tools sometimes enable them to identify the original reading. When sufficient numbers of these text-critical issues have been decided based on the examination of this internal evidence, scholars can then identify the manuscripts that most frequently preserve these correct readings. These generally more reliable manuscripts will be given preference in making text-critical decisions in which firm conclusions cannot be reached based on other evidence.

Textual critics have often argued that manuscripts should be "weighed rather than counted."[40] The process of "weighing" includes consideration of the general trustworthiness of a specific text. The Alands explained: "[T]he peculiar traits of each manuscript should be duly considered."[41] Although the critic cannot blindly follow any single manuscript or group of manuscripts, "certain combinations of witnesses may deserve a greater degree of confidence than others."[42] These opinions prompted the Alands to assign manuscripts to

---

38. Westcott and Hort, *Introduction to the New Testament*, 31. This dictum was one of only two written by the authors in all caps to express importance.

39. See Westcott and Hort, *Introduction to the New Testament*, 32–33. Similarly, Ehrman has argued that "witnesses *known* to produce an inferior text when the case can be decided with a high degree of certainty (on the 'internal' grounds discussed below), are also more likely to produce an inferior text where the internal evidence is more ambiguous" (*Studies in the Textual Criticism of the New Testament*, 5; emphasis original).

40. Metzger and Ehrman, *Text of the New Testament*, 302; Aland and Aland, *Text of the New Testament*, 280.

41. Aland and Aland, *Text of the New Testament*, 281.

42. Aland and Aland, *Text of the New Testament*, 281.

five different categories. These categories are helpful for a provisional estimate of the general quality of a text (though we can develop a more accurate assessment for the portions of the NT already treated in the published Editio Critica Maior volumes). Manuscripts in Category I are "Manuscripts of a very special quality which should always be considered in establishing the original text."[43] The manuscripts in this category not only include the very early ones, the papyri and the majuscules of the 3rd and 4th centuries, but also later manuscripts that have been found to preserve original readings consistently, such as the 9th-century minuscule 33 and the 10th-century minuscule 1739.[44] These considerations have led most reasoned eclectics to show some preference for a group of manuscripts often referred to as the Alexandrian group.

Scholars can also measure the quality of a manuscript by noting the number of obvious errors, such as nonsense and singular readings. Nonsense readings are those that make no sense at all and must be mistakes. For example, Matt 2:16 says that King Herod was tricked "by the magi." However, the scribe of W (032) made an obvious, nonsensical error when he wrote that Herod was tricked "by the wedding ceremonies."[45] Singular readings are readings that appear in only one early manuscript (papyrus or majuscule) and are assumed to be scribal mistakes.[46] Since so many copies of the Greek NT have survived, we ordinarily expect the original reading to be preserved in more than just one manuscript.

However, one must be careful about assuming that higher numbers of nonsense and singular readings imply that the manuscript is always unreliable. In some cases, a clumsy scribe copied a superb exemplar, and the high quality of the exemplar is preserved at important points despite the scribe's ineptitude. For example, Zuntz pointed out that $\mathfrak{P}^{46}$ is "by no means a good manuscript" since "the scribe committed very many blunders."[47] Nevertheless, after a very careful comparison of $\mathfrak{P}^{46}$'s readings with those of other manuscripts, Zuntz concluded: "The excellent quality of the text represented by our oldest manuscript, $\mathfrak{P}^{46}$, stands out again."[48] This sounds like a direct contradiction until Zuntz explains:

> As so often before, we must here be careful to distinguish between the very poor work of the scribe who penned it and the basic text which he so poorly rendered. $\mathfrak{P}^{46}$ abounds with scribal blunders, omissions, and also additions. . . . Once they have been discarded, there remains a text of outstanding (though not absolute) purity.[49]

---

43. Aland and Aland, *Text of the New Testament*, 106.

44. Aland and Aland, *Text of the New Testament*, 317. The Alands noted that although the scholars of the 19th century were enamored with the majuscules, and scholars for most of the 20th century were most impressed by the papyri, in more recent scholarship, "a whole group of minuscules is advancing claims for equal recognition, and with equal justification" (129).

45. I.e., γαμων was written for μαγων. We will later see (section 7.1.2) that this was the result of a common scribal error involving the accidental transposition of the letters of a word (metathesis).

46. For definitions of singular and subsingular readings, see Westcott and Hort, *Introduction to the New Testament*, 230.

47. Zuntz, *Text of the Epistles*, 18.

48. Zuntz, *Text of the Epistles*, 212.

49. Zuntz, *Text of the Epistles*, 212–13.

Judgments about the quality of different witnesses and different groups of witnesses are made largely based on internal evidence. The results of this analysis of internal evidence then become criteria for evaluating the external evidence. This poses serious problems for claims that external evidence is "the most objective" and thus to be prioritized.[50] Conclusions drawn from the supposed quality of witnesses are only as reliable as the analysis of internal evidence used to measure that quality. Thus, one should not assume that external evidence is necessarily more reliable than internal evidence. In any given case, either external or internal evidence may carry more weight depending on the nature of the textual variant.

Epp has voiced strong reservations about a preference for the "best quality" manuscripts since such an assessment is "ambiguous and relative."[51] He challenged: "'Best' in what sense? 'Best' in whose judgment? 'Best' by what standards?" Elliott has repudiated the principle of preferring the best manuscripts and referred to Westcott and Hort's preference for the early majuscules ℵ and B as the "cult of the 'best' manuscripts."[52] Although preference for the readings of the best manuscripts can be a helpful guide, the principle must be applied cautiously and with an awareness of the many subjective decisions that led to the appraisal of particular manuscripts as having the highest quality.

The researcher may scan the attestations for each variant unit to find the manuscripts that the Alands identified as belonging to "Category I." These are (01) ℵ, A (02; except in the Gospels), B (03), 057, 33 (except in the Gospels), 1175, 1241 (in General Epistles), 1243 (in General Epistles), 1739 (in Paul and General Epistles), 2053, 2062, 2344 (in General Epistles and Revelation), and 2427, as well as some other manuscripts that preserve relatively small portions of the NT.

The Alands also identified some manuscripts as belonging to "Category II," which they described as "manuscripts of a special quality" and "of importance for establishing the original text," even though these manuscripts had more "alien influences" than those belonging to Category I.[53] Category II manuscripts include: C (04), D^p (06), E^a (08), F^p (010), I (016), L^e (019), T (029), Θ (038), Ψ (044), 048, 33 (in the Gospels), 36 (in Acts), 81, 256 (in Paul), 322 (in General Epistles), 323 (in General Epistles), 442, 579 (in Mark and Luke), 892, 1067 (in General Epistles), 1292 (in General Epistles), 1342 (in Mark), 1409 (in Acts and General Epistles), 1506 (in Paul), 1611 (in Revelation), 1735 (in General Epistles), 1739 (in Acts), 1841 (in Revelation), 1852 (in General Epistles), 1854 (in Revelation), 1881, 1962, 2050, 2127 (in Paul), 2298 (in General Epistles), 2329, and 2464.

We may conveniently tabulate the number of Category I and II witnesses for each reading for Matt 18:15 by using the table from step 1 and placing Category I witnesses in bold type and underlining Category II witnesses:

50. See footnote 4 in this chapter.
51. Epp, "Traditional 'Canons,'" 99.
52. J. K. Elliott, "Can We Recover the Original Text of the New Testament? An Examination of the Role of Thoroughgoing Eclecticism," in *Essays and Studies in New Testament Textual Criticism*, EFN 3 (Cordova: Ediciones el Almendro, 1992), 27–28.
53. Aland and Aland, *Text of the New Testament*, 106.

Table 6.6. Preferred Witnesses in Matt 18:15

	2nd c.	3rd c.	4th c.	5th c.	6th c.	7th c.	8th c.	9th c.
1. ἁμαρτήσῃ εἰς σέ				D	N O Σ 078		E L	F G H Δ Θ 28 565 892
2. ἁμάρτῃ εἰς σέ				W				33 1424
3. ἁμαρτήσῃ			ℵ B					
4. ἁμάρτῃ								

Remember that this table includes only witnesses that date to the 9th century or prior. Some later witnesses may belong to Category I or II, and these should be added to the chart if they appear in the attestation. In this case, however, no other witnesses need to be added.

Reading 1 has three Category II witnesses (L Θ 892), and reading 2 has one Category II witness (33). However, since reading 3 has two Category I witnesses, this distribution supports reading 3.

As more volumes of the Editio Critica Maior appear, it will be possible to classify the best manuscripts for the various books of the NT with great accuracy and precision. Tommy Wasserman suggests that researchers should prefer the reading that "is supported by witnesses that have the initial text as their closest potential ancestor."[54] The "initial text" is the reconstructed hypothetical text from which all the surviving witnesses descended.[55] The Coherence-Based Genealogical Method, which is used to establish the text in the Editio Critica Maior volumes, shows probable genealogical relationships between texts through stemmata for NT books and corpora. The charts of textual flow for the portions of the NT treated in the published volumes of the Editio Critica Maior (Acts and the Catholic Letters) are now available. At the INTF website (uni-muenster.de/INTF/en/index.html), click "Databases," then "ECM Acts"; then select "Phase 4" in the left-hand column, and then "Coherence and Textual Flow." At the bottom of that page, you will find the "General Textual Flow." Make sure that the "Chapter" setting is "All." Then click "A" to display the textual flow with the hypothetical initial text. Click on "Z" to display all witnesses in the textual flow. The top portion of the flowchart will show the texts believed to be the closest to the initial text, the ancestor of all known texts. These are called the close A-related witnesses, or witnesses with A as their first potential ancestor.[56]

---

54. Tommy Wasserman, "Criteria for Evaluating Readings in New Testament Textual Criticism," in Ehrman and Holmes, *Text of the New Testament in Contemporary Research*, 605.

55. Michael W. Holmes, "From 'Original Text' to 'Initial Text': The Traditional Goal of New Testament Textual Criticism in Contemporary Discussion," in Ehrman and Holmes, *Text of the New Testament in Contemporary Research*, 653.

56. Used with permission of the Institute for New Testament Textual Research (INTF), University of Münster. Due to space constraints, the textual flow below resulted from unclicking "Z." This removes from the textual flow those witnesses in which the specific text in Acts (Acts 1:1 in this example) is no longer extant.

Figure 6.1. Witnesses to Acts Most Closely Related to the Initial Text

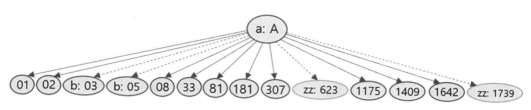

One cannot immediately tell from the flowchart how closely the various descendants are related to the initial text. For this information, click the encircled "a: A" at the top of the flowchart. A new table will appear that ranks the closest witnesses to the initial text in descending order and specifies the percentage of shared variant units on which the two witnesses agree.

Unfortunately, the textual flow for the Gospels is not currently available, so we cannot yet use this approach for our sample variant unit, Matt 18:15. However, using tools developed for the Editio Critica Maior volume titled *Parallel Pericopes (Special Volume Regarding the Synoptic Gospels)*, the researcher can identify the closest relatives of the initial text in the Synoptic Gospels in another way. At the INTF website, click "Databases," then "Manuscript Clusters" under the right-hand column titled "Links," then "Parallel Pericopes Mss. Clusters." In the Manuscript box, type "A" (the siglum for the initial text). Make sure that "Synoptic Gospels," "Simple Grouping," and "Show Further Relations" are also selected. Click "GO!" The results identify six manuscripts whose texts are more similar to the initial text than to the MT: B (03), 892, L (019), ℵ (01), C (04), and Δ (037). These texts likely belong to the same textual group. Three of these witnesses (L Δ 892) support reading 1. Two of these witnesses (B and ℵ) support reading 3. Notice, although many scholars assume that ℵ and B are the best manuscripts of the Gospels, 892 and L (019) are actually superior to ℵ in the Synoptic Gospels in the variant units covered by the *Parallel Pericopes* volume. Consider also that continued work on the Editio Critica Maior will enable scholars to refine and improve the Alands' classifications. For example, the Alands placed 892 and L in Category II and Δ in Category III (an independent text). However, the *Parallel Pericopes* data suggests that these manuscripts should be classified as belonging to Category I for the Synoptic Gospels.

With the benefit of this data, we can improve our table by highlighting the witnesses closest to the initial text:

Table 6.7. Witnesses Closest to the Initial Text in the Synoptic Gospels

	2nd c.	3rd c.	4th c.	5th c.	6th c.	7th c.	8th c.	9th c.
1. ἁμαρτήσῃ εἰς σέ				D	Ν Ο Σ 078		Ε L	F G H Δ Θ 28 565 **892**
2. ἁμάρτῃ εἰς σέ				W				<u>33</u> 1424
3. ἁμαρτήσῃ			ℵ B					
4. ἁμάρτῃ								

6.3. CRITERION 3: Prefer readings found in multiple early witnesses

This criterion or principle was applied in textual decisions at least as early as the time of Origen (early 3rd c.). On a few occasions, Origen categorized readings as belonging to "few," "many," or "most" manuscripts available to him.[57] Although he sometimes rejected the reading found in most manuscripts based on other principles,[58] in other cases, he followed the reading found in the majority of manuscripts.[59] This does not mean that Origen would affirm the MT approach if he were alive today. Origen rarely appealed to the majority reading, and when he did, he also appealed to other supporting evidence. Furthermore, the only manuscripts available to Origen were, from the modern perspective, very early manuscripts. Origen did not belong to an era in which the majority of manuscripts had been produced a millennium or more after the original and often differed from the earliest available manuscripts.

Scholars generally do not follow the reading of even the oldest available manuscripts if only one early witness has that reading. Ordinarily, one would expect the original reading to be preserved in more than one early manuscript. Singular readings (readings that appear

---

57. B. M. Metzger, "Explicit References in the Works of Origen to Variant Readings in New Testament Manuscripts," in *Biblical and Patristic Studies in Memory of Robert Pierce Casey*, ed. J. N. Birdsall and R. W. Thomson (Freiburg: Herder, 1963), 86–87; F. Pack, "Origen's Evaluation of Textual Variants in the Greek Bible," *ResQ* 4 (1960): 143–44; Eldon J. Epp, "The Eclectic Method in New Testament Textual Criticism: Solution or Symptom?," *HTR* 69 (1976): 216.

58. See, for example, Origen's discussion of the variants in John 1:28 (*Comm. Jo.* §80) in which he prefers the reading of the minority of manuscripts.

59. Epp ("Eclectic Method," 216) referred to Origen's practice as "an adumbration of the much more modern canon underlying the 16th-century phrase, *textus receptus* or 'text received by all' a canon that in reality declares that the reading supported by the largest number of manuscripts is to be accounted original." Epp noted that Origen did not consistently follow the canon and sometimes even rejected the reading of all the manuscripts known to him. However, he argued that "the canon of a majority reading is latent in his comments." Donaldson ("Explicit References to New Testament Variant Readings," 1:101–2, 106–7) has shown that the majority reading was not as important a criterion for Origen as Pack's earlier research had suggested. Ordinarily, Origen does not attempt to quantify support for specific readings. He merely notes that "some copies" have one reading and "other copies" another.

in only one witness) even in a very early manuscript are generally regarded as the result of a scribal error, and careful examination of singular readings confirms that assessment. One of the "twelve basic rules for textual criticism" followed by the Alands is

> The principle that the original reading may be found in any single manuscript or version when it stands alone or nearly alone is only a theoretical possibility. Any form of eclecticism which accepts this principle [that the original reading may be found in a single witness] will hardly succeed in establishing the original text of the New Testament; it will only confirm the view of the text which it presupposes.[60]

When the earliest manuscripts unanimously agree on a particular reading, the probability that the reading is original increases. Samuel Tregelles expressed the principle in his "Introductory Notice" to the first volume of his *Greek New Testament*:

> If the reading of the ancient authorities in general is unanimous, there can be but little doubt that it should be followed, whatever may be the later testimonies; for it is most improbable that the independent testimony of early MSS., versions, and Fathers should accord with regard to something entirely groundless.[61]

Preference for readings found in multiple early witnesses follows the same reasoning as the legal principle in Deut 19:15: "A fact must be established by the testimony of two or three witnesses" (cf. Deut 17:6; Matt 18:16; 2 Cor 13:1; 1 Tim 5:19; Heb 10:28). The testimony of multiple witnesses is usually more trustworthy than the testimony of a single witness.

Although preference for readings found in multiple early witnesses is reasonable, text-critical issues cannot be decided by a simple majority of the early witnesses. The surviving early witnesses are only a very, very small fraction of the witnesses that circulated in the first millennium of the transmission of the text. The numbers of early witnesses now available are much too small to constitute a statistically valid sample size.[62] Statements in the early church fathers often confirm this. Their descriptions of the readings of the majority of manuscripts available to them often do not match the readings preserved in the majority of manuscripts available today. For example, in his *Commentary on Matthew* (§134), Origen notes that most manuscripts of Luke 23:45 state that the sun was darkened (καὶ ἐσκοτίσθη ὁ ἥλιος), but a few other manuscripts state that the sun was eclipsed (τοῦ ἡλίου ἐκλιπόντος).[63] However, of the Greek manuscripts from the 8th century and earlier that

---

60. Aland and Aland, *Text of the New Testament*, 281.

61. Samuel Prideaux Tregelles, *Matthew and Mark*, vol. 1 of *The Greek New Testament* (London: Samuel Baxter and Sons, 1857), ii.

62. Gerd Mink ("Contamination, Coherence, and Coincidence," 146) correctly commented, "Nearly all manuscripts from the first millennium are lost. What we have from the early phases of transmission is not likely to be representative of the text in those times; therefore, we have to rely on later sources to trace older variants."

63. See Heine, trans., *Commentary of Origen on the Gospel of St Matthew*, 2:745–46.

are available today, five ($\mathfrak{P}^{75}$ ℵ B C L) support the latter reading and only three (A D W) support the former reading. What Origen claimed was the majority reading now appears to be the minority reading.[64]

We may now examine again the witnesses for the various readings in Matt 18:15.

Table 6.8. Early Witnesses to Matt 18:15

	2nd c.	3rd c.	4th c.	5th c.	6th c.	7th c.	8th c.	9th c.
1. ἁμαρτήσῃ εἰς σέ				D	N O Σ 078		E L	F G H Δ Θ 28 565 **892**
2. ἁμάρτῃ εἰς σέ				W				33 1424
3. ἁμαρτήσῃ			ℵ B					
4. ἁμαρτῃ								

We can quickly see that reading 1 is supported by most of the included manuscripts from the 9th century and earlier. This is also true if we push the time frame back a few centuries. This criterion, however, does not prefer *majority* readings, as was explained earlier. Rather, readings with earlier support from *multiple* witnesses are to be preferred. Based on this criterion, reading 4 may be excluded as a serious candidate for the original reading. Since reading 2 lacks support from multiple witnesses until the 9th century, readings 1 and 3 are to be preferred.

6.4. Summarizing the External Evidence

We can summarize our findings for our sample variant unit now and attempt to assess the evidence.

Table 6.9. Summary of the External Evidence for Matt 18:15

Evaluation of External Evidence for Variant Unit in Matt 18:15	
Criterion	*Preferred Reading(s)*
1. Prefer readings that can be shown to be early.	3, 1, 2 (in descending order)
a. Reevaluate the date assigned to readings found in early witnesses from various regions.	None of the readings can be shown to significantly predate their earliest surviving witness
b. Reevaluate the date assigned to readings shared by early witnesses that are not closely related to each other.	None of the readings can be shown to significantly predate their earliest surviving witness

---

64. Of course, the number of manuscripts available to Origen may not have been a statistically valid sample size either. The majority readings in the environs in which Origen studied did not necessarily reflect the majority of readings in the rest of the world at that time.

2. Prefer readings in witnesses that are known to be reliable and accurate.	1 and 3 (no preference)
3. Prefer readings found in multiple early witnesses.	1 and 3 (no preference)

Reading 3 is best supported by the external evidence since it is preferred by criterion 1 and stands equal to reading 1 in two other criteria. Criteria 1a and 1b did not prompt any adjustment to our tentative dating of the readings. The criteria for evaluating the external evidence show that the original reading is probably not reading 2 or 4. We must now evaluate the internal evidence.

7

EVALUATION OF INTERNAL EVIDENCE

As mentioned earlier, internal evidence relates to evidence that emerges from the readings themselves. Westcott and Hort conveniently divided internal evidence into two subcategories. "Transcriptional evidence" considers the practices of ancient scribes with special attention to the kinds of changes that scribes were most likely to make either accidentally or intentionally. Transcriptional evidence seeks to eliminate any readings that probably resulted from common scribal changes. "Intrinsic evidence" relates to the style, grammar, vocabulary, and theology of the specific NT author and seeks to understand what the author would ordinarily be expected to write. Transcriptional evidence focuses on *scribes*, their practices, and especially the kinds of errors that they most frequently made. Intrinsic evidence focuses on *authors* and their tendencies.

7.1. Transcriptional Evidence

When beginning Greek students are introduced to important principles of NT textual criticism, they often memorize a series of rules such as "Prefer the shorter reading" and "Prefer the more difficult reading." These were not intended to be hard and fast rules that can be universally and mechanically applied. When text critics of previous centuries formulated these criteria for evaluating variants, they usually gave a series of important, even necessary, qualifications. For example, in an essay in 1725, Johann Albrecht Bengel summarized an old canon for textual criticism using the Latin expression *proclivi scriptioni praestat ardua*, which may be translated, "the difficult reading is to be preferred to the easy reading."[1] But by "difficult," Bengel merely meant a more obscure, unclear, less elaborate, or less polished reading, certainly not one that made no sense or was impossible in its context. He defined the "easy reading" as one that was highly polished, more elaborate, or more explanatory.[2]

---

1. The preference for the most difficult reading was previously expressed by Erasmus (1516), Jean Le Clerc (1516), and John Mill (1707). See Epp, "Traditional 'Canons,'" 105.
2. See Admonitions 13 and 15, Bengel, *New Testament Word Studies*, 1:xviii.

Similarly, Griesbach elevated to new importance an old canon that stated that "the shorter reading is to be preferred."[3] However, Griesbach offered numerous clarifications and qualifications of this canon. His full explanation stated:

> The shorter reading (unless it lacks entirely the authority of the ancient and weighty witnesses) is to be preferred to the more verbose, for scribes were much more prone to add than to omit. They scarcely ever omitted anything on purpose, but they added many things; certainly they omitted some things by accident, but likewise not a few things have been added to the text by scribes through errors of the eye, ear, memory, imagination, and judgement. Particularly, the shorter reading is to be preferred, even though according to the authority of the witnesses it may appear to be inferior to the other,—
>
> (a) if at the same time it is more difficult, more obscure, ambiguous, elliptical, hebraizing, or solecistic;
> (b) if the same thing is expressed with different phrases in various manuscripts;
> (c) if the order of words varies;
> (d) if at the beginning of pericopes;
> (e) if the longer reading seems to be a gloss or interpretation, or agrees with the wording of parallel passages, or seems to have come from lectionaries.[4]

After reading Griesbach's extensive qualifications of the canon, one might be tempted to quip, "But I thought the shorter reading was to be preferred! I wish that Griesbach would apply this principle to his own writing!" Yet, Griesbach went on to offer even more qualifications. He identified numerous circumstances in which the *longer* reading was to be preferred to the shorter one. Griesbach was not attempting to sound erudite by droning on and on with unnecessary verbosity. He simply realized that very short principles for establishing the original reading are ordinarily misleading principles. They are very unlikely to aid in the recovery of the original text. Since preference for the shorter or longer reading depends on many other factors, several scholars have suggested that textual critics focus on those other factors rather than the relative length of the readings.[5]

---

3. This canon had been articulated earlier by Le Clerc (1516), Bengel (1725), and Johann Jakob Wettstein (1730). See Epp, "Traditional 'Canons,'" 106–7. Griesbach emphasized this canon by making it the first in his list of fifteen canons.

4. Johann Jakob Griesbach, *Novum Testamentum Grace: Textum ad fidem codicum versionum et partum*, 2nd ed., 2 vols. (London: Elmsly, 1796–1806), 1:lx–lxi. The wording of the canon here is a slight adaptation of the paraphrase in Metzger and Ehrman, *Text of the New Testament*, 166–67.

5. See J. David Miller, "The Long and Short of *lectio brevior potior*," *BT* (2006): 11–16; Stephen C. Carlson, *The Text of Galatians and Its History*, WUNT 2.385 (Tübingen: Mohr Siebeck, 2015), 90; Malik, *P.Beatty III (P47)*, 114–15; Farnes, *Simply Come Copying*, 16, 202–3.

7.1.1   Methods for Discovering the Tendencies of Ancient Scribes

In order to assess transcriptional evidence, the text critic must have an accurate understanding of the tendencies of ancient scribes. At least three different methods have been used to develop profiles of the kinds of changes that scribes were most prone to make as they copied their exemplar: the anecdotal method, the singular reading method, and the close-copy method.

Anecdotal Method

The most common method by far over the last several centuries offered descriptions of the most frequent changes based on the general impressions of the textual critics who had worked closely with a variety of manuscripts. The description of this approach as the anecdotal method is not intended to be derogatory. The scholars who developed many of the criteria for assessing transcriptional evidence had extensive first-hand experience in transcribing ancient manuscripts and comparing variants. They did truly impressive work without the benefit of many of the tools now available to modern scholars. Yet, the fact remains that their descriptions of scribal tendencies were not based on carefully quantified statistical data, and their characterizations often overgeneralized the work of ancient scribes. In other words, earlier generations of scholars did not maintain detailed records of the kinds of errors or changes that individual copyists made in order to determine precisely which kinds of changes were most common. Their descriptions of scribal changes often did not account for differences in scribal practice at different places, different times, or for the production of manuscripts for different purposes.[6]

Singular Reading Method

This method carefully examines readings in a manuscript that are not shared by any known manuscript of the Greek NT.[7] These unique readings are often (and in this method sometimes presumed to be[8]) scribal errors committed by the scribe who copied the manuscript. Singular readings are usually identified by comparing the apparatuses of the critical editions with the most detailed lists of supporting manuscripts for variant readings.[9] The

---

6. James R. Royse, *Scribal Habits in Early Greek New Testament Papyri*, NTTS 36 (Leiden: Brill, 2008), 3–4.

7. F. J. A. Hort may have been the first to apply this method. He recognized that some of the singular readings in a manuscript were "individualisms," that is, readings "originating from the scribe or one of his immediate predecessors," as opposed to those which appeared in "the ancestral text" and are now only singular readings because so few of the earliest manuscripts still exist (*Introduction to the New Testament in the Original Greek*, 232). Hort suggested that these individualisms enable scholars to "form an estimate of the degree of general accuracy attained by the scribe of a given document, and also of the kinds of mistakes to which he was prone" (p. 232).

8. Ernest Cadman Colwell, *Studies in Methodology in Textual Criticism of the New Testament*, NTTS 9 (Grand Rapids: Eerdmans, 1969), 108.

9. In his very thorough application of the singular reading method to the papyri, Royse used the apparatuses of ten different critical texts. See Royse, *Scribal Habits*, 65.

researcher can then tabulate how many of the scribe's errors involved omission, addition, transposition, harmonization to the content of a parallel passage, etc. As a huge improvement over the old anecdotal method, this method produces objective and quantifiable data. For example, Royse's application of the method to the early Greek papyri of the NT demonstrated that all six of the papyri he examined omit text more frequently than they add text. Four of these six papyri omitted text two or three times more often than they added text.[10] Several other studies related to other manuscripts have generally confirmed that accidental omission was more common than addition.[11] Royse concluded that the old canon, "the shorter reading is to be preferred," should be replaced with the opposite canon, "the longer reading is to be preferred."[12]

Several scholars have pointed out some weaknesses in the singular reading method. Some argue that understanding the habits and tendencies of a scribe requires analyzing the entire manuscript rather than focusing solely on its singular readings.[13] "Habits" necessarily occur frequently, and it would not be surprising if more than one scribe made the same mistake at the same point in the text, if these "habits" truly represent the practices of ancient scribes in general. Furthermore, as has long been recognized, a singular reading is not necessarily the creation of the scribe who copied the manuscript containing it. The scribe may have merely copied that reading from his exemplar whose scribe may have copied it from his exemplar, etc. Since the number of Greek manuscripts of the NT still available today is only a small percentage of those that existed throughout history, today's singular reading may not have been a singular reading at all a thousand years ago.

Close-Copy Method

The surest method for identifying scribal habits examines parent-child manuscripts, that is, cases in which an extant manuscript is a clear copy of another extant manuscript. The identified copy of an extant manuscript is called the *Abschrift*[14] and the parent

---

10. Royse, *Scribal Habits*, 719.

11. Peter M. Head, "Observations on Early Papyri of the Synoptic Gospels, Especially on the 'Scribal Habits,'" *Bib* 71 (1990): 240–47; Kyoung Shik Min, *Die früheste Überlieferung des Matthäusevangeliums (bis zum 3./4. Jh.): Edition und Untersuchung*, ANTF 34 (New York: de Gruyter, 2005); Juan Hernández Jr., *Scribal Habits and Theological Influences in the Apocalypse: The Singular Readings of Sinaiticus, Alexandrinus, and Ephraemi*, WUNT 2.218 (Tübingen: Mohr Siebeck, 2006). However, Paulson found that in Matthew, Vaticanus's singular readings added more words than it omitted, and Ephraemi had more instances of addition than omission (Gregory S. Paulson, *Scribal Habits and Singular Readings in Codex Sinaiticus, Vaticanus, Ephraemi, Bezae, and Washingtonianus in the Gospel of Matthew* [Wilmore, KY: GlossaHouse, 2018], 128–31).

12. See, however, Royse's important qualifications to his suggested canon (*Scribal Habits*, 735).

13. Barbara Aland, "Kriterien zur Beurteilung kleinerer Payrusfragmente des Neuen Testaments," in *New Testament Textual Criticism and Exegesis: Festschrift J. Delobel*, ed. Adelbert Denaux, BETL 161 (Leuven: Peeters, 2002), 1–13.

14. Consequently, the examination of parent and child manuscripts and the differences between them is called the *Abschrift* method. For a helpful introduction to this approach, see Farnes, *Simply Come Copying*, 24–42.

manuscript is called the exemplar or *Vorlage*. So far, scholars have identified twenty-three probable *Abschriften*.[15] A related method examines similarities and differences in identified sibling manuscripts (manuscripts believed to be direct copies from the same nonextant exemplar). When multiple sibling manuscripts exist, scholars can reconstruct the now-lost exemplar with a high degree of accuracy and then compare the copies to the reconstructed parent in a manner similar to the *Abschrift* method.[16]

Unfortunately, like in several other areas of text-critical research, a lot of work remains to be done to complete the task. In order to arrive at the best understanding of ancient scribal habits, this method needs to be thoroughly applied to all *Abschriften* and sibling manuscripts in their entirety. Ideally, the method should examine not only the text of these manuscripts but their other shared features as well.[17]

A few scholars have described the close-copy method as "looking over the scribe's shoulder" as he goes about his work. This is not entirely true, of course. This method cannot determine with absolute certainty whether a difference found between a copy and its parent or sibling was due to the scribe's grogginess, a change he intentionally made, or one that he found in a second exemplar that he occasionally consulted. However, the close-copy method is as close as modern scholars can come to looking over a scribe's shoulder.

The method faces several limitations. First, of the thousands of manuscripts of the Greek NT available today, only a relatively few *Abschriften* or sibling manuscripts exist. The number is not large enough to consider them a truly representative sample. Second, the *Abschriften* all date from the 9th to the 16th century, and our earliest sibling copies date from the 6th century. Scribal tendencies in this later period may be different from those in the earliest and most important phase of copying the Greek NT.[18] Third, some subjectivity is involved in deciding if a manuscript is a true *Abschrift* or a sibling to an extant manuscript.

The discussion of scribal tendencies here will avoid appeal to anecdotal evidence and will focus on the tendencies that have been confirmed by the best recent studies. It will also avoid hard and fast rules that urge preference for a specific kind of reading. Some of these rules must be heavily qualified to reflect actual scribal practices; so, they are not truly helpful guides. Our discussion will use the standard categories of "unintentional changes" and "intentional changes." However, the distinction between these is not as neat and clear-cut as we might like. Even in cases in which we can explain what

---

15. Farnes, *Simply Come Copying*, 24.

16. For an excellent introduction and application of this method, see Elijah Hixson, *Scribal Habits in Sixth-Century Greek Purple Codices*, NTTSD 61 (Leiden: Brill, 2019).

17. For example, Hixson (*Scribal Habits*, 77) examined orthography, unit delimitation, *kephalaia* (chapters in MSS), *titloi* (subheadings in *kephalaia*), and the Eusebian apparatus in the three sister manuscripts that he researched.

18. David C. Parker, "Scribal Tendencies and the Mechanics of Book Production," in *Textual Variation: Theological and Social Tendencies? Papers from the Fifth Birmingham Colloquium on the Textual Criticism of the New Testament*, ed. H. A. G. Houghton and David C. Parker, TS 3.6 (Piscataway, NJ: Gorgias, 2008), 179.

a particular scribe did, we can seldom know with any certainty why the scribe did it. We cannot possibly psychoanalyze an ancient scribe and identify the motives behind the scribe's actions.[19]

Before delving into the discussion, one more caveat is necessary. Discussions of scribal tendencies often offer a portrait of a stereotypical scribe and work with the assumption that all or most other scribes were very similar. However, a careful look at individual manuscripts quickly reveals that scribes were different, sometimes very different. Think about it. *Different* scribes with *different* skill levels from *different* places at *different* times copied the Greek NT. Colwell rightly emphasized that scribes were individuals and "each has his own pattern of errors."[20] He elaborated, "One scribe is liable to dittography, another to the omission of lines of text; one reads well, another remembers poorly; one is a good speller; etc., etc."[21]

In his recent study, Hixson examined three 6th-century copies (022, 023, 042) of a shared exemplar, which were likely produced by separate scribes approximately at the same time and at the same location. He found that the skill levels of the scribes varied, and each was prone to making distinct alterations to the exemplar's text, whether accidentally or intentionally.[22] The scribe of 023 was very conservative. Although he made slightly more insignificant changes (nonsense readings and spelling differences) to the text than the scribe of 042 did, he was the least likely of the three scribes to introduce significant changes to the text (like substitutions, harmonizations, or editorial readings). The scribe of 042 made significant changes to the text 7.11 times across 10 equivalent folios. The scribe of 022 made 4.49 significant changes over an equivalent amount of text. The scribe of 023 made only 1.36 significant changes over an equivalent amount of text. Thus, the scribe of 022 made over twice the number of significant changes made by the scribe of 023, and the scribe of 042 made over five times the number of significant changes.[23]

Several scribes produced copies with these significant differences even though all copied the same exemplar around the same time, apparently in the same scriptorium and probably with comparable training. Thus, we have little reason to believe that different scribes with different backgrounds, from different places and different eras, would have identical tendencies. Consequently, rather than speaking of the tendencies of an imagined stereotypical scribe, it is far better to seek to understand the tendencies of the individual scribe who copied a specific manuscript. This is required by Hort's insightful principle that "KNOWLEDGE OF DOCUMENTS SHOULD PRECEDE FINAL JUDGMENT UPON READINGS."[24]

---

19. Parker (*Introduction to the New Testament Manuscripts*, 152–53) shares a similar concern.

20. Colwell, *Studies in Methodology*, 114.

21. Colwell, *Studies in Methodology*, 114. Colwell acknowledged that he gleaned this insight from Alphonse Dain, *Les manuscrits* (Paris: Belles-Lettres, 1949), 46.

22. Hixson, *Scribal Habits*, 250–65.

23. See Hixson's discussion of the "Relative Tendencies of Each Scribe" in *Scribal Habits*, 251–54.

24. Westcott and Hort, *Introduction to the New Testament in the Original Greek*, 31. Hort placed the principle in all caps for emphasis.

7.1.2 Common Errors of Ancient Scribes[25]

Alexander Pope mused that "To err is human."[26] Scribes were obviously human, and they naturally made mistakes and imprudent decisions. The conditions under which they performed their work sometimes exacerbated their mistakes in copying. The ancient procedures commonly used for hand-copying a book are described in ancient literature, portrayed in ancient artwork, and can sometimes be inferred from the copies themselves. Surprisingly, scribes did not ordinarily use writing desks or tables for their copying until the Middle Ages. Instead, they copied as they sat on a stool, a bench, or even cross-legged on the floor while they held their copy material in their lap.[27] Writing in this posture for hours on end was terribly uncomfortable. A formula that appears on the end of many ancient manuscripts of classical works complains: "Writing bows one's back, thrusts the ribs into one's stomach, and fosters a general debility of the body."[28]

Neilos, the scribe who copied lectionary 299 in the 12th century, left numerous marginal notes; these have been helpfully gathered, transcribed, and translated by A. C. Myshrall.[29] The scribe's comments provide helpful insights into the challenges of the ancient scribe who desired to copy the NT faithfully. In the notes, Neilos sometimes prayed that the Lord would enable him to copy accurately despite his weaknesses. He specifically mentioned the challenges that fatigue, drowsiness, stupidity, and nearsightedness posed to a scribe as he copied. Here is a sample of the marginal notes:

"Christ, guide my works."

"Unclean hands: spare, Lord, spare this most holy writing."

"Spare, Lord, spare the one who is completely slow."

"The one who writes tends toward errors."

"Woe also to those writing errors."

"In haste, for laziness leads to a lack of attention."

"I am very tired with a heavy head, and what I write I do not know."

In one note, Neilos confesses that he is "very drowsy and foolish." Myshrall found that many of the references to the scribe's fatigue appear in sections that are marked by more

---

25. Parts of this section treating common errors of ancient scribes are based on Quarles and Kellum, *40 Questions about the Text and Canon*, 42–46. Used with permission.

26. Alexander Pope, "An Essay on Criticism," in *The Major Works*, ed. Pat Rogers (Oxford: Oxford University Press, 2006), 33.

27. Bruce M. Metzger, "When Did Scribes Begin to Use Writing Desks?," in *Historical and Literary Studies: Pagan, Jewish, and Christian,* NTTS 8 (Grand Rapids: Eerdmans, 1968), 123–37.

28. Bruce M. Metzger, *Manuscripts of the Greek Bible: An Introduction to Palaeography* (New York: Oxford University Press, 1981), 20.

29. Lectionary 299 is the Gospel lectionary text that was written over the erased New Testament text of Codex Zacynthius. All the following quotations of Neilos's notes are from Myshrall, "Introduction to Lectionary 299," 197–99.

frequent errors, poor handwriting, and extensive erasures where the scribe had to recopy text due to mistakes that he later caught.[30] These marginal notes are a window into the struggles of the scribe.

Unintentional Changes

Scribes sometimes introduced changes into the text by accident. Common errors committed by ancient scribes fall into four major categories: errors in spelling, errors of sight, errors of hearing, and errors in memory. When evaluating transcriptional evidence, researchers should carefully consider if variants may have occurred because of one (or more) of these common errors.

Scribes frequently changed the spelling of Greek words, especially those containing certain vowels or combinations of vowels (diphthongs). Scholars refer to the differences in spelling as orthographic variations. Although Greek words are usually spelled uniformly in modern editions of the Greek NT, the spelling of words in the Greek NT was not standardized until the Middle Ages. Prior to that time, scribes in various places and during different time periods often used distinct spellings. Vaticanus offers an example of how spelling preferences changed over time. After six or seven centuries, the ink of the codex began to fade. A 10th- or 11th-century scribe attempted to preserve the text of the codex by tracing over each letter (a process known as "reinking"). However, the scribe apparently disliked the frequent use of the moveable nu (ν) in the text (placement of a nu at the ending of a word when the preceding letter is a vowel, and the next word begins with a vowel). He often chose not to reink the moveable nu. Although Vaticanus and Sinaiticus are both 4th-century manuscripts, probably copied within only a few decades of each other, the two texts use different spellings. Vaticanus prefers to use ει in many words in which Sinaiticus uses ι and vice versa.[31] This is an example of itacism. Itacism (or "iotacism") refers to the evolution of Greek pronunciation in which the distinctions in sound between ι, ει, η, οι, and υ were lost, and these vowels and diphthongs were increasingly all pronounced like ι.[32]

Westcott and Hort argued that the original authors of the NT books probably spelled words differently from one another and that even the same author likely spelled words differently in a single NT book.[33] They were correct about this. For example, Matthew's Gospel appears to have used two different spellings for the word "Jerusalem" (Ἱεροσόλυμα and Ἱερουσαλήμ).[34] Although this may be puzzling to modern English speakers, spelling in American English was not standardized until the publication of Noah Webster's

---

30. Myshrall, "Introduction to Lectionary 299," 200.

31. Paulson found that scribe A of Sinaiticus changed ει to ι 338 times in Matthew alone. The scribe who copied Matthew in Vaticanus changed ι to ει 73 times. See Paulson, *Scribal Habits*, 14–15, 38–39, 41–42, 46–47, 125–26, 268–93.

32. BDF §§22–25.

33. Westcott and Hort, *Introduction to the New Testament in the Original Greek*, 304, 308.

34. In addition, Ἱεροσόλυμα is sometimes treated as fem. sg. (2:3) but sometimes as neut. pl. (4:25; 15:1). For the different spellings, compare 2:3 and 23:37. All three of these spellings and forms

American Spelling Book in 1783. The famous American explorer William Clark who, together with Meriwether Lewis, mapped the Louisiana Purchase, spelled the name of the Sioux tribe no less than twenty-seven different ways in his journals![35] Even today, American dictionaries approve two different spellings of some words such as adapter/adaptor and doughnut/donut.

In most cases, orthographic variation is considered an insignificant variation since it rarely changes the meaning of a passage. However, sometimes orthographic variation does affect the meaning of the text. For example, the scribe of Codex Sinopensis (O or 023) sometimes changes an ει to η. This may be due to the fact that the diphthong and vowel were pronounced identically. Still, the change of αιτησει to αιτηση in Matt 7:21 (probably unintentionally) converts a future indicative to an aorist subjunctive. Similarly, the change of βληθεισῃ to βληθηση in Matt 13:47 turns an aorist passive participle feminine singular dative form into a future passive indicative second person singular form.[36] In this case, the scribe almost certainly did not intend to change the grammatical form since the new form makes no sense in the context.

In addition to these vowel changes, scribes sometimes substituted similar-sounding consonants for one another. Scribes tended to substitute one consonant for another within the same classification, i.e., one velar/guttural consonant for another velar/guttural or one dental consonant for another dental. For example, the scribe of 𝔓46 sometimes changes a δ to a ζ, a τ to a δ, and a θ to a τ. The scribe also changes a κ to a χ.[37]

Another common form of error involves errors of sight. In errors of sight, a scribe sometimes confused one Greek letter for another that was similar in appearance. Some of the letters that were most easily confused in the majuscule script are (1) C, Є, Θ, O; (2) Γ, Τ, Π; (3) ⅄, Δ, ⅄; and (4) H, N. Confusion of letters was exacerbated by fading ink or other damage in the exemplar, dim lighting, or poor eyesight. The witnesses to 1 Tim 3:16 present one of the best-known examples of letter confusion. The earliest manuscripts and church fathers identify Jesus as "the one who . . ." (OC), but many later manuscripts (and later corrections) refer to him as "God" (using the abbreviation Θ̄C̄).[38] The reference to Jesus' incarnation in the verse understandably prompted a Christian scribe to mistakenly read the O as a Θ. Another example of this confusion of O for a Θ is seen in Matt 5:4, where the scribe who produced Δ (037) accidentally wrote ΠЄΝΟΟΥΝΤЄC (which is not a word) instead of ΠЄΝΘΟΥΝΤЄC ("those who are mourning").

---

appear in other Greek writers. See Charles L. Quarles, *Matthew*, Exegetical Guide to the Greek New Testament (Nashville: B&H Academic, 2017), 24; BDF §§ 39, 56.

35. Donald Jackson, "Some Books Carried by Lewis and Clark," *Bulletin of the Missouri Historical Society* 16 (1959): 11–13.

36. For the list of changes from the exemplar (where all three copies still exist) in 023, see Hixson, *Scribal Habits*, 117.

37. For the specific examples, see Royse, *Scribal Habits*, 244.

38. This form, known as a *nomen sacrum*, was very common in the early manuscripts. For a helpful discussion of the *nomina sacra*, see Larry W. Hurtado, *The Earliest Christian Artifacts: Manuscripts and Christian Origins* (Grand Rapids: Eerdmans, 2006).

Some errors of sight were the result of the scribe's focus moving back and forth from the exemplar to his copy. As the scribe turned from the exemplar to his copy and then back again, he could pick his copying back up in the wrong spot. If he jumped back to a spot too early in the exemplar and started copying again, it would result in *dittography*, that is, copying twice what should have been copied only once. If he jumped back to a spot too late in the exemplar and started copying again, it would result in *haplography*, that is, skipping a section of the text that should have been copied. Both kinds of mistakes that resulted from the shifting focus are most common when words or lines ended with the same letter or combination of letters (homoeoteleuton)[39] or began with the same letter or combination of several letters (homoeoarcton).

An example of haplography due to homoeoteleuton appears in Matt 5:19–20. Matthew 5:19 ends with the phrase τῶν οὐρανῶν, and Matt 5:20 ends with the same phrase. Codex Bezae (D or 05) completely omits 5:20. Apparently, when the scribe completed copying the final line of 5:19 and turned back to the exemplar, he accidentally returned to the phrase at the end of 5:20 and picked up copying there.

Haplography due to homoeoarcton probably explains the omission of fourteen words (καρδίας σου καὶ ἐν ὅλη τῇ ψυχῇ σου καὶ ἐν ὅλη τῇ ἰσχύϊ σου) from Luke 10:27 in 𝔓45. This example is a bit more complicated since the papyrus breaks off after the first few letters in each line at this point, and the text must be reconstructed based on the estimated line length. In Royse's reconstruction, the scribe skipped from the κα in καρδίας to the κα in the καὶ that appears immediately after τῇ ἰσχύϊ σου.[40]

In other cases, the scribe's eye accidentally skipped, either forward or backward, to an identical word, syllable, or even single letter in the near context. Scholars refer to this error as a leap "from same to same." Scribe A of Codex Sinaiticus (א or 01) accidentally omitted the words τοῖς οὐκ ἐκ περιτομῆς in Rom 4:12. Since the omitted phrase is immediately preceded by περιτομῆς, this is a clear example of haplography due to parablepsis. The scribe was apparently copying phrase by phrase (or word by word) at this point and after writing the first περιτομῆς in his copy, he accidentally continued his copying from the second περιτομῆς in his exemplar.[41] The same scribe provides an example of dittography by a leap backward from "same to same" in 1 Thess 2:13–14, copying the text from the words παρ᾽ ἡμῶν τοῦ θεοῦ in 2:13 through the words ἐκκλησιῶν τοῦ θεοῦ in 2:14 twice. That is, he leaped from the . . . ῶν τοῦ θεοῦ in 2:14 back to the same combination in the previous verse.[42] The scribe seems to have struggled to concentrate on his work in this section for some reason. In his second copying of this section, the scribe introduced three changes into the text. Furthermore, both versions of the section include what appears to be an example of haplography due to homoeoteleuton. The scribe omitted ἀληθῶς in καθὼς ἀληθῶς ἐστιν, seemingly leaping from the first ως to the second ως.[43]

---

39. Sometimes spelled "homoioteleuton."

40. See Royse, *Scribal Habits*, 139n176, for a detailed explanation of this hypothesis.

41. Dirk Jongkind, *Scribal Habits of Codex Sinaiticus*, TS 3.5 (Piscataway, NJ: Gorgias, 2007), 206–7.

42. Jongkind, *Scribal Habits of Codex Sinaiticus*, 207–8.

43. Jongkind, *Scribal Habits of Codex Sinaiticus*, 208.

Sometimes scribes accidentally skipped a few letters of a word as they copied. An example is the scribe of Θ (038) who accidentally skipped the letters δε of the word ἀδελφῷ (to a brother) in Matt 5:22. As a result, the insult "dimwit" ('Ρακά) was now directed, not to a brother but ἀλφῷ ("to a leper").[44] The scribe behind L (019) accidentally skipped the ην when writing γαλήνη in Matt 8:26. As a result, one reads that the sea became a great weasel instead of a great calm![45] Obviously, this change was completely unintentional. Scribes were not comics trying to get laughs. They were attempting to accurately copy what most of them recognized as Holy Scripture. But their eyes sometimes failed them as they copied.

Another common scribal change was metathesis, which involved transposing the order of letters or words.[46] Since Greek uses the case endings of nouns to indicate their grammatical function in the sentence (in contrast to the use of word order, as in English), the transposition of words often has no effect on the meaning of the text. For example, in Matt 2:3, several of our earliest codices refer to the ruler as ὁ βασιλεὺς Ἡρῴδης. The majority of Greek manuscripts, however, use the order Ἡρῴδης ὁ βασιλεὺς, perhaps influenced by the order in Matt 2:1. Both the orders are appositional constructions identifying Herod as king. Even highly detailed commentaries on the Greek text of Matthew understandably ignore this variant unit.

However, in some instances, changes in word order do affect meaning. In Heb 10:38, several early witnesses read ὁ δὲ δίκαιος μου ἐκ πίστεως ζήσεται. In this reading, the μου modifies the substantival adjective δίκαιος. The phrase "my righteous one" refers to the believer who belongs to God and perseveres in his faith. However, one Greek manuscript (and some old Latin and Syriac witnesses) follows the standard LXX text here and uses the word order ὁ δὲ δίκαιος ἐκ πίστεως μου ζήσεται. In this reading, μου modifies πίστεως and refers to God's faithfulness rather than the believer's faith. In this example, the difference in word order does affect exegesis. The exegete will need to determine the word order intended by the author of Hebrews in order to discover the precise meaning of the verse.

Scribes made other mistakes in copying. For example, since the earliest manuscripts were written in *scriptio continua* in which majuscule letters were written one after the other without breaks between words, later scribes might divide the letters into words differently.[47] However, this and other errors in sight occurred too infrequently to be counted among the "common" errors.

Scribes were also prone to make accidental changes in their copy due to errors of hearing. This involved replacing one word with a similar-sounding word. Some of these errors of hearing may have resulted from the leader of a scriptorium reading an exemplar aloud while other scribes copied. However, most errors of hearing are probably just the result of

---

44. See E. A. Sophocles, J. H. Thayer, and H. Drisler, *Greek Lexicon of the Roman and Byzantine Periods (from B.C. 146 to A.D. 1100)* (New York: C. Scribner's Sons, 1900), 121.

45. See John Lowndes, *A Modern Greek and English Lexikon* (London: Black, Young, and Young, 1837), 162.

46. A previously discussed example is the transposition of the μ and γ in the text of Matt 2:16 in W (032), which resulted in μάγων (magi) becoming γάμων (marriage feasts).

47. For two good examples, see Aland and Aland, *Text of the New Testament*, 282.

a single scribe copying an exemplar on his own. When a person produces a hand copy of a document, they typically look at a word or phrase, then say that word or phrase in their mind (or even aloud) as they read it and write it in their copy. Researchers describe this phenomenon as "subvocalization." Studies have confirmed that subvocalization is a normal part of the reading process by measuring minute movements of the larynx and the muscles used in speech while subjects read silently. Subvocalization also plays an important role in short-term memory including the act of remembering the text that the scribe just read and then reproducing it on the page of his copy.[48] In other words, even when copying visually, speech and hearing still play a part in the process. Because of the role that hearing plays in the process, copyists can easily substitute a new word for a similar-sounding word. In modern English, writers sometimes substitute homophones for one another—even when they are able to identify the distinct meanings of the different spellings accurately. They may write "there" even though they intend to use the third-person plural possessive pronoun "their." Ordinarily, a proofreader can quickly determine when a writer has accidentally used a homophone because one word will not make sense in context, but the other homophone will fit the context perfectly. Ancient scribes made similar mistakes, and ordinarily they are just as easily identified since most errors of hearing result in a nonsense reading.

On rare occasions, however, either of the two similar-sounding words makes sense in context. The similar-sounding variants show that an error of hearing occurred, but it may be more difficult to determine which of the two readings was intended by the author. One of the more difficult examples is the variation of διώκωμεν and διώκομεν in Rom 14:19. Since the distinction in the pronunciation of the long o (ὦ μέγα) and the short o (ὂ μικρόν) faded over time, the two verb forms sounded nearly identical. However, the two forms have different meanings. The former is a hortatory subjunctive by which Paul urges the Romans to join him in pursuing the things that produce peace. The latter is an indicative by which Paul simply explains that he and others are pursuing the things that produce peace. The decision between these two variants is a difficult one. This variant unit is the only one in the entire Epistle to the Romans that receives a "D" rating in the UBS[5] indicating that the editorial committee "had great difficulty in arriving at a decision."[49]

An error of hearing probably explains several of the variants in Matt 18:15. Scribes appear to have been confused by the similar sounds of ηση and εἰς σέ. If the original text were ἁμαρτήσῃ εἰς σέ, as the external evidence explored in Chapter 6 suggests, a scribe who had just copied the two final syllables of the verb could easily turn back to the prepositional phrase in his exemplar and mistakenly assume that he had just copied that phrase due to the almost identical sound. This would result in the variant ἁμαρτήσῃ. The variants ἁμαρτήσῃ and ἁμάρτῃ εἰς σέ would also be pronounced almost identically by many scribes. These variants do not seem to be the result of a scribe's conscious effort to revise the text. They are a product of a simple error of hearing.

---

48. B. A. Levy, "Role of Articulation in Auditory and Visual Short-Term Memory," *Journal of Verbal Learning and Verbal Behavior* 10 (1971): 123–32; J. Locke and F. Fehr, "Subvocalization of Heard or Seen Words Prior to Spoken or Written Recall," *American Journal of Psychology* 8 (1972): 63–68.

49. UBS[5], 3*.

Scribes also accidentally introduced changes when making copies due to errors in memory. When the scribe turned away from the exemplar to write the text on his copy, he had to mentally recall the text that he had just seen. As explained above, most recalled the text by saying it (rather than seeing it) in their minds. The more text the scribe attempted to copy at once, the greater the likelihood that his memory might fail him. The lapse in memory could result in an accidental change in word order or replacing a word with a synonym (if the scribe knew Greek well). If the scribe knew a parallel passage better than the one that he was copying, he could accidentally conform the text to that parallel. If the scribe best remembered similar text from the preceding context that he had already copied, that too might unconsciously influence his recall.

Here are a couple of examples of changes that seem to reflect these mechanisms. Although changes in word order were sometimes intentional, an example in Matt 18:8 seems to be the result of a lapse of memory: Sinaiticus, Vaticanus, several minuscules, and a few Latin manuscripts have the reading εἰσελθεῖν εἰς τὴν ζωὴν κυλλὸν ἢ χωλόν. However, most other Greek manuscripts and several early versions have the order εἰσελθεῖν εἰς τὴν ζωὴν χωλὸν ἢ κυλλὸν. There seems to be no good motivation for scribes to change the order intentionally. Two features of the construction may have exacerbated confusion with regard to the order. The transposed adjectives are close synonyms since both κυλλός and χωλός may refer to deformities or handicaps related to either the hand or the foot, and the two adjectives also have very similar sounds.

An example of accidentally replacing a word with a synonym appears in John 8:26. Nearly all manuscripts use the present active infinitive of λαλέω (λαλεῖν). However, Codex Washingtonianus (W 032) uses the aorist active infinitive of λέγω instead (εἰπεῖν). The change was probably an unconscious substitution.

Intentional Changes

For our purposes, "intentional changes" do not necessarily refer to attempts to change the wording of the *original* text. In many instances, the scribe was intentionally changing the text of the exemplar but probably believed that he was restoring the original text that one of his predecessors had not accurately copied. Bart Ehrman acknowledged this:

> Later scribes who were producing our manuscripts, on the other hand, were principally interested in copying the texts before them. They, for the most part, did not see themselves as authors who were writing new books; they were scribes reproducing old books. The changes they made—at least the intentional ones—were no doubt seen as improvements of the text, possibly made because the scribes were convinced that the copyists before them had themselves mistakenly altered the words of the text. For the most part, their intention was to conserve the tradition, not to change it.[50]

---

50. Bart D. Ehrman, *Misquoting Jesus: The Story Behind Who Changed the Bible and Why* (New York: HarperCollins, 2005), 215. In context, it appears that "later" at the beginning of the quote above functions as an adverb, not an adjective modifying "scribes." In other words, Ehrman is not referring

Several NT manuscripts offer insights into the work of scribes who corrected manuscripts. Codex Sinaiticus has an unusually high number of corrections. The text was corrected at approximately 27,305 different places![51] Some corrections were made by the original scribes who copied various sections of the codex before it left the scriptorium. Many others were made by later generations of correctors. Sinaiticus had at least seven correctors.[52] These correctors attempted to fix the mistakes made by the original scribes in several ways. They inserted text that had been accidentally omitted, removed text that resulted from accidental dittography, and replaced some words. Sometimes the correctors attempted to conform the text to the readings that they found in their own preferred exemplar. Scribes not only made corrections in older manuscripts; they also corrected readings they found in the exemplar by choosing to write in their copy a reading other than the reading of the exemplar.

Thus, scribes recognized the need to make corrections in earlier manuscripts. Many of the intentional changes in the readings of their exemplar were the copyist's effort to correct mistaken readings and restore the presumed reading of the original. What modern scholars describe as intentional changes were often the results of a scribe's text-critical decisions. The following questions will help the researcher recognize these scribal changes:

- ***Does the reading seem to be an attempt to clarify the meaning?***

The copyists of some manuscripts may have been more concerned about communicating the meaning of the exemplar to their readers than always preserving the exact wording of the exemplar. In some cases, the client who commissioned the copy may have instructed the scribe to produce a text that clarified difficult constructions or used synonyms for rare terms. In these scenarios, the goal of the copyist was similar to that of modern editors producing paraphrases or readers' editions of the Bible.

Ordinarily, scribes viewed their assignment as simply copying their exemplar as accurately and faithfully as possible. Even when scribes sought to clarify the text, their approaches to clarification were very modest. One common clarification simply involved supplying a noun to serve as the subject of a sentence. This addition explicated what was already implicit in the text. For example, strong evidence supports the reading that introduces Matt 22:20 with καὶ λέγει αὐτοῖς. The subject "Jesus" is implied by v. 18. However, over a dozen manuscripts including three majuscules (05 019 038) insert ὁ Ἰησοῦς (ordinarily in *nomen sacrum* form) in v. 20. The insertion clarifies the text without changing its meaning in any way. Such changes are especially common at the beginning of one of the assigned readings (lections) in the church calendar since these readings sometimes

---

to scribes who copied the NT late in the history of transmission. Rather, the phrase refers to scribes who began their work after the NT authors had completed theirs.

51. Parker, *Codex Sinaiticus*, 79. Although no manuscript contains more corrections, some did have more correctors. Codex Bezae had at least a dozen different correctors. See Parker, *Codex Bezae*, 34–49, 123–65.

52. These correctors are referred to as ca, cb, cc, cc*, and cpamph. However, cb was a group of at least three different scribes. See Parker, *Codex Sinaiticus*, 80.

began after the portion of the text that identified the implied subject of the verb(s) at the beginning of the reading. This was probably a factor in the insertion of the name "Jesus" in various manuscripts at Matt 4:18; 8:5; 14:22, etc. Each of these passages stands at the beginning of an assigned lection in the Christian calendar.[53] A similar phenomenon probably explains the presence of εἶπε δὲ ὁ κύριος in the Greek text of Luke 7:31 in Erasmus's edition of the Greek NT.[54] The expression εἶπεν ὁ κύριος was one of six standard formulas used to introduce church lessons.[55]

Some clarifications were explanations originally placed in the margin of the text and later copied into the text. An obvious example of the insertion of a marginal note into the main text appears in minuscule 3. Marginal notes often commented on variant readings and introduced their comments with statements such as "in many of the manuscripts, this is what is found: . . ." The text of 2 Cor 8:5 in minuscule 3 has the insertion "in many manuscript copies, this is what is found: and not like we hoped." Desiderius Erasmus argued that this example shows the need to engage in textual criticism since this "particularly fine manuscript" contained this instance of "several words being transferred by an illiterate scribe from the margin to the body of the text."[56]

- ### *Does the reading seem to be an attempt to improve the style or grammar?*

Scribal changes are sometimes efforts to explain obscure terms, fill out truncated constructions, and smooth out awkward expressions. For example, Mark 7:2 reads: "And when they [the Pharisees] saw some of his disciples, that they are eating with defiled hands, that is with unwashed hands. . . ." Some readers apparently felt that the present indicative ἐσθίουσιν "they are eating" was awkward so they removed the "that" (ὅτι) and the verb and substituted the participle ἐσθίοντες (though Mark's expression is a common idiom of Hellenistic Greek).[57] Some readers noticed that Mark's long sentence was incomplete so they supplied verbs such as κατεγνωσαν ("they condemned"; 05) and εμεμψαντο ("they

---

53. These verses began the readings for the third day of the first week of Pentecost and the fourth and ninth Sundays after Pentecost Sunday, respectively. For a detailed list of the readings assigned for specific dates, see the appendix in Scrivener, *Plain Introduction to the Criticism of the New Testament*, 1:80–89.

54. Luke 7:31 began the reading assigned for the sixth day of the third week of the new year (which began Sept. 1).

55. See Parker, *Introduction to the New Testament Manuscripts*, 99. The ECM Catholic Letters uses the symbol Λ after a reading to indicate that the variant was influenced by a lectionary incipit (a standard formula used to introduce the daily reading). See ECM 4.2:3.

56. Guy Bedouelle, ed., *Collected Works of Erasmus*, vol. 83 (Toronto: University of Toronto, 1998), 105. See the excellent discussion in Elijah Hixson, "When a Marginal Note Becomes the Text," *Evangelical Textual Criticism (blog)*, October 19, 2022, http://evangelicaltextualcriticism.blogspot.com.

57. This is an example of the "present retained in indirect discourse." See Daniel B. Wallace, *Greek Grammar Beyond the Basics: An Exegetical Syntax of the New Testament* (Grand Rapids: Zondervan, 1996), 537–39.

found fault"; 017 021 028 etc.).[58] Due to this tendency, we should generally be suspicious of readings that are more highly polished.

▪ *Does the reading seem to be an attempt at harmonization?*

Scribes occasionally harmonized a passage to a parallel passage in another Gospel. Harmonization is the probable cause of one of the variants in Matt 18:15. Unlike the variants that are best explained as resulting from confusion in sound, the variant ἁμάρτῃ matches the form of the verb in Luke 17:3. The change in verbal form closely conforms Matthew's ἐὰν δὲ ἁμαρτήσῃ ὁ ἀδελφός σου to Luke's ἐὰν ἁμάρτῃ ὁ ἀδελφός σου.

Some of the best examples of harmonization to a parallel are found in Luke's version of the Model Prayer (Luke 11:2–4).[59] Scribes appear to be more familiar with Matthew's version (Matt 6:9–13)[60] and adapt Luke's version to Matthew's at several points. Although the earliest manuscripts, such as 𝔓[75], Vaticanus, and Sinaiticus, and other early witnesses (Marcion, Origen, Tertullian), address the prayer simply to the Father (Πάτερ), the vast majority of later manuscripts address it to our Father who is in heaven (Πάτερ ἡμῶν ὁ ἐν τοῖς οὐρανοῖς). In 𝔓[75], Vaticanus, and several early versions, Luke's form of the prayer does not contain the third petition, "Your will be done on earth as it is in heaven." However, almost all later manuscripts match Matthew here. Luke's version sought forgiveness "for our sins" (τὰς ἁμαρτίας ἡμῶν). However, Codex Bezae and a few other witnesses match Matthew here as well: "our debts" (τὰ ὀφειλήματα). The earliest manuscripts of Luke end the prayer with "Do not lead us into temptation." However, most other manuscripts end the prayer with "but deliver us from the evil one."

Some scholars suggest that this harmonization was intentional. Metzger, for example, refers to "an exceedingly strong temptation to assimilate the Lukan text to the much more familiar Matthean form."[61] Some scribes do seem to have intentionally conformed Luke's version of the prayer to Matthew's version. In Codex Bezae, for example, Luke's version of the Model Prayer matches Matthew's in great detail.[62] However, in many cases, the adaptation is not thorough and systematic enough to lead to a strong suspicion of intentional harmonization. Naturally, some scribes were more familiar with one Gospel than another. During the memory phase of the copying process (between reading the exemplar and writing on the copy), the readings of the more familiar Gospel may have influenced the scribe's memory of the text being copied. Even some of the changes to Luke's version of the Model Prayer may have emerged in this way. Most manuscripts do not change Luke's

---

58. Neither verb is used elsewhere in Mark. The incomplete sentence is an example of anacoluthon, in which the lengthy parenthesis caused the author "to forget the original construction and substitute another for it in resuming" (BDF §467).

59. For a helpful discussion of the history of research on harmonization, see Cambry G. Pardee, *Scribal Harmonization in the Synoptic Gospels*, NTTSD 60 (Leiden: Brill, 2019).

60. Note that the quotation of the Model Prayer in Didache 8.2 follows Matthew's version.

61. Metzger, *Textual Commentary*, 130.

62. The only differences are (1) the scribe omitted the ὡς in Matt 5:10 (which was added by corrector 1); (2) the scribe adds the phrase εφ ημας before ελθετω σου η βασιλεια in Luke 11:2; and (3) three insignificant orthographic differences.

δίδου, τὸ καθ᾽ ἡμέραν, or τὰς ἁμαρτίας to Matthew's δός, σήμερον, or τὰ ὀφειλήματα like Codex Bezae does. Many early scribes knew Matthew's version of the prayer by heart and this may have unconsciously influenced their copying of Luke's version until gradually, in the earliest centuries of copying, Luke's version was changed to be more similar to Matthew's. The inconsistent and haphazard nature of harmonization in many texts is easily explicable if the harmonization is often unintentional.[63]

Matthew's Gospel was the most well-known of the Gospels in the early church. Speaking in the broadest terms, most scribes tended to harmonize either Mark or Luke to Matthew when conforming a text in the Gospels to a parallel. In the most thorough study of the topic to date, Cambry Pardee concluded:

> These two facts, that manuscripts of Matthew were subject to harmonization the least frequently and that the text of Matthew served as the source of harmonistic influence the most frequently, show that the Gospel of Matthew was the dominant horizon of expectation by which most scribes read and copied the Gospels. Matthew was copied the most frequently and its manner of presenting gospel material became the cognitive exemplar of many scribes and the source of most reflexive harmonization in the manuscripts.[64]

However, we must not assume that all scribes tend to harmonize Mark and Luke to Matthew. Some scribes (like the scribe of 𝔓[88])[65] tend to harmonize Matthew to Luke, and others tend to harmonize Matthew to Mark (like the scribe of 042).[66] Pardee observed: "Far from being predictable, assimilation occurs in all directions, in manuscripts of all three Synoptics (and all four Gospels), and in all manuscripts from all around the Mediterranean world."[67]

Harmonization often involves conforming a reading to the immediate context or to another passage in the same Gospel rather than conformity to a parallel in another Gospel. In John 8:20, nearly all manuscripts read καὶ οὐδεὶς ἐπίασεν αὐτόν (no one seized him). However, minuscule 28 (cf. 544) reads καὶ οὐδεὶς ἐπέβαλεν ἐπ᾽ αὐτῷ τὰς χεῖρας (no one laid hands on him). The scribe is apparently recalling similar wording from the previously copied John 7:30. The two different expressions both begin with the same two words and are basically synonymous. Another example of conformity to the context may appear in Matt 19:4. Vaticanus (B 01), Koridethi (Θ 038), and several minuscules and early versions refer to God as the Creator (ὁ κτίσας). However, most manuscripts refer to God as

---

63. Parker (*Introduction to the New Testament Manuscripts*, 340) correctly observes that "Harmonisation is not consistent, and it does away with differences in what seems a very haphazard manner."

64. Pardee, *Scribal Harmonization in the Synoptic Gospels*, 433.

65. Pardee, *Scribal Harmonization in the Synoptic Gospels*, 436.

66. Hixson (*Scribal Habits*, 243–44) noted that almost two-thirds of the harmonizations in the text of Matthew in 042 "are instances in which the scribe conformed the text of Matthew to Markan parallels. . . . The harmonizations to Markan parallels are diverse in type, indicating that harmonization was the scribe's primary vice."

67. Pardee, *Scribal Harmonization in the Synoptic Gospels*, 20.

the Maker (ὁ ποιήσας). The latter reading probably conforms the divine title to the term ἐποίησεν used to describe God's activity in creation in the LXX text of Gen 1:27, which is quoted in this verse.

- ### Does the reading seem to be a conflation of other variants?

Scribes were often aware of variant readings because they had access to multiple copies that differed from each other or because variant readings were identified in the margin of their exemplar. Scribes who were unable to decide which reading was most likely the original sometimes placed both readings in the text. For example, the earliest Greek manuscripts of Acts 6:8 and important versional evidence describe Stephen as "full of grace." However, later majuscules and most minuscules describe Stephen as "full of faith." Majuscule E (08), minuscule 1884, and one Latin manuscript (50) conflate the two readings so that Stephen is "full of grace and faith."[68] Similarly, in Acts 20:28, some early manuscripts refer to the "church of God," while others refer to the "church of the Lord." Most minuscules combine the two readings to form "church of the Lord and God."[69] In general, readings that seem to combine multiple variants into a single reading are probably the work of copyists rather than the original author.

- ### Which reading seems initially difficult but makes better sense after further study?

As explained earlier, when scribes encountered a reading that did not appear to make sense in the context, they often assumed that their exemplar contained a scribal error, and they attempted to correct the text to what they assumed must have been the original reading. Most scribes could not devote hours and hours to such questions. They simply had too much text waiting to be copied. Their need to complete the copy sometimes prompted hasty decisions. If they had the time to consult other exemplars and/or ancient commentaries on the text and carefully analyze the style, grammar, vocabulary, and theology of the author, they might have decided that the reading that seemed awkward or difficult on the surface actually made perfect sense. Thus, textual critics should prefer readings that initially seem difficult but make better sense after further study.

Some resources summarize this principle in a manner that is dangerously simplistic: "The more difficult reading is to be preferred." However, important qualifications are necessary. Edward Hobbs insightfully argued that if a text has enough points of variation and the harder reading is always followed, "you will end up with an unintelligible text."[70] Metzger and Ehrman note that preference for the more difficult reading is relative since

---

68. See also 044, which conflates these two and still another reading (cf. 617): πιστεως χαριτος πνευματος και δυναμεως.

69. Metzger (*Textual Commentary*, 425) describes this reading as "obviously conflate, and therefore secondary."

70. Edward Hobbs, "Prologue: An Introduction to Methods of Textual Criticism," in *The Critical Study of Sacred Texts*, ed. Wendy D. O'Flaherty, Berkeley Religious Studies Series 2 (Berkeley: Graduate Theological Union, 1979), 19.

"a point is sometimes reached when a reading must be judged so difficult that it can have arisen only by accident in transcription."[71] In other words, some readings are so difficult as to be virtually impossible. Readings that make no sense at all are best assumed to be the result of scribal error. However, before rejecting a reading as too difficult, the textual critic should be rather certain that the reading makes no sense. Careful reflection will sometimes lead to a discovery that the reading that is difficult on the surface is only difficult because of the misunderstanding of the interpreter.

For example, in Luke 4:44, the oldest manuscripts state that Jesus was preaching in the synagogues of Judea (τῆς Ἰουδαίας). Later manuscripts state that Jesus was preaching in the synagogues of Galilee. At first glance, nearly every interpreter will assume that this latter reading must be correct. The immediately preceding context (Luke 4:31) places Jesus in Capernaum of Galilee. The very next verse after 4:44 (5:1) places Jesus on the shores of Lake Gennesaret (the Sea of Galilee). Furthermore, the parallels to this passage in Matt 4:23 and Mark 1:39 describe Jesus preaching in the synagogues of Galilee. Obviously, the original reading was "of Galilee." Case closed! But more in-depth study leads to the discovery that Luke often uses the term Judea in the "broader Hellenistic sense"[72] to refer to the entirety of Palestine, the "land of the Jews," that was encompassed in the kingdom of Herod the Great (Luke 1:5; 6:17; 7:17; 23:5; Acts 2:9; 10:37; 11:1, 29; 15:1). This area included not only the Roman province of Judea but also Samaria, Galilee, and large portions of Perea and Syria. One can understand an ancient scribe or even a modern textual critic wrongly assuming that the oldest manuscripts must be mistaken and confidently "correcting" the text to "of Galilee." If most modern readers were scribes, they would have made the same faulty assumption! Without the benefit of a concordance or a computer program that enabled them to identify and quickly examine each of Luke's usages, the scribes would probably have overlooked the fact that Luke uses the term "Judea" with a slightly different sense than Matthew and Mark and in a sense different from the scribes' own common usage.

- *Which reading best explains the origin of the other readings?*

The original reading is the one from which all other readings were derived either directly or indirectly. Thus, the reading that best explains how all others developed is probably original. This criterion is one of the oldest[73] and most important criteria for identifying the original reading. Epp observed that this criterion "commonly is considered preeminent among all criteria, external and internal, and decisive in those cases where it is applicable."[74] For example, in the case of the two variants in Luke 4:44 discussed above, we

---

71. Metzger and Ehrman, *Text of the New Testament*, 303.

72. John Nolland, *Luke 1–9:20*, WBC 35A (Dallas: Word, 1989), 25. Cf. def. 2 in "Ἰουδαία," BDAG, 477.

73. Canon XXIV in Gerhard von Mastricht's list from 1711 reads: "When the origin of variant readings is known, a variant reading generally disappears." Gerhard von Mastricht, *Η ΚΑΙΝΗ ΔΙΑΘΗΚΗ, NOVUM TESTAMENTUM GRAECUM* (Amsterdam: H. Wetstein, 1711), 12.

74. Epp, "Traditional 'Canons,'" 93. Epp later notes (p. 94) that Tischendorf described this criterion as "the foremost among all rules."

can easily explain why ancient scribes would have changed "of Judea" to "of Galilee," but it is much more difficult to explain why they would have changed "of Galilee" to "of Judea."

This step in the application of reasoned eclecticism is sometimes called the "local genealogical method" since the goal is to produce a stemma or genealogy of the variant readings showing which readings were derived from another reading. A variety of relationships are hypothetically possible. For example, in a variant unit that has four variants, any of the five relationships below is conceivable.

Figure 7.1. Examples of Potential Genealogies of Variants

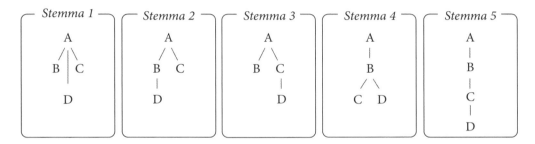

In practice, we will sometimes find that two or more stemmata seem to provide reasonable explanations for the origin and development of the variants. How then do we decide which explanation is best? The decision must be made based on how convincing the explanation is for each relationship depicted in the stemma. The number of generations in the stemma is generally irrelevant. In other words, we should not prefer Stemma 1 to Stemma 5 simply because the explanation in Stemma 1 requires only one generation and the explanation in Stemma 5 requires five generations. What matters is how persuasive the case is for the relationship represented by each arrow in the stemma. Any weak link in the proposed stemma may cast doubt on reading A being the best explanation for the other readings.

We may return to our example in Luke 4:44. We compared just two variants above, but this variant unit in fact has multiple variants for the genitive modifier: τῆς Ἰουδαίας (synagogues of Judea), τῆς Γαλιλαίας (synagogues of Galilee), τῶν Ἰουδαίων (synagogues of the Jews), and αὐτῶν (their synagogues). In the pattern of Stemma 1, all the other variants can be explained as presumed corrections of the reading τῆς Ἰουδαίας. The rationale for each correction would be the same as explained earlier. Many scribes noted that Jesus was in Galilee during this episode of his ministry (Luke 4:31; 5:1) and apparently assumed that "Judea" referred exclusively to the southern part of Palestine, not including Samaria, Galilee, Perea, or Idumea. Some scribes harmonized the text to the parallels in Matt 4:23 and Mark 1:39 changing the reading to "of Galilee." Others assumed that the original reading must have referred to the Jewish people rather than the territory of Judea and "corrected" the reading to "of the Jews." But this reduces the expression to a redundancy since the synagogues in which Jesus might preach in Galilee were obviously Jewish synagogues. For this very reason, the expression "synagogues of the Jews" is not used elsewhere in the NT. Still other scribes assumed that "of Judea" must be mistaken and replaced it with "their" under the influence of texts such as Luke 4:15 (cf. Matt 4:23; 8:35; 10:17; 12:9; 13:54; 22:34; Mark 1:23, 39). Thus, we can offer a compelling explanation for the development of the variant readings using Stemma 1 in which "of Judea" is reading A.

However, before assuming that this is the best explanation, we should consider other alternatives. For the reasons explained above, it is highly probable that "of Galilee" is an attempt to correct "of Judea." It is very difficult to explain why the reading "of Judea" would have developed from any of the other variants except for possibly "of the Jews." If a scribe changed "of the Jews" to "of Judea," the change was probably accidental. Although a scribe could have seen "of the Jews" as oddly redundant, he would probably have regarded "of Judea" as even more problematic in context and a poor suggestion for a "correction." Perhaps a very early, inattentive scribe miscopied τῶν Ἰουδαίων as τῆς Ἰουδαίας. However, it is unlikely that τῶν Ἰουδαίων is the original reading since (1) it is redundant, (2) it is never used elsewhere, and (3) it has support in only one 5th-century majuscule and a late lectionary. One could argue that τῶν Ἰουδαίων is a clarification of the reading αὐτῶν. The scribe may have wanted to identify specifically whose synagogues these were. Yet, scribes would probably not have felt the need to offer such a clarification here since they made no similar clarification to the expression ταῖς συναγωγαῖς αὐτῶν earlier in Luke 4:15. Even the two manuscripts that have τῶν Ἰουδαίων in Luke 4:44 (W *l*387) preserve the αὐτῶν in 4:15. Thus, we can propose this stemma.

Figure 7.2. Proposed Stemma of Variants in Luke 4:44

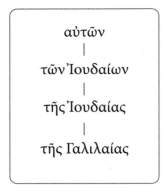

Although the proposal is plausible, it is much less probable than our first explanation. We had nagging doubts about most of the steps in the genealogy. Furthermore, this stemma identifies the original reading as one that is not attested until it appears in one minuscule and several lectionaries beginning in the 9th century. And the proposal identifies the two readings that are best attested in the earliest witnesses as the last two readings to emerge! The real problem with this stemma is not that it requires more stages to explain the development of all the variants. The true difficulty is that each of these stages fails to offer satisfactory explanations for the development of one variant from another reading.

7.2. Intrinsic Evidence

While the examination of transcriptional evidence focuses on the question, "What changes were scribes most likely to make?", the examination of intrinsic evidence focuses on the question, "What was the author most likely to have written?" The examination of intrinsic evidence seeks to identify (1) the reading that is most consistent with the author's grammar, style, and vocabulary, (2) the reading that best fits the immediate context, and (3) the reading that is most compatible with the author's theology. Although the identification of this second element is always relevant, the identification of the first and third depends on having an adequate sample size. The Epistle of Jude, for example, is so brief that we may not be able to confidently assess its normal grammar, style, and vocabulary or attain a comprehensive understanding of the author's theology. However, the four Gospels, Acts, the Pauline corpus, Hebrews, and Revelation are lengthy enough to make generally reliable assessments of a specific author's tendencies.

7.2.1 Which Reading Is Most Consistent with the Author's Grammar, Style, and Vocabulary?

Modern scholars have a significant advantage over earlier generations of textual critics in assessing an author's grammar, style, and vocabulary. Today, we can examine and quantify an author's use of particular constructions with a few keystrokes in a good biblical languages program on our computers. We saw an example of this modern advantage in examining an author's vocabulary above in the discussion of the variant unit at Luke 4:44; along with the difficulty and explanatory power of the proposed original reading, our arguments for it rest on an informed understanding of Luke's use of the phrase "of Judea" (τῆς Ἰουδαίας). In other cases, grammar, syntax, or style need to be investigated.

A variant unit appears in Jas 1:12 of the UBS[5]. Although 𝔓[74], ℵ, A, B, and other manuscripts and versions lack a stated subject for the verb ἐπηγγείλατο, some manuscripts supply the subject ὁ θεός after the verb, and many others supply the subject ὁ κύριος after the verb. Which reading is most consistent with James's style? A search for indicative verbs that lack an explicit subject locates numerous examples. In five of these examples, God is the implied subject (Jas 1:18; 2:5, 11; 4:8, 10). Interestingly, Jas 2:5 contains the same construction as Jas 1:12, a relative pronoun followed by ἐπηγγείλατο τοῖς ἀγαπῶσιν αὐτόν. A few manuscripts (e.g., 1505, 2495, 1243) supply a noun identifying God in Jas 2:5, but the evidence for this reading is very meager. That example confirms that some scribes were uncomfortable with the absence of an explicit subject and felt compelled to add it. In other words, an examination of James's style shows that the author was quite comfortable with referring to divine activity without using an explicit divine reference and that scribes sometimes felt compelled to supply such a reference to eliminate any perceived ambiguity in the text. This evidence supports the editors of the UBS[5] in selecting the verb without the explicit subject as the preferred reading.

7.2.2 Which Reading Best Fits the Immediate Context?

The original reading is presumably one that fits well in the context. Later copyists were less likely than the author to understand the author's train of thought. Incongruities in a passage are more likely the result of scribal changes than an author's failure to communicate reasonably.

This principle is helpful in an evaluation of a variant unit in Rom 4:19. Several of our earliest witnesses state that Abraham considered (κατενόησεν) his own body to have already died.[75] In this case, the preceding participial phrase is probably concessive ("even though he did not weaken in faith") and the following participial clause is probably causal ("since he was about a hundred years old"). However, many other witnesses state that Abraham did *not* consider (οὐ κατενόησεν) his own body to have already died, the exact opposite of the other reading. In this case, the preceding participial phrase is causal ("because he did not weaken in faith") and the following participial clause is concessive ("even though he was about a hundred years old").

One reading portrays Abraham's faith as one that was fully aware of the difficulties that would seem to prevent the fulfillment of God's promise to him. The other reading portrays Abraham's faith as dismissing those difficulties. Which of these readings best suits the context? The original context of the passage to which Paul refers (Gen 17:15–16) shows that Abraham did, in fact, consider both his and Sarah's inability to conceive a child in their old age to be significant: "Abraham fell facedown. Then he laughed and said to himself, "Can a child be born to a hundred-year-old man? Can Sarah, a ninety-year-old woman, give birth?" (CSB). Furthermore, Paul's appeal to the example of Abraham demonstrates Abraham's awareness of the circumstances that would seem to prevent the fulfillment of God's promise. This is why Abraham needed to be "strengthened in his faith" (Rom 4:20) by becoming "fully convinced that what He had promised He was also able to perform" (HCSB). Most importantly, Paul uses Abraham's belief that God is able to bring life out of death (Isaac's birth despite the deadness of Abraham's body and Sarah's womb) as a paradigm for the Christian belief "in Him who raised Jesus our Lord from the dead" (cf. Rom 4:24–25, HCSB). Thus, the flow of Paul's argument best supports the reading that lacks the negative (οὐ).

7.2.3 Which Reading Best Fits with the Author's Theology?

Although we should allow for some development in an author's theology over a significant period of time, we should expect general consistency in the theological views expressed by an author in a single writing or even in several different writings from the same general time period. The NT authors do not contradict themselves. Like most thoughtful authors, they communicate a coherent theology. Thus, when considering the question, "What is this author most likely to have written?," it is helpful to consult other statements

---

75. The adverb ἤδη is probably original. Even if not, this temporal relationship is implied by the perfect participle.

by the same author on the same topic. The reading that best fits with the author's theology (when it is properly understood!) is most likely the original reading.

In Rom 9:4, several early and important witnesses have the singular noun ἡ διαθήκη (𝔓⁴⁶ B D F G it^(ar, b) Cop^(sa, bo) eth). However, many more witnesses (including important witnesses such as ℵ and 1739) have the plural reading αἱ διαθῆκαι. Based on his view of covenant(s) in Romans and other Pauline writings, which form would Paul have been expected to use?

Paul believed that God had made multiple covenants with Israel. Galatians 3:15 refers to God's covenant with Abraham. Galatians 4:24 then refers to two different covenants with Israel. One of these covenants was issued from Mount Sinai, the law of Moses. The other covenant was the Abrahamic covenant, which Paul closely associates with the promise of the Spirit and of freedom, important features of the new covenant. In his letters to the Corinthians, Paul refers to the new covenant, which was enacted by Jesus' death (1 Cor 11:25; 2 Cor 3:6), and which fulfills Jer 31:33 by writing God's law on the hearts of his people (2 Cor 3:3) and Ezek 36:27 by placing God's Spirit in them to produce a life of obedience (2 Cor 3:6). Paul indicates that this new covenant was also given to "Israel" in Rom 11:27. Ephesians 2:12 refers to God's covenants with Israel as "covenants (pl.) of promise." In light of this theology of the covenants articulated elsewhere by Paul, we would expect Paul to describe Israel as the recipient of "the covenants (pl.)." Thus, the committee of the UBS⁵ chose the plural as the original reading and gave it a B rating.

This reading also seems to be the reading that best fits the context in terms of style. If we adopt the plural reading, Rom 9:4 contains a carefully constructed couplet characterized by assonance and symmetry with close correspondence between **ἡ υἱοθεσία/ἡ νομοθεσία**, **ἡ δόξα/ἡ λατρεία**, and **αἱ διαθῆκαι/αἱ ἐπαγγελίαι**. The assonance and symmetry are disrupted with the singular reading. Scribes who changed the plural to a singular probably did so under the influence of the preceding singular nouns in the series while overlooking the couplet form.

7.3. Exploring Other Potentially Relevant Evidence

Although the discussion above treats many of the categories of evidence useful in the application of reasoned eclecticism, sometimes other pieces of evidence can be important as well. Brainstorm for other categories of evidence that might affect your text-critical decision. Sometimes, other variant units in close proximity to the variant unit you are examining will give new insight into the factors that influenced some of the variants. Sometimes paratextual features in a manuscript such as asterisks, obeli, marginal notes, or the Eusebian section and canon numbers offer helpful clues for identifying the original reading. If a specific witness seems to be especially important for your decision, it is worthwhile to consult good-quality images of that manuscript to verify that the apparatus of your critical edition is correct.

For example, in the variant unit that we examined in our previous example, I suggested that scribes probably changed the plural αἱ διαθῆκαι in Rom 9:4 to the singular ἡ διαθήκη to match the other singular nouns in the series. If so, the scribes may have done the same thing with the plural αἱ ἐπαγγελίαι at the end of the verse. If they made the same change there, this would provide compelling evidence supporting the tendency to conform all the nouns in the series to the same singular number. Interestingly, three (D F G) of the four majuscules that have the singular form of the third noun in the series also use the singular form of the final noun in the series. When I consult the CNTTS Apparatus (Revised), the most detailed apparatus of Romans currently available,[76] I find that $\mathfrak{P}^{46}$ and B are the only early witnesses listed as supporting a singular form for the third noun (ἡ διαθήκη) but a plural form for the final noun (ἐπαγγελίαι). However, I notice that $\mathfrak{P}^{46}$ is qualified with the superscript [vid], a manuscript notation that indicates "an apparent reading." The NA edition uses the superscript "vid" to indicate "that the reading attested by a witness cannot be determined with absolute certainty."[77] This reading is worth checking out. Fortunately, good images of $\mathfrak{P}^{46}$ are available through the New Testament Virtual Manuscript Room for scholars who are granted expert access. When I consult the images, I discover that the right-hand side of the page containing Rom 9:4 is broken off, and we must reconstruct what came between ἐπαγγελι at the end of line 16 and the πατέρες that begins line 17. I notice that the transcription that accompanies the images reconstructs the missing text at the end of the line as "[αι] [ων οι]," thus supporting the information in the CNTTS Apparatus. But, I wonder, how did the transcriber determine whether the iota was originally present to form the nominative plural feminine ending? Such decisions are often made based partly on the amount of space or number of characters in a line. Yet, the iota is such a small slender character that it would not significantly impact the line length. When I consult the NA[27], I find that the editors listed $\mathfrak{P}^{46vid}$ as a witness for the *singular* form of the noun. Thus, the editors of the NA[27] and the transcriber (together with the CNTTS Apparatus) disagree regarding the form of the noun in $\mathfrak{P}^{46}$.

　　I then examine the number of letters per line on this page of the manuscript. Of the twenty-seven lines on this page of $\mathfrak{P}^{46}$, the shortest lines (lines 1, 11, 13) have 28 characters, the longest line (line 5) has 35 characters, and the average line length (excluding line sixteen whose probable length we are seeking to calculate) is 30.85 characters. Based on considerations of line length alone, the singular form επαγγελια is slightly more probable than the plural form. Line 16 contains either 33 or 34 characters depending on the presence or absence of a final iota in the form ἐπαγγελία(ι). Only *two* of the twenty-six lines (again, excluding line sixteen whose probable length we are seeking to calculate), have 34 or more characters. *Twenty-four* of the twenty-six lines consist of precisely 33 characters or less. Only *one* line (line 3) has precisely 34 characters. *Three* lines (lines 14, 18, and 26) have precisely 33 characters. The probability that line 16 contains the plural form is slightly lower than the probability that it contains the singular form. That probability decreases when I consider that the scribe of $\mathfrak{P}^{46}$ sometimes uses spaces between words and often grants as much space on the line to an iota as to wider characters. Thus, I suspect that the editors of the NA[27] correctly assessed the reading of $\mathfrak{P}^{46}$. However, the evidence is insuf-

---

76. As of June 20, 2024, prior to the publication of the ECM volume containing Romans.
77. NA[28], 59*.

ficient to determine with any confidence whether 𝔓⁴⁶ used the singular or plural form of "promise." Our analysis demonstrates that no one can verify an inference of either of the two readings from the extent of the lacuna since other examples of 33- and 34-character lines appear elsewhere on the page. Consequently, 𝔓⁴⁶ᵛⁱᵈ should not be cited as a witness to *either* form. The NA²⁸ wisely eliminated 𝔓⁴⁶ᵛⁱᵈ from its list of witnesses supporting the singular form.[78]

What have we learned from these additional investigations? We may have only one early witness (B) that uses a singular form of διαθήκη without also using a singular form of ἐπαγγελία. These additional steps (consulting another variant unit in the series, consulting images of an important manuscript, and calculating line lengths of this page of the manuscript) increase confidence in the decision initially reached after applying the normal principles.

7.4. Weighing the Evidence

Once the analysis described in the preceding pages is complete, we must weigh the evidence. Unfortunately, not all the evidence will necessarily support the same conclusion. Often, some evidence will support one reading while other evidence supports another. Hence the necessity of weighing competing evidence.

Some textual critics advise prioritizing the external evidence when it is at odds with internal evidence.[79] Others suggest prioritizing the internal evidence instead.[80] A wiser approach is to give the most weight to the lines of evidence that are most compelling when all the principles have been properly considered.

Sometimes the external evidence, especially as it has been traditionally assessed, is very evenly balanced.[81] In these cases, internal evidence may be the determining factor

---

78. The editors of the NA (cf. NA²⁷, 55*, and NA²⁸, 59*) state: "When an inference is drawn from the extent of a lacuna, it is carefully verified that the manuscript cannot be cited equally well for other readings in the tradition." By "extent of a lacuna," the editors are referring to the amount of text that might fit in the portion of the page that is missing or obscured. The change to the apparatus for this variant unit in NA²⁸ reflects their adherence to the stated principle.

79. E.g., Porter and Pitts, *Fundamentals of New Testament Textual Criticism*, 101: "External evidence, most textual critics agree, should take priority in making text-critical judgments, because it is the most objective tangible evidence that we have for the textual history of the NT. Too often in text-critical discussions—even among reasoned eclectics, and especially by thoroughgoing eclectics—internal evidence has overturned external considerations." But the claim that external evidence is generally less subjective and more reliable than internal evidence is problematic. See the discussion of external evidence in chapter 6 above.

80. Elliott, "Thoroughgoing Eclecticism." Léon Vaganay and Christian-Bernard Amphoux recommend beginning with "verbal criticism" that bases decisions on knowledge of common scribal changes (transcriptional evidence) then turns to "external criticism" that bases decisions on genealogical relationships "once the examination of the errors of textual transmission has proved inconclusive" (*An Introduction to New Testament Textual Criticism*, trans. Jenny Heimerdinger, 2nd ed. [Cambridge: Cambridge University Press, 1991], 62).

81. See, for example, the assessments of the variants in Rom 1:1; 4:22; 5:2; 7:20; 8:34; 11:31; 14:5 in Metzger, *Textual Commentary*, 446, 452, 455, 458, 465, 468.

in the decision. Sometimes the intrinsic evidence will best support one variant, but the transcriptional evidence will best support another. Rather than considering this to be a "fifty-fifty split" that makes the entirety of the internal evidence irrelevant, the text critic should attempt to determine which line of evidence is most persuasive and prefer the reading supported by it.

In some cases, the external evidence will support one reading, but the internal evidence will support another. In those cases, further study may resolve the apparent contradiction. For example, Metzger's *Textual Commentary* on the variant unit at the end of Rom 14:12 states that the external evidence supports the inclusion of the τῷ θεῷ but the internal evidence favors its omission since "it is easy to understand why, if the words were originally absent from the text, copyists would have supplied them in order to clarify the reference of the verb."[82] The editors represented "the balance of external and internal considerations" by including the phrase in brackets with a C rating.

But is the evidence truly balanced? The external evidence in favor of the inclusion of τῷ θεῷ is very persuasive. The only early Greek writer identified as omitting the phrase is Polycarp. However, the truncated reference to Rom 14:10, 12 in Pol. *Phil.* 6.2 is from memory, and Polycarp's memory was not entirely accurate and precise. The reference to v. 10 changes Paul's πάντες γάρ παραστησόμεθα to καὶ πάντας δεῖ παραστῆναι and τῷ βήματι τοῦ θεοῦ to τῷ βήματι τοῦ Χριστοῦ (influenced by his memory of 2 Cor 5:10).[83] The reference to v. 12 drops the ἡμῶν in ἕκαστος ἡμῶν, changes περὶ ἑαυτοῦ to ὑπὲρ αὐτοῦ, and converts δώσει to δοῦναι. Since Polycarp changed the judgment seat of God to the judgment seat of Christ, he naturally dropped the reference to giving an account "to God" specifically.

A closer look at the Greek manuscripts of Rom 14:12 that omit τῷ θεῷ suggests that the same factor that prompted Polycarp to drop τῷ θεῷ also probably prompted some of the scribes to do so. Many manuscripts conformed Rom 14:10 to 2 Cor 5:10 by changing the reference to the judgment seat of God to the judgment seat of Christ. This made the reference to giving an account "to God" in Rom 14:12 awkward and inconsistent with the preceding context. Several of the manuscripts that omit "of God" in Rom 14:12 refer to the judgment seat of Christ in 14:10 (6 424² 1881).[84] But several important manuscripts that omit the τῷ θεῷ, such as B F G 1739 and 2200, do refer to the judgment seat of God in Rom 14:10. The absence of the τῷ θεῷ in these texts may be an intentional omission (perhaps motivated by a desire to reduce redundancy resulting from the repeated uses of the noun θεός in 14:10 and 12), an accidental omission, or the result of contamination in which the scribe consulted two or more exemplars in their copying.[85] Although we can easily explain

---

82. Metzger, *Textual Commentary*, 469.

83. Zuntz (*Text of the Epistles*, 224) refers to this as the "ancient harmonistic variant" and says that it was shared by Marcion and thus "it originated so early and asserted itself so persistently, one wonders how the original wording could be traced and appreciated."

84. 424² refers to the second corrector. This manuscript is by far the most heavily corrected of all the minuscules. The corrections tend to conform the text to that of Family 1739, which includes 6, 424, and 1881.

85. The "harmonistic variant" dates to the first half of the 2nd century and is early enough to have influenced even an ancestor of B.

why scribes would have supplied the τῷ θεῷ in Rom 14:12, we can also offer a plausible explanation for their omission of the phrase. Thus, the transcriptional evidence does not actually counter the external evidence in the manner that Metzger believed.

Further, there is more to internal evidence than merely transcriptional evidence. The other aspect of internal evidence, intrinsic evidence, weighs decidedly in favor of the reading τῷ θεῷ. Although 2 Cor 5:10 (cf. 2 Tim 4:1) refers to the judgment seat of Christ, Paul more frequently refers to God (the Father) as the judge to whom sinners must give an account (Rom 2:16; 3:6; 1 Cor 5:13; 2 Thess 1:5). Paul's basic argument in this text is that sinners must not judge and condemn one whom God has (judged and) accepted (Rom 14:3). The prerogative to judge belongs to God since he is the Lord over his servants (Rom 14:4). The inferential particle ἄρα at the beginning of Rom 14:12 indicates that the verse is an inference from the preceding quotation of Isa 49:18. Paul's point is that every person will ultimately acknowledge God's lordship by bowing before him and confessing him. Since only one's lord is worthy to judge a person, people must give an account to God, not to other people. Thus, the context strongly implies the inclusion of τῷ θεῷ. That is the very climax to which Paul's argument has been building.

If, after more careful study, the tension remains, we will be forced to adopt the reading that has the stronger support, even by a slim margin, despite reservations. The UBS[5] used the letter D to indicate that the editorial committee had "great difficulty in arriving at a decision."[86] An even greater level of uncertainty is indicated by a diamond, ♦. The diamond is used in variant units for which "no final textual decision seemed possible."[87]

---

86. UBS[5], 9*.
87. UBS[5], 9*.

Part Three

————

THE PRACTICE OF REASONED ECLECTICISM

Newspaper editor Arthur Brisbane said in a lecture in 1911: "Use a picture. It's worth a thousand words."* The old adage seems to apply to textual criticism. Although discussions of methods and theories are necessary and important, textual criticism may be difficult to understand until one has the opportunity to see practical examples of it.

Although Part Two applied the principles of textual criticism to many different variant units, it is especially helpful to see how the different steps in the method of reasoned eclecticism may each be applied to an individual textual challenge. Thus, Part Three will walk through the application of the entire method addressing three important variant units in Matt 16:2b–3, John 1:18, and Col 1:12.

* The now famous quote was reported in the article "Speakers Give Sound Advice," *Syracuse Post Standard*, March 28, 1911.

EXAMPLE A

MATTHEW 16:2b–3

A.1. Preliminary Considerations

A.1.1 Identify the Variant Readings

The UBS[5] brackets the words ὀψίας γενομένης λέγετε· εὐδία, πυρράζει γὰρ ὁ οὐρανός· καὶ πρωΐ· σήμερον χειμών, πυρράζει γὰρ στυγνάζων ὁ οὐρανός. τὸ μὲν πρόσωπον τοῦ οὐρανοῦ γινώσκετε διακρίνειν, τὰ δὲ σημεῖα τῶν καιρῶν οὐ δύνασθε in Matt 16:2b–3. These brackets indicate that, although the editors regard the words as part of the text, the presently available evidence is not sufficient to make this "completely certain."[1] The superscript 1 after the closing bracket refers us to the text-critical apparatus where we find this:

> {C} Ὀψίας γενομένης ... οὐ δύνασθε; (*with minor variants; see* Lk 12:54–56) C D L W Δ Θ *f*[1] 33 180 205 565 597 700 892 1006 1010 1071 1241 1243 1292 1342 1424 1505 *Byz* [E F G H N O Σ] *Lect* it[a, aur, b, c, d, e, f, ff1, ff2, g1, l, q] vg syr[p, h] cop[bopt] eth geo slav Eusebian Canons Chrysostom; Juvencus Hilary Jerome Augustine // *omit* ℵ B X *f*[13] 157 579 syr[c, s] cop[sa, meg, bopt] arm Origen; mss[acc. to Jerome] REB EU

The witnesses before the double slash marks (//) support the inclusion of the bracketed text. The witnesses listed after the double slash marks support the omission of the bracketed text.

A.1.2 Analyze the Nature of the Differences Between the Variants

Although the apparatus notes some minor variation exists in the texts that include Matt 16:2b–3, the two variants treated in the apparatus are simply the inclusion or omission of the bracketed words. One might assume that a choice between these two variants is a simple one. However, the C rating indicates that the editorial committee "had difficulty in deciding which variant to place in the text."[2] A survey of twenty-six critical commentaries on Matthew in English and German published since 1968 found that ten support

---

1. UBS[5], 7*.
2. UBS[5], 8*.

the inclusion of the bracketed text, ten support its omission, and the remaining six were undecided. Thus, this variant unit is worthy of more thorough study.[3]

A.1.3 Reflect on the Implications for the Text's Meaning

If the bracketed text is included, Jesus contrasted the Pharisees and Sadducees' ability to predict the weather based on the appearance of the sky with their inability to discern the signs of the eschatological seasons—the indications that the messianic era had arrived. The statement is a stern indictment of the spiritual blindness of the group. If the text is omitted, Jesus responded to the group's request for a sign with an immediate refusal that castigated the group as belonging to an evil and adulterous generation.

Although the variant unit does not have a huge impact on the meaning of the pericope, this variant unit, consisting of thirty-one words, is important since it is the longest in the current major critical editions of the Gospel of Matthew.[4]

A.2. External Evidence

A.2.1 Criterion 1: Prefer readings that can be shown to be early

Our tables categorizing the witnesses for each variant by century will separate the manuscripts of the Greek NT from the early church fathers due to the differing nature of these two sources of evidence as explained earlier.

Table A.1. Manuscripts of the Greek New Testament

Variant	2nd c.	3rd c.	4th c.	5th c.	6th c.	7th c.	8th c.
Inclusion of Matt 16:2b–3				C D W			E L
Omission of Matt 16:2b–3			ℵ B				

Table A.2. Early Church Fathers

Variant	2nd c.	3rd c.	4th c.	5th c.	6th c.	7th c.	8th c.
Inclusion of Matt 16:2b–3			Eusebian Canons Chrysostom Juvencus Hilary	Jerome Augustine			
Omission of Matt 16:2b–3		~~Origen~~		MSS known by Jerome			

---

3. For more detailed analyses of this variant unit, see Charles L. Quarles, "Matthew 16.2b–3: New Considerations for a Difficult Textual Question," *NTS* 66 (2020): 228–48; and Quarles, "Usefulness of Pre-genealogical Coherence," 424–46.

4. Codex Bezae has an even longer variant reading consisting of fifty-seven words after Matt 20:28. However, that variant does not have strong external evidence and is not a serious candidate for the original reading.

The two earliest Greek manuscripts of this passage lack Matt 16:2b–3. Furthermore, Origen's commentary on Matthew does not mention the content of Matt 16:2b–3. However, Origen's commentary was not intended to be an exhaustive treatment of the Gospel, and Origen skips words, clauses, and whole verses in his exposition, even when it is obvious that these verses were present in Origen's text of Matthew.[5] In addition, both manuscripts that most closely resemble Origen's text of Matthew (1 and 1582) contain the longer reading. In light of these factors, Origen cannot be confidently claimed as a witness to the shorter reading.

Eusebius's Canons were developed in the early 4th century and they constitute the earliest witness for the longer reading in Matthew. Eusebius assigned the section number 162 (ρξβ) and the canon number 5 (ε) to Matt 16:2b–3 to indicate that the verse had a parallel in Luke 12:54–56 (sec. 161).[6] In addition to the 4th-century fathers listed in the apparatus that refer to the longer reading, Basil of Caesarea mentions the passage in *Hexaemeron* 6:4. No church father mentions that any manuscripts lack the longer reading until Jerome in the early 5th century. His *Comm. Matt.* 3.16 (16:2) says that the longer reading was absent in most manuscripts available to him.

Although our two earliest majuscules both support the shorter reading, their witness is balanced by the widespread support for the longer reading by the church fathers from the same period. Thus, the two readings may be of equal antiquity as far as we can discern from the available evidence so far.

ADDITIONAL CONSIDERATION 1: Reevaluate the date assigned to readings found in early witnesses from various regions

Table A.3. Geographical Distribution[7]

	North	Northeast	East	Southeast	Southwest	Northwest
Inclusion of Matt 16:2b–3	Basil	syr$^{p, h}$ Chrysostom	**Eusebius** Jerome	cop$^{bo pt}$	Augustine	**It** Vg **Juvencus Hilary**
Omission of Matt 16:2b–3		syr$^{c, s}$		cop$^{sa, meg,}$ bo^{pt}		

The wide geographical distribution of texts with the longer reading in the 4th and 5th centuries suggests that the reading may be considerably earlier than the earliest extant witnesses that support it. The distribution suggests that the longer reading dates to at least as early as the 3rd century. Thus, even if Origen is treated as a witness to the shorter reading (which we have already questioned), the longer reading would be of equal antiquity with the shorter reading. The evidence suggests that the longer reading is earlier than the shorter reading if Origen's silence is excluded as testimony for the shorter reading.

---

5. For examples, see Quarles, "Matthew 16:2b–3," 240n30.

6. For an introduction to Eusebius's system, see NA^{28}, 85*–86*, 89*–94*.

7. The bold font marks witnesses dating to the mid-4th century or earlier.

ADDITIONAL CONSIDERATION 2: Reevaluate the date assigned to readings shared by early witnesses that are not closely related to each other

Since the ECM data on Matthew is not currently available, we will assess the relationship between texts using two approaches: utilizing the ECM data on Mark and the ECM data on parallel pericopes (Matthew). The ECM data on Mark shows that the two early witnesses to the shorter reading (ℵ and B) agree on 90.33 percent of readings and ℵ is B's third closest relative. In the *Parallel Pericopes* data, ℵ is B's closest relative and agrees on 84.6 percent of readings.

The levels of agreement between the early witnesses to the longer reading are tabulated below.

Table A.4. Percentages of Agreement Between Witnesses to the Longer Reading (Mark)

ECM Mark	W	C	D	L	Δ	MT
W	–	73.67	67.99	74.8	73.13	77
C	73.67	–	71.09	88.97	87.97	87
D	67.99	71.09	–	71.17	69.10	73
L	74.8	88.97	71.18	–	87.74	85
Δ	73.13	87.97	69.10	87.4	–	85
MT	77	87	73	85	85	–

Table A.5. Percentages of Agreement Between Witnesses to the Longer Reading (Parallel Pericopes)

Parallel Pericopes (Matthew)	W	C	D	L	Δ
W	–	<93.1	<72.8	<93.1	<93.1
C	<90.4	–	<72.8	<90.4	<90.4
D	<72.8	<72.8	–	<72.8	<72.8
L	<85.2	<85.2	<72.8	–	<85.2
Δ	<92.3	<92.3	<72.8	<92.3	–

Because the longer reading is shared by texts of approximately the same era that are not closely related, the reading probably predates these texts by potentially several generations of copies. This suggests that the longer reading predates the shorter reading.

A.2.2 CRITERION 2: Prefer readings in witnesses that are known to be reliable and accurate

Since the ECM of Matthew is not currently available, we may rely on the Alands' classifications of manuscripts to help identify the most reliable and accurate witnesses. The

Alands described the manuscripts in their Categories I and II as "manuscripts of a very special quality" and "manuscripts of a special quality," respectively. However, all papyri and majuscules through the 3rd and 4th centuries were included. Thus, the inclusion of some texts is due primarily to their antiquity and not necessarily because of their reliability.

Table A.6. Category I and II Witnesses

Variant	Aland Category I	Aland Category II
Inclusion of Matt 16:2b–3		C L Θ 33 892 1342
Omission of Matt 16:2b–3	ℵ B	13

Alternatively, we could use the ECM Mark data to assess the accuracy of these witnesses with the expectation that this level of accuracy in Mark may extend to Matthew also. In the "General Textual Flow" of Mark, I click on "A" (for the Initial Text) to display the witnesses that most closely resemble the text reconstructed for the ECM.[8]

Figure A.1. Witnesses to Mark Most Closely Related to the Initial Text

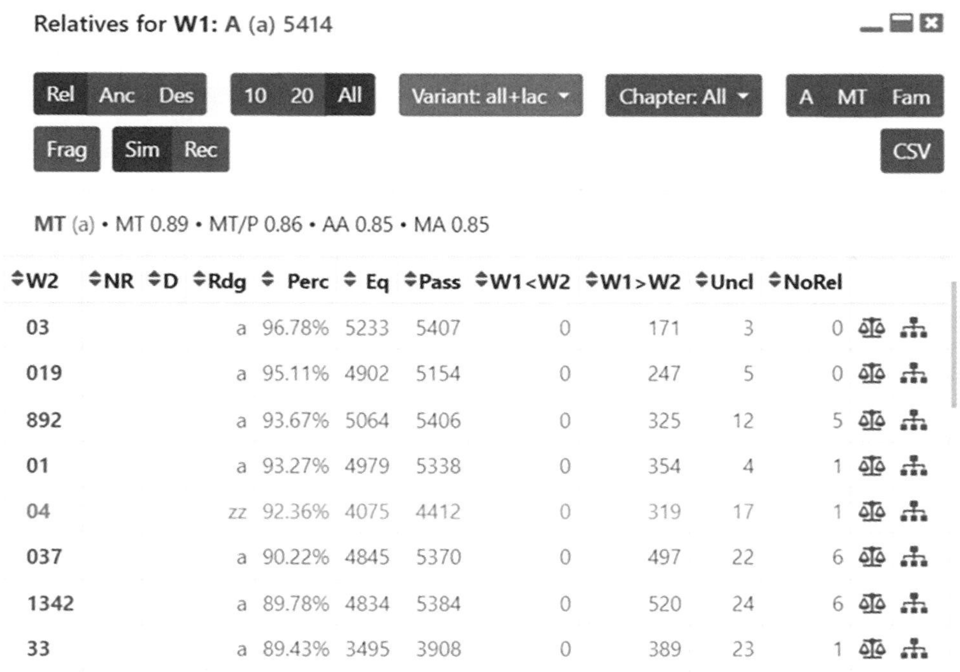

Relatives for W1: A (a) 5414   ▬ ◼ ❌

Rel	Anc	Des		10	20	All		Variant: all+lac ▾		Chapter: All ▾		A	MT	Fam
Frag	Sim	Rec												CSV

MT (a) • MT 0.89 • MT/P 0.86 • AA 0.85 • MA 0.85

⇕W2	⇕NR	⇕D	⇕Rdg	⇕ Perc	⇕ Eq	⇕Pass	⇕W1<W2	⇕W1>W2	⇕Uncl	⇕NoRel		
03			a	96.78%	5233	5407	0	171	3	0	⚖	⛓
019			a	95.11%	4902	5154	0	247	5	0	⚖	⛓
892			a	93.67%	5064	5406	0	325	12	5	⚖	⛓
01			a	93.27%	4979	5338	0	354	4	1	⚖	⛓
04			zz	92.36%	4075	4412	0	319	17	1	⚖	⛓
037			a	90.22%	4845	5370	0	497	22	6	⚖	⛓
1342			a	89.78%	4834	5384	0	520	24	6	⚖	⛓
33			a	89.43%	3495	3908	0	389	23	1	⚖	⛓

---

8. Used with permission of the Institute for New Testament Textual Research (INTF), University of Münster. For an explanation of the different features of this table, see the "Short Guide to the CGBM-Mark (Phase 3.5)" by Klaus Wachtel and revised by Greg Paulson (https://ntg.uni-muenster.de/pdfs/Short_Guide_CBGM_Mark_KW.pdf).

This data suggests that at least L (019) 892 and C (04) should also be placed in Category I and possibly Δ (037) 1342 and 33. All six of these texts support the longer reading. Contrary to initial impressions, the number of high-quality texts that support the longer reading tips the scales in favor of the longer reading.

A.2.3 CRITERION 3: Prefer readings found in multiple early witnesses

Both readings appear in multiple 4th-century witnesses, whether majuscules or early church fathers. Thus, this criterion does not favor either reading. In the 5th century, Jerome indicates that most witnesses known to him supported the shorter reading. However, a greater number of presently extant early witnesses support the longer reading.

A.2.4 Summarizing the External Evidence

Table A.7. Evaluation of the External Evidence

Evaluation of External Evidence for Variant Unit in Matt 16:2b–3	
Criterion	*Preferred Reading(s)*
1. Prefer readings that can be shown to be early.	1 or 2 (no preference)
a. Reevaluate the date assigned to readings found in early witnesses from various regions.	1
b. Reevaluate the date assigned to readings shared by early witnesses that are not closely related to each other.	1
2. Prefer readings in witnesses that are known to be reliable and accurate.	1
3. Prefer readings found in multiple early witnesses.	1 or 2 (no preference)

A.3. Internal Evidence

A.3.1 TRANSCRIPTIONAL EVIDENCE: Prefer the reading *least* likely to have resulted from common scribal changes.

Which reading did NOT ***likely result from common errors related to sight, hearing, or memory?***

The only unintentional error that might plausibly explain the omission of the longer reading is haplography due to parablepsis. The eyes of the scribe may have shifted from the γεν in γενομένης in 16:2b to the γεν in γενεὰ πονηρά.[9] However, this would not explain

---

9. John Nolland, *The Gospel of Matthew*, NIGTC (Grand Rapids: Eerdmans, 2005), 646.

the deletion of the ὀψίας. It would require either the original scribe to have deleted the word without consulting his exemplar or a later scribe who used the text with the nonsensical ὀψίας to have done so. Thus, neither variant seems to have resulted from a common unintentional change to the text.

Which reading did NOT likely result from the scribe's effort to correct a perceived error, clarify the meaning, improve the style or grammar, harmonize to a parallel or the context, or conflate variants?

Some scholars have suggested that the longer reading was added to assimilate Matthew to the parallel in Luke 12:54–56.[10] However, these two passages have more differences than similarities and are unlikely candidates for scribal harmonization.

Some scholars have suggested that scribes purposefully deleted the reference to the meteorological signs since they were not reliable weather predictors in the region where the text was copied, perhaps far from the location where Jesus spoke them.[11] However, an examination of discussions of meteorological signs in the ancient Mediterranean world demonstrates that the signs discussed in the longer reading in Matthew were more widely applicable than those discussed in Luke 12:54–56 since the discussion in Luke assumes a location directly to the east of the Mediterranean Sea. However, no manuscripts omitted the passage in Luke or revised it to make it universally applicable. Thus, it is doubtful that Matthew was revised for that purpose.

The most plausible explanation for an intentional scribal change is the hypothesis that a scribe omitted the longer reading in order to conform Matt 16:1–4 to the parallel in Matt 12:38–39. Harmonization to context or harmonization to similar material within a single Gospel is more common than harmonization of Gospel material to a synoptic parallel. The omission of the longer reading brought the latter passage into nearly perfect agreement with the passage that the scribe had already copied earlier. Thus, the transcriptional evidence seems to favor the longer reading.

Which reading initially seems difficult but makes better sense after further study?

Reading 2 seems to present no difficulty for a scribe. If a difficulty existed, we would expect variation in Matt 12:39 too since that earlier verse so closely matches Matt 16:4. However, no significant variation occurs there.

On the other hand, scribes could have found reading 1 to be difficult for several reasons. For example, they may have been puzzled by the shift in topic from the messianic sign requested by the Pharisees and Sadducees to meteorological signs to signs of the times.

---

10. See Metzger, *Textual Commentary*, 33.

11. Scrivener (*Plain Introduction to the Criticism of the New Testament*, 2:326–27) offered this explanation, and numerous commentaries on Matthew have adopted Scrivener's view. See, for example, W. D. Davies and Dale Allison, *Matthew 8–18*, vol. 2 of *The Gospel according to St. Matthew*, ICC (London: T&T Clark, 1991), 581n12.

Which reading best explains the origin of other readings?

In scenarios involving simple omission or addition, detailed studies of each manu-script are necessary to determine if the individual scribes responsible for each witness to a reading more frequently added or omitted material and under what circumstances. Fortunately, Greg Paulson examined scribal tendencies exhibited in the singular readings within the Gospel of Matthew in our five early witnesses, ℵ, B, C, D, and W.

Tendencies in the witnesses to reading 1. The scribes of C and W have a roughly equiva-lent number of omissions and additions (8 and 10 respectively in C; 11 and 9 respectively in W).[12] Surprisingly, Paulson found that the singular readings in D included a significantly higher number of omissions than additions (31 and 23 respectively).[13]

Tendencies in the witnesses to reading 2. Paulson found that the scribe of ℵ "omits more than adding, and omits greater units of words than what is displayed in the additions."[14] The scribe of B omits more frequently than he adds (though his additions are longer by word count).[15] However, the largest omission in the singular readings in Matthew is 13 words in ℵ and 2 words in B. Thus, the omission of 31 words would be unusually large. Given the tendencies of these various scribes to either add or omit, reading 1 seems less likely to have resulted from a scribal change. However, since no additions or omissions of comparable length appear in any of the singular readings examined in these manuscripts, these findings do not significantly aid our search for the original reading in this variant unit.

A.3.2 INTRINSIC EVIDENCE: Prefer the reading that the author was *most* likely to have written.

Which reading is most consistent with the author's grammar, style, and vocabulary?

The shorter reading is very consistent with Matthew's style since it mirrors the state-ment in Matt 12:38–39 as discussed above. On the other hand, the omission of Matt 16:2b–3 would be a very simple and easy change for a scribe to make as well.

The longer reading contains several features that are marks of Matthew's style and would be difficult for a scribe to imitate. The reading begins with a genitive absolute, a construction remarkably common in Matthew. Furthermore, the precise expression ὀψίας γενομένης is twice as common in Matthew as in double tradition material (material shared by Matthew and Luke). The parallels between evening and morning as well as fair and stormy weather are reminiscent of the parallelism so frequent elsewhere in Matthew that it "typifies Matthew's style."[16] The longer reading contains the lexeme διακρίνω. Elsewhere

---

12. Paulson, *Scribal Habits*, 70.

13. Paulson, *Scribal Habits*, 103.

14. Paulson, *Scribal Habits*, 43.

15. Paulson, *Scribal Habits*, 58.

16. Robert H. Gundry, *Matthew: A Commentary on His Handbook for a Mixed Church under Persecution*, 2nd ed. (Grand Rapids: Eerdmans, 1994), 323–24.

Matthew inserts words from the κρι-word group in paralleled material eleven different times. It is also interesting that the logion mentions evening before morning. If the saying had been created by a later scribe, one would have expected morning to be mentioned before evening, the view of the day in the Greco-Roman world. The order in the longer reading displays a distinctively Jewish view of the day. Many of these Matthean features are so subtle that it is doubtful a later scribe could have been conscious of them. Even a scribe who sought to purposefully imitate Matthew's style would probably not have been capable of composing a reading so thoroughly Matthean.

Consequently, both readings are consistent with Matthew's style. However, since the Matthean traits of the shorter reading would be very easy for a scribe to produce but the extensive Matthean features of the longer reading are inimitable, the intrinsic evidence strongly favors the longer reading.

Which reading best fits the immediate context?

As explained earlier, some scribes may have felt that reading 1 was awkward in this context due to a perceived shift in the topic of the Pharisees and Sadducees' question and the topic of Jesus' reply. However, the statement in Matt 16:2b-3 captures the irony of the situation quite well. The members of these sects can correctly interpret signs in the sky, but when messianic signs signaling the dawn of the messianic era have appeared under their very noses, they have failed to understand their significance. Both readings fit the immediate context equally well.

Which reading best fits with the author's theology?

Both readings suit Matthew's theology. The parallel in Matt 12:38–39 demonstrates the consistency of reading 2 with Matthew's theology. However, Matthew's Gospel stresses the spiritual blindness of the Pharisees. Jesus instructs them to "go and learn" (Matt 9:13), questions whether they have even read the Law (Matt 12:5), and refers to the scribes and Pharisees as blind guides who lead the blind to their own demise (Matt 15:14; 23:16, 19, 24, 26). Thus, reading 1 highlights a prominent Matthean theme that is absent in reading 2.

A.4. Exploring Other Potentially Relevant Evidence

An in-depth analysis of this variant unit should involve the examination of high-resolution color images of the important witnesses supporting each reading. Manuscripts with the longer reading sometimes mark the reading with asterisks and/or add marginal notes. The marginal reading in 1424 states: "The things marked by use of the asterisk are not contained in other manuscripts nor in the Jewish Gospel." This Jewish Gospel (Judaikon) was a revision of the Greek Gospel of Matthew that abridged Matthew at many points. Some figures in the early church appear to have mistaken this Jewish Gospel for the original Gospel of Matthew, which was believed to have been first written in Hebrew or Aramaic. This suggests the possibility that the longer reading may have been omitted due to its absence in the Jewish Gospel and the presumption that it was not originally part of Matthew's composition.

Another interesting study relates to the use of the Eusebian section and canon numbers in manuscripts with the shorter reading. The section numbers marked various sections of the Gospels at a time before chapter or verse divisions. The canon numbers indicated if the section had a parallel in another Gospel(s) and, if so, which Gospel(s). The section and canon numbers in manuscripts with the longer reading are very consistent. However, the section and canon numbers in this section of Matthew in the manuscripts with the shorter reading vary widely. The evidence from the Eusebian apparatus—in particular, the inconsistent manner in which it is adjusted—suggests that the shorter reading is the result of a scribe intentionally omitting the longer reading, though it was present in his exemplar: Since Eusebius's system originally included the longer reading, it had to be adjusted when applied to manuscripts that lacked that reading. The copyists were using exemplars that contained the longer reading, and each scribe independently adjusted the apparatus to accommodate the omission. Since they had no previous model to follow, they adjusted the apparatus in their own different ways.

This hypothesis is supported by changes to the Eusebian apparatus in one of the two earliest witnesses to the shorter reading, codex ℵ. In the original Eusebian apparatus, the longer reading is marked as section 162 with the canon number 5 (expressed by the Greek stigma) to show it has a parallel in Luke. Then Matt 16:4 was marked as section 163 with the canon number 6 (expressed by the Greek epsilon) to show it had a parallel in Mark 8:12–13. In ℵ, 162 is shifted to Matt 16:4 (and correctly marked with canon 6). Section 163 is shifted to Matt 16:6 and marked with canon 2 to show that it appears in all three Synoptic Gospels. However, a close look at the apparatus at Matt 16:6 shows that the scribe originally wrote the canon number 6 (stigma) then erased the stigma and changed the canon number to 2 (beta). This adjustment suggests that the Eusebian apparatus in ℵ was taken from a manuscript that included the longer reading and that the scribe of ℵ had to adapt the Eusebian system without a previous model. Since an exemplar of ℵ contained the longer reading, the existence of the longer reading prior to the earliest witnesses to the shorter reading is confirmed.

Other helpful research might explore discussions of signs for predicting the weather in the ancient Mediterranean world to test the theory that the longer reading was omitted by scribes in environments where the principles were not applicable.

A.5. Weighing the Evidence

In this case, the external and internal (both transcriptional and intrinsic) evidence supports the longer reading. Thus, there is no need to attempt to assess which body of evidence is the most compelling. This detailed examination of the variant unit suggests that the evidence for the longer reading is stronger than the editorial committee for the UBS[5] concluded. In light of the current assessment, the longer reading deserves an A (or at least a B) rating.

EXAMPLE B

John 1:18

B.1. Preliminary Considerations

B.1.1 Identify the Variant Readings

In the UBS[5], John 1:18 reads: θεὸν οὐδεὶς ἑώρακεν πώποτε· μονογενὴς θεὸς[5] ὁ ὢν εἰς τὸν κόλπον τοῦ πατρὸς ἐκεῖνος ἐξηγήσατο. The superscript 5 following θεὸς guides us to the presentation of variants in the apparatus:

{B} μονογενὴς θεός 𝔓[66] ℵ* B C* L syr[p, hmg] geo[2] Origen[gr 2/4] Didymus Cyril[1/4] // ὁ μονογενὴς θεός 𝔓[75] ℵ[2] 33 cop[bo] Clement[2/3] Clement[from Theodotus 1/2] Origen[gr 2/4] Eusebius[3/7] Basil[1/2] Gregory-Nyssa Epiphanius Serapion[1/2] Cyril[2/4] // ὁ μονογενὴς υἱός A C[3] W[supp] Δ Θ Ψ 0141 *f*[1] *f*[13] 28 157 180 205 565 579 597 700 892 1006 1010 1071 1241 1243 1292 1342 1424 1505 *Byz* [E F G H] *Lect* it[a, aur, b, c, e, f, ff2, l] vg syr[c, h, pal] arm eth geo[1] slav Irenaeus[lat 1/3] Clement[from Theodotus 1/2] Clement[1/3] Hippolytus Origen[lat 1/2] Letter of Hymenaeus Alexander Eustathius Eusebius[4/7] Serapion[1/2] Athanasius Basil[1/2] Gregory-Nazianzus Chrysostom Theodore Cyril[1/4] Proclus Theodoret John-Damascus; Tertullian Hegemonius Victorinus-Rome Ambrosiaster Hilary[5/7] Ps-Priscillian Ambrose[10/11] Faustinus Gregory-Elvira Phoebadius Jerome Augustine Varimadum REB BJ // μονογενὴς υἱὸς θεοῦ it[q] Irenaeus[lat 1/3]; Ambrose[1/11] vid // ὁ μονογενὴς vg[ms] Ps-Vigilius[1/2]

B.1.2 Analyze the Nature of the Differences Between the Variants

The apparatus in the UBS[5] presents five variant readings for John 1:18. Two of the readings appear only in ancient versions or the writings of the early church fathers and lack support from any existing Greek manuscript.[1] These will be excluded from this discussion.

---

1. Regarding the latter of these two readings, D. A. Fennema ("John 1.18: 'God the Only Son,'" *NTS* 31 [1985]: 132n12) correctly stated, "The failure of this reading [ὁ μονογενὴς] to appear in any Greek manuscript of the Fourth Gospel precludes its originality."

Three variants remain for us to consider: (1) μονογενὴς θεός, (2) ὁ μονογενὴς θεός, and (3) ὁ μονογενὴς υἱός. The adjective μονογενής is consistent in all three variants. The variant readings may be broken down into two variant units. One unit concerns the presence or absence of the definite article. The other variant unit relates to the noun that follows μονογενής: θεός (which we will call reading 1) versus υἱός (reading 2). To keep the discussion as simple as possible, we will focus only on determining the noun that followed μονογενής.

B.1.3 Reflect on the Implications for the Text's Meaning

John 1:18 contains a prime example of a theologically significant variant unit.[2] Some manuscripts describe Jesus as (the) μονογενὴς θεός, which has been translated "only God" (ESV), "the unique one who is himself God" (NLT), and "the One and Only Son, who is himself God" (NIV, cf. CSB, NASB). Many manuscripts describe Jesus as the μονογενὴς υἱός, the "only begotten Son" or "one and only Son" (KJV, HCSB; cf. RSV). Is John describing Jesus' divine sonship, more clearly affirming his deity, or both? The answer depends partly on questions of word meaning and syntax, but largely depends on which variant the interpreter selects.

B.2. External Evidence

B.2.1 CRITERION 1: Prefer readings that can be shown to be early

The following tables show the manuscripts of the Greek NT and the early church fathers who support each reading, categorized by the approximate century in which the testimony was produced. The tables treat only sources from the first eight centuries and earlier whose testimony can be confidently determined. Note that the witness C[3] was excluded from the table. Although C (04 Codex Ephraemi) is a 5th-century manuscript, C[3] refers to a correction in the manuscript by the second of two correctors. This second corrector probably did his work in Constantinople in the 9th century. Codex W is a 5th-century manuscript. However, as the superscripted "supp" indicates, this portion of John's Gospel is "a portion of a manuscript supplied by a later hand where the original is missing, usually representing a different text-type."[3] Appendix I of the NA[28] shows that this supplement contained John 1:1–5:11. To find the probable date of this supplement, we must refer to other sources. Recent scholars generally date the supplement to the 7th century based on Kenyon's analysis of the script. However, Henry Sanders has offered compelling

---

2. F. J. A. Hort (*Two Dissertations* [Cambridge: Macmillan, 1876], ix), who conducted extensive research on this variant unit for a seventy-two-page dissertation, wrote: "I should hardly have cared to spend so much time on the enquiry . . . had I been able to regard it as unimportant. To any Christian of consistent belief it cannot be indifferent what language St John employed on a fundamental theme."

3. UBS[5], 26*.

evidence that the supplement is actually older than the rest of the manuscript, and a recent examination of the manuscript generally supports Sanders's claims.[4]

Table B.1. Manuscripts of the Greek New Testament

Variant	2nd c.	3rd c.	4th c.	5th c.	6th c.	7th c.	8th c.
μονογενὴς θεός		𝔓66 𝔓75	ℵ B	C			L
μονογενὴς υἱός			W^{supp}	A		~~W^{supp}~~	E

Table B.2. Early Church Fathers

Variant	2nd c.	3rd c.	4th c.	5th c.	6th c.	7th c.	8th c.
μονογενὴς θεός	Clem$^{2/3}$	Or$^{gr\ 2/4}$	Gregory-Nyssa Epiphanius Eusebius$^{3/7}$	Cyril$^{3/4}$ Didymus			
μονογενὴς υἱός	Ire$^{2/3}$ Clem$^{1/3}$	Hippolytus Letter of Hymenaus Alexander Eustathius Athanasius Gregory-Nazianzus Tertullian	Eusebius$^{4/7}$ Chrysostom Victorinus-Rome Ambrosiaster Hilary Ambrose Faustinus Gregory-Elvira Phoebadius	Theodore Proclus Theodoret Jerome Augustine Varimadum			John-Damascus

The earliest manuscripts of the Greek NT support the reading θεός. However, the early and widespread support of the early church fathers for the reading υἱός suggests that the readings are equally old.[5]

ADDITIONAL CONSIDERATION 1: *Reevaluate the date assigned to readings that appear in early witnesses from various regions*

Here we will organize the witnesses of known provenance in terms of their location in relationship to the Mediterranean Sea. The UBS[5] apparatus includes church fathers from the mid-5th century and earlier. Since our concern is the early geographical distribution of the readings, we will mark with bold-type witnesses from the mid-4th century and earlier.

---

4. Sanders, *New Testament Manuscripts in the Freer Collection*, 134–39. In April 2024, I was permitted to examine W (032) using a digital microscope in visible, ultraviolet, and near-infrared light. My examination led me to conclude that Sanders's hypothesis is probable.

5. Hort, (*Two Dissertations*, 8) came to this same conclusion, though he wrote before the discovery of 𝔓66 and 𝔓75.

Table B.3. Early Geographical Distribution

	North	Northeast	East	Southeast	Southwest	Northwest
μονογενὴς θεός	Basil Gregory-Nyssa	syr^P	**Origen** Eusebius Epiphanius	𝔓66 𝔓75 **Clement** Didymus Cyril Serapion Coptic		
μονογενὴς υἱός	Basil Gregory-Nazianzus Theodore	syr^c **Eustathius** Chrysostom Theodoret	Eusebius Hegemonius Jerome	**Clement** Alexander Cyril Serapion	**Tertullian** Augustine	it vg **Irenaeus** **Hippolytus** Victorinus-Rome Hilary Ambrose Faustinus Gregory-Elvira Phoebadius

Some readers may be puzzled by the placement of Origen in the East since he is often associated with Alexandria. However, the bulk of Origen's writings are from his time in Caesarea. This includes most of his commentary on the Gospel of John, in which all four of his references to John 1:18 that have been preserved in Greek appear.

Since the 2nd- and 3rd-century references to this verse in the church fathers are so important, consulting each reference may be helpful.[6] A careful examination of the uses in the writings of Eusebius reveals some of the difficulties in quantifying citations in the early church fathers. In his quotations of John 1:18, Eusebius uses μονογενὴς θεός three to five times,[7] μονογενὴς υἱός three to six times, depending on whether we include truncated quotations and quotations in which some features have been adapted to fit a new grammatical context.[8] In one important quotation, Eusebius uses μονογενὴς υἱός immediately followed by the variant reading μονογενὴς θεός.[9] Eusebius uses both phrases in clear quotations of John 1:18 interchangeably and in close proximity in his commentary on Isaiah. Apparently, Eusebius was familiar with both readings and was uncertain which to choose.

As far as we can tell from the extant evidence, the two readings had a roughly equivalent distribution in the 2nd and 3rd centuries. Reading 1 dominated in the East, and

---

6. This may be done most easily by searching for the two constructions in the Thesaurus Linguae Graecae database (https://stephanus.tlg.uci.edu/index.php) using the Text Search tool. However, this feature of the website is available only to subscribers or by access provided by an institutional library.

7. Eusebius, *Eccl. theol.* 3.6.3; *Comm. Isa.* 1.41; and *Comm. Ps.* 23.820 (without the definite article). Cf. *Comm. Isa.* 2.51.10.

8. Eusebius, *Eccl. theol.* 1.20.16; 2.23.6; *Comm. Isa.* 1.41. In addition, *Eccl. theol.* 1.20.17 appears to be a truncated quotation, and *Eccl. theol.* 1.20.6 is a quotation in which the case of the phrase has been adjusted to fit the context.

9. Eusebius, *Eccl. theol.* 1.8.4. The UBS^5 seems to have counted this quotation in support of the μονογενὴς υἱός reading since it was mentioned first and the μονογενὴς θεός reading was introduced as an alternative to it (using ἤ).

reading 2 dominated in the West. However, in the 4th century and later, reading 2 enjoyed wider geographical distribution. It appears that reading 1 was either unknown or had been rejected in the West sometime prior to the middle of the 5th century. Several of the witnesses to reading 1 come from Egypt. These include the papyri, Clement, and potentially Origen. However, the claim that the reading is a local reading with only Egyptian support is exaggerated.[10] The early witnesses to reading 1 (5th c. or earlier) include Gregory in Cappadocia (Asia Minor) and Epiphanius in Cyprus.

As noted in chapter 6, using the early church fathers to date readings is somewhat problematic since (1) their writings have gone through the same process of copying and recopying that the NT has, and (2) they sometimes cite the Bible loosely or from memory.[11] Nevertheless, reading 2 ("only Son") probably dates as early as the time of the copying of the papyri that support reading 1 since "there is virtually no other way to explain its predominance in the Greek, Latin, and Syriac traditions, not to mention its occurrence in fathers such as Irenaeus, Clement, and Tertullian, who were writing before our earliest surviving manuscripts were produced."[12]

ADDITIONAL CONSIDERATION 2: *Reevaluate the date assigned to readings shared by early witnesses that are not closely related to each other*

Our most helpful data for discerning the relationships between texts comes from the application of the Coherence-Based Genealogical Method (CBGM) used for the Editio Critica Maior volumes. Unfortunately, the data on the rate of agreement between texts for all the variant units in John is not presently available.

Our next best option is to check the rate of agreement between the witnesses for each reading in the Gospel of Mark since Mark is the only Gospel for which detailed data is available. This is not ideal. For various reasons, texts that seem to be closely related in one Gospel may not be in another. Thus, when data for John is available, our conclusions here should be reevaluated.

The data for Mark is available at the INTF website: http://uni-muenster.de/INTF/en/datenbanken/index.html. Under "Links," select "ECM Mark." Then select "Comparison of Witnesses." One can then compare witnesses in Mark. Neither $\mathfrak{P}^{66}$ nor $\mathfrak{P}^{75}$ contains portions of Mark, so we may begin with the earliest witnesses for each reading that do contain Mark and compare them. A more convenient way to see relationships between texts is to select MARK PHASE 3.5 in the header. Then select "Coherence and

---

10. Cf. Bart D. Ehrman, *The Orthodox Corruption of Scripture: The Effect of Early Christological Controversies on the Text of the New Testament.* New York: Oxford University Press, 1996, 79.

11. For helpful discussions of some of the challenges faced in using patristic evidence in textual criticism, see Fee, "Use of the Greek Fathers," 351–56; and Houghton, "Use of the Latin Fathers," 392–98.

12. Ehrman, *Orthodox Corruption of Scripture,* 79. Hort's extensive study (*Two Dissertations,* 8) similarly concluded: "As far as external testimony goes, θεός and υἱός are of equal antiquity: both can be traced far back into the second century."

Textual Flow." Scroll down the page to "General Textual Flow." Select "Chapter: All." The resulting stemma has 03 (Vaticanus) at the top. This means that Vaticanus is the extant manuscript that contains the text most likely to be the earliest ancestor of all other extant texts of Mark.[13] In the stemma, all the witnesses supporting reading 1 are closely related. To see how closely related they are, click the Gregory-Aland number for the manuscript. Be sure that "Rel," "All," and "Sim" are selected. This displays a Table[14] for which the top portion is:

Figure B.1. Witnesses to Mark Most Closely Related to Vaticanus (03)

Relatives for W1: 03 (a) 5527

| Rel | Anc | Des | | 10 | 20 | All | Variant: all+lac ▾ | | Chapter: All ▾ | | A | MT | Fam |
| Frag | Sim | Rec | | | | | | | | | | | CSV |

MT (a) • MT 0.84 • MT/P 0.82 • AA 0.81 • MA 0.81

⇕W2	⇕NR	⇕D	⇕Rdg	⇕ Perc	⇕ Eq	⇕Pass	⇕W1<W2	⇕W1>W2	⇕Uncl	⇕NoRel		
019			a	92.19%	4851	5262	132	226	47	6	⚖	⛓
892			a	90.58%	5001	5521	138	299	74	9	⚖	⛓
01			a	90.33%	4923	5450	139	329	51	8	⚖	⛓
04			zz	88.82%	4003	4507	108	305	79	12	⚖	⛓
037			a	86.87%	4762	5482	133	475	91	21	⚖	⛓
1342			a	86.65%	4765	5499	130	491	96	17	⚖	⛓
33			a	85.50%	3420	4000	108	366	88	18	⚖	⛓

Most of the other texts that have reading 1 (01 04 019 33) have relatively high levels of agreement with Vaticanus. Minuscule 33 may be an exception. The rate of agreement between Vaticanus and 33 (85.5 percent) is not much higher than Vaticanus's level of agreement with the MT ("MT 0.84" in the chart, i.e., 84 percent). By closing the window and clicking 33 in the stemma, a table showing 33's closest relatives is displayed. The table shows that 33 agrees with the MT in 89 percent of its variant units. This is significantly more frequent agreement with the MT than possessed by any other witnesses supporting reading 1 (019: 86.63 percent; 04: 86.36 percent; 03: 85.5 percent; 01: 84.90 percent). Thus, 33 seems to fit the criterion of not being closely related to the other witnesses. However, 33 does not fit the criterion of being "early." Remember that the goal here is to establish

---

13. By selecting "A" to the right of "Chapter: All," one can display the stemma that would result if a nonextant text were the earliest ancestor of all extant texts.

14. Used with permission of the Institute for New Testament Textual Research (INTF), University of Münster.

the antiquity of readings. If a reading is shared by two manuscripts of roughly the same date whose texts have little relationship to one another otherwise, the reading is probably considerably older than those texts (unless it resulted from contamination or multiple emergence with coincidental agreement). However, since 33 dates to the 9th century, it does not serve to push the antiquity of the reading earlier than what was already established by its appearance in our earliest majuscules.

The three witnesses supporting reading 2 that are from the 8th century or earlier are A, W[supp], and E. W[supp] is a quire containing John 1:1–5:11. Most modern scholars believe that it was added to the manuscript to replace damaged or lost pages. This supplement has a unique textual character and data is not currently available for a detailed comparison of W[supp] with A and E.[15] Kenyon has argued that W[supp] is two centuries or more later than A, while Sanders has argued that W[supp] is older than W and dates to the second half of the 4th century. If one follows Kenyon's date, the relationship between A and W[supp] will not have any bearing on the date of the reading. If, however, one accepts Sanders's date, and if one were able to show that A and W[supp] are not closely related, then the data would suggest that the reading is at least several generations of copies earlier than either W[supp] or A.[16]

Codex E (07) was not among the manuscripts included in the apparatus of the ECM of Mark. Retrieving the data for it and for Codex A (02) in the Manuscript Clusters tool (http://intf.uni-muenster.de/TT_PP/PP_Clusters.html) shows that in the parallel pericopes of the Synoptic Gospels, A and E are not close relatives. Both agree with the MT more frequently than they agree with each other. However, since E is an 8th-century manuscript, the shared reading would not significantly predate Codex A anyway. Thus, this examination does not suggest that either reading must have existed significantly earlier than our earliest witnesses to it.

B.2.2 Criterion 2: Prefer readings in witnesses known to be reliable and accurate

Since the CBGM has not been applied to the Gospel of John and a general textual flow for the Gospel of John is not available, we will rely on the Alands' categorizations of the manuscripts. We can conveniently highlight the Category I and II manuscripts. Remember that Category I manuscripts are those "of a very special quality which should always be considered in establishing the original text."[17] Category II manuscripts are high-quality manuscripts that are contaminated by some inferior readings.

---

15. Sanders (*New Testament Manuscripts in the Freer Collection*, 131) traced all the agreements between W and the six chief uncials in this first quire of John and found that W[supp] agreed with ℵ 104 times, A 114 times, B 143 times, and L 138 times (agreements with C and D were significantly lower due to lacuna in those MSS).

16. Megan Burnett recently compared the text of the first quire of John in W to the text in twenty other manuscripts, critical editions, and textual families. She found that W[supp] and A (02) agreed in only 57.85 percent of variant units. Thus, W[supp] and A should not be considered close relatives. Burnett, *Codex Washingtonianus*, 70.

17. Aland and Aland, *Text of the New Testament*, 106.

Table B.4. Category I and II Witnesses

Variant	Aland Category I	Aland Category II
μονογενὴς θεός	$\mathfrak{P}^{66}$ $\mathfrak{P}^{75}$ ℵ B	C L
μονογενὴς υἱός	[W^{supp}]	

Although six important early witnesses support reading 1, none of the Alands' Category I and II manuscripts support reading 2. Reading 2 is supported by only three Greek manuscripts from the first eight centuries of Christian history. Codices A and E belong to Category V in the Gospels. The Alands placed W in Category III. However, they did not offer a separate evaluation of W^{supp}. Sanders's comparisons of texts show that W^{supp} is very similar to B and L. Thus, it should be classified as a reliable text, and therefore I've included it in brackets under Category I in Table B.4. Nevertheless, reading 1 is supported by a group of witnesses that is generally recognized as more reliable.

Alternatively, we could use the ECM Mark data again to assess the accuracy of these witnesses with the expectation that this level of accuracy in Mark may extend to John also. In the "General Textual Flow" of Mark, click on "A" (for the Initial Text) to display the witnesses that most closely resemble the text reconstructed for the ECM.[18]

Figure B.2. Witnesses to Mark Most Closely Related to the Initial Text

Relatives for W1: A (a) 5414 　　　　　　　　　 ▬ ◰ ✖

Rel　Anc　Des　　10　20　All　　Variant: all+lac ▾　　Chapter: All ▾　　A　MT　Fam

Frag　Sim　Rec　　　　　　　　　　　　　　　　　　　　　　　　　　CSV

MT (a) • MT 0.89 • MT/P 0.86 • AA 0.85 • MA 0.85

⇕W2	⇕NR	⇕D	⇕Rdg	⇕ Perc	⇕ Eq	⇕Pass	⇕W1<W2	⇕W1>W2	⇕Uncl	⇕NoRel		
03			a	96.78%	5233	5407	0	171	3	0	⚖	🔬
019			a	95.11%	4902	5154	0	247	5	0	⚖	🔬
892			a	93.67%	5064	5406	0	325	12	5	⚖	🔬
01			a	93.27%	4979	5338	0	354	4	1	⚖	🔬
04			zz	92.36%	4075	4412	0	319	17	1	⚖	🔬
037			a	90.22%	4845	5370	0	497	22	6	⚖	🔬
1342			a	89.78%	4834	5384	0	520	24	6	⚖	🔬
33			a	89.43%	3495	3908	0	389	23	1	⚖	🔬

---

18. The following figure is used with permission of the Institute for New Testament Textual Research (INTF), University of Münster.

In Mark, the four majuscules supporting reading 1, which Aland ranked in Categories I and II (ℵ, B, C, L), all resemble the ECM text more closely than the MT. Minuscule 33 also supports reading 1. Of the witnesses to reading 2, 037 (Δ), 892, and 1342 preserve texts that closely resemble the ECM text. Minuscule 892 is impressive since it is the third closest relative to the ECM text, behind B and L. Thus, five very reliable texts support reading 1 but three reliable texts support reading 2.

B.2.3 CRITERION 3: Prefer readings found in multiple early witnesses

Five witnesses from the 5th century or earlier support reading 1. Only one or two (depending on the date of W^supp) support reading 2. If W^supp belongs to the 7th century, as most modern scholars assume, and if one restricts "multiple early witnesses" to manuscripts of the Greek NT, reading 2 fails to satisfy this criterion. However, the date of W^supp deserves careful reconsideration,[19] and the attestation to this reading in early Christian literature suggests that many early manuscripts that have not survived also contained this reading. Both readings obviously appeared in multiple early manuscripts.

B.2.4 Summarizing the External Evidence

Table B.5. External Evidence

Evaluation of External Evidence for Variant Unit in John 1:18	
Criterion	*Preferred Reading(s)*
1. Prefer readings that can be shown to be early.	1
a. Reevaluate the date assigned to readings found in early witnesses from various regions.	1 and 2 of equal antiquity
b. Reevaluate the date assigned to readings shared by early witnesses that are not closely related to each other.	NA
2. Prefer readings in witnesses that are known to be reliable and accurate.	1
3. Prefer readings found in multiple early witnesses.	1 or 2 (no preference)

In summary, the external evidence generally favors reading 1. The oldest and best manuscripts support this reading and show that the reading can confidently be traced back to the 2nd century. On the other hand, the testimony of the early church fathers and the wide geographical distribution suggest that reading 2 can also be traced back to the 2nd century.

---

19. See footnote 59 on p. 16 above.

B.3. Internal Evidence

B.3.1 TRANSCRIPTIONAL EVIDENCE: Prefer the reading *least* likely to have resulted from common scribal changes

Which reading did NOT *likely result from common errors related to sight, hearing, or memory?*

In the examination of transcriptional evidence, the basic question is, "What changes were the scribes most likely to make?" Variants that are easily explained as the result of common scribal changes are especially suspect. Thus, we should begin by asking if one or more of the variants may have resulted from the confusion of letters similar in appearance, the confusion of similar sounds, etc.

The early manuscripts of John that support reading 1 ($\mathfrak{P}^{66}$ $\mathfrak{P}^{75}$ $\aleph$ B C) all use the *nomen sacrum* for God ($\overline{\Theta C}$). The *nomen sacrum* for "son" ($\overline{YC}$) differs by only a single letter. Scribes familiar with the more frequent expression "one and only Son" could have misread the unique expression "one and only God" and written the more familiar expression in their copy. This could have been an error of sight if the theta were smudged, unclearly copied, fading, etc. However, given the dissimilarity in the appearance of the theta and upsilon in majuscule script, the replacement was more likely intentional.

Which reading did NOT *likely result from the scribe's effort to correct a perceived error, clarify the meaning, improve the style or grammar, harmonize to a parallel or the context, or conflate variants?*

Reading 2 may have resulted from a scribe harmonizing to a parallel or to the context. The expression μονογενὴς υἱός appears in John 3:18 and a similar expression that uses the same vocabulary appears in 3:16 and 1 John 4:9. John also uses the adjective μονογενής independently. Furthermore, the noun "son" is implied in the construction in John 1:14. Reading 1 probably did not result from an effort to harmonize since the exact expression μονογενὴς θεός is not used elsewhere in Johannine literature (or the NT or LXX).

Which reading initially seems difficult but makes better sense after further study?

The scribe(s) who changed the wording of John 1:18 probably viewed the change as a correction that restored the presumed original reading. A change from θεός to υἱός would be natural, especially in the 2nd century, in which Christians began to describe Jesus as "begotten by God" (Justin, *1 Apol.* 23). This soon influenced the interpretation of μονογενής so that it was assumed to mean "only begotten" (Latin: *unigenitus*).[20]

Ehrman argued that orthodox scribes intentionally changed "Son" to "God." He wrote: "It appears, though, that some scribes—probably located in Alexandria—were not content

---

20. Tertullian, *Against Praxeas* 7.1.

even with this exalted view of Christ [Jesus as God's only Son], and so they made it even more exalted [Jesus as the only God]."[21] However, Erhman's theory is improbable.[22] If the scribes intentionally made this perceived improvement, one would expect them to make the same change in other texts that originally referred to Jesus as the "one and only Son" (John 3:16, 18; 1 John 4:9). But such a change does not appear in a single extant manuscript.

Because scribes were probably familiar with the more common expression "only Son" and because "only God" does not appear elsewhere in the NT, reading 1 is the more difficult reading from the scribe's perspective. Hort correctly stated that reading 1 is "unlikely to be suggested to a scribe by anything lying on the surface of the context, or by any other passage of Scripture."[23] Metzger correctly suggested that reading 2 is the easier reading and "the result of scribal assimilation to Jn 3.16, 18; 1 Jn 4.9."[24]

Which reading best explains the origin of other readings?

Since reading 1 is the more difficult reading and could not have resulted from a harmonization, reading 1 probably explains the origin of reading 2 better than reading 2 explains the origin of reading 1.

B.3.2 INTRINSIC EVIDENCE: Prefer the reading that the author was *most* likely to have written

Rather than treating the three questions related to intrinsic evidence separately, for this variant we will entertain all three questions at once. Our goal is to determine which reading best fits the context and is most consistent with John's normal style, vocabulary, and theology.[25]

Answering these questions requires a clear understanding of the meaning of the adjective μονογενής. English readers familiar with some older translations may assume that the adjective means "only begotten." However, this adjective is not derived from the verb

---

21. Ehrman, *Misquoting Jesus*, 162.

22. In his detailed study, Paul McReynolds ("John 1:18 in Textual Variation and Translation," in *New Testament Textual Criticism: Its Significance for Exegesis; Essays in Honour of Bruce M. Metzger*, ed. Eldon J. Epp and Gordon D. Fee [Oxford: Clarendon, 1981], 114) stated even more bluntly, "That any scribe would have changed υἱός to θεός defies imagination."

23. Hort, *Two Dissertations*, 8. Hort added, "The always questionable suggestion of dogmatic alteration is peculiarly out of place here" (p. 9). Hort argued that, with the exception of Epiphanius ("that very peculiar person"), no ancient writer appealed to the expression μονογενὴς θεός in a doctrinal dispute. He concluded: "The single fact that μονογενὴς θεός was put to polemical use by hardly any of those writers of the fourth century who possessed it, either as a reading or as a phrase, shews how unlikely it is that the writers of our earliest extant MSS. were mastered by any such dogmatic impulse in its favour as would overpower the standing habits of their craft" (p. 10). Hort also demonstrated the ancient writers holding to a very wide variety of Christologies were willing to use the expression: "This great variety of belief among those who have received μονογενὴς θεός into their theological vocabulary suggests at once that its utility is not that of a weapon of offence or defence" (p. 27).

24. Metzger, *Textual Commentary*, 169.

25. On the meaning of the adjective, see Gerard Pendrick, "Μονογενης," *NTS* 41 (1995): 587–600.

γεννάω ("beget" or "conceive") but from the noun γένος ("kind" or "class"). The adjective describes something or someone as the only one of its kind or class, hence "unique." It does not refer to begetting. On the other hand, when used of human beings rather than objects, the adjective normally does identify the person as an only child. This is true in the NT, the LXX, and extrabiblical literature.[26]

If this is the meaning of the adjective in John 1:18, reading 2 undoubtedly fits the style of the Gospel of John and the context of the Prologue very well. The expression μονογενὴς υἱός appears in John 3:18 and a similar expression that uses the same vocabulary appears in 3:16 (τὸν υἱὸν τὸν μονογενῆ). A similar expression appears again in 1 John 4:9 (τὸν υἱὸν αὐτοῦ τὸν μονογενῆ). John also uses the adjective μονογενής independently. In John 1:14, Jesus is described as μονογενοῦς παρὰ πατρός ("the unique one [who came] from the Father"). The adjective is substantival even though it lacks the definite article. Since God is described as "Father" in the construction rather than merely "God" (cf. 1:6), the text strongly implies Jesus' identity as the Son of the Father. Thus, the translation "only Son" is appropriate even though the noun υἱός is not used. The adjective is probably intended to emphasize that Jesus' divine sonship is unique. This uniqueness prevents readers from assuming that Jesus is a child of God who was spiritually conceived by God like ordinary believers (John 1:12–13).

However, taking the adjective as referring to an only son does not necessarily mean that reading 2 is original. The Prologue to John's Gospel also affirms Jesus' full deity. His deity was explicitly affirmed in the statement "the Word was God" (1:1) and by the reference to the Word's eternality and agency in creation (1:2). He is portrayed as the tabernacle in which the glory of God resides (1:14). Furthermore, he is described as "full of grace and truth," a description drawn from Exod 34:6 that recalls the manifestation of God's glory and character to Moses. Thus, the Logos of John 1:14 is both the only Son (in relationship to the Father) and God who manifests the divine glory and character.

Although both Jesus' deity and divine sonship are affirmed in John 1:1–18, the emphasis is primarily on his identity as God. Nowhere earlier in the Prologue is Jesus *explicitly* called the Son. Divine sonship is implied only by the substantival use of μονογενής and the reference to God as Father in 1:14. Consequently, if reading 2 is original, the title "only Son" clarifies the relationship to the Father implied in 1:14 by adding the noun.

If reading 1 is original, the construction may be interpreted in two different ways. First, the adjective μονογενής may be substantival, identifying Jesus as the Father's only Son (as in 1:14). If so, the noun θεός is appositional and emphasizes Jesus' full deity. This view was suggested by Hort,[27] has been recently defended by Fennema,[28] and was adopted by the translators of many modern English versions such as the NIV and CSB ("the one and only Son, who is himself God") and NRSV and NASB ("God the only Son").

---

26. This is the consistent usage in the New Testament. Six of the nine usages of the adjective in the LXX refer to an only son or daughter (Judg 11:34; Tob 3:15; 6:11; 8:17; Ps 24:16; Pss. Sol. 18:4).

27. Hort, *Two Dissertations*, 16–18.

28. Fennema, "John 1.18: 'God the Only Son,'" 124–35.

Ehrman protests that this syntax is impossible: "When is an adjective *ever* used substantively when it immediately precedes a noun of the same inflection? No Greek reader would construe such a construction as a string of substantives, and no Greek writer would create such an inconcinnity. To the best of my knowledge, no one has cited anything analogous outside of this passage."[29] Although this construction is certainly very unusual (and this rarity could be confusing to a scribe), the preceding context has prepared the careful reader to understand it. The substantival use of the anarthrous μονογενοῦς in 1:14 prompts the reader to see the adjective as substantival in 1:18 as well. If the adjective is substantival, the noun θεός is necessarily appositional.

Second, the adjective μονογενής may function as an attributive adjective, a far more common function for adjectives followed by nouns of the same case, gender, and number. If so, the sense is "only God" (ESV).[30] Ehrman insists that the construction μονογενὴς θεός must mean "only God" but that such a sense is implausible:

> The problem, of course, is that Jesus can be the unique God only if there is no other God: but for the Fourth Gospel, the Father is God as well. Indeed, even in this passage the μονογενής is said to reside in the bosom of the Father. How can the μονογενὴς θεός, the unique God, stand in such a relationship to (another) God?

Ehrman's statement implies that if John originally wrote μονογενὴς θεός, he would have affirmed the existence of two separate deities, the Father and the Son, a God and another God. However, this objection fails to persuade. In fact, the objection seems to assert the very opposite of what the title would mean in the context of Johannine Christology. If the expression μονογενὴς θεός means "only God," it is probably used by John to prevent readers from misunderstanding the Prologue as teaching some sort of polytheism. The expression "only God" recalls the statement in the Shema that "the Lord is one" and the many affirmations of Yahweh's uniqueness such as "there is no other" (Deut 4:35, 39; 1 Kgs 8:60; Isa 45:5, 6, 14, 18, 21; 46:9; Dan 3:29). John elsewhere uses similar constructions to emphasize God's uniqueness. For example, John 5:44 refers to God with the construction τοῦ μόνου θεοῦ ("the only God"). John 17:3 describes God as τὸν μόνον ἀληθινὸν θεόν ("the only true God"). Similarly, 1 John 5:20 describes God as ὁ ἀληθινὸς θεός, a construction in which the definite article is probably monadic and asserts that he is the one true God. In light of the OT background and other Johannine statements, μονογενὴς θεός would be an expression affirming the deity of Jesus while also strongly affirming monotheism. Contrary to Ehrman's argument, Jesus' identity as the "only God" would by no means deny the deity of the Father, especially since Jesus explicitly asserts, "I and the Father are one" (John 10:30).

---

29. Ehrman, *Orthodox Corruption of Scripture*, 81.

30. The adjective means "only" or "unique" without any reference to a son or daughter in three of the ten occurrences in the LXX (Pss 21:21; 34:17; Wis 7:22). Pss 21:21 and 34:17 refer to the psalmist's "only life" (in parallel with ψυχή). Wisdom 7:22 uses the adjective to describe the "uniqueness" of personified Wisdom who is "an emanation of the pure glory of the Almighty" (NETS). Since John's Gospel seems to exhibit a Wisdom Christology, this text may have influenced the expression μονογενὴς θεός in John 1:18.

In either the interpretation "the only Son who is God" or the interpretation "the only God," the concluding verse of the Prologue matches the themes of the initial verse of the Prologue. Both portray Jesus as the expression of God ("Word" and "he has expressed him"), affirm Jesus' identity as God ("the Word was God" and "the only God"), and describe Jesus' relationship to God the Father ("the Word was with God" and "is at the Father's side").[31] The context thus seems to favor reading 1.

Ehrman acknowledged that reading 1 better fits the context. He wrote:

> The word θεός itself occurs some seven times in the passage, the word υἱός never. It may be that the context has decided the issue for some scribes, who conformed the passage to the terminology *ad loc.*[32]

However, it seems more probable that John's original expression was well-suited to the context than that it had to be conformed to the context by a later scribe.

B.4. Exploring Other Potentially Relevant Evidence

Other lines of evidence may be important factors in deciding between these variants. We need better data about the relationships between the early texts of the Gospel of John. Detailed data, like that produced for the ECM volumes, would yield more confident conclusions in the analysis of external evidence. Additionally, further research on the date of the first quire of John in W (032) is necessary. If the standard date for this quire (7th or 8th century) is accepted, no early Greek manuscript of the NT supports reading 2.[33]

B.5. Weighing the Evidence

The external evidence best supports reading 1 since this reading is supported by the earliest witnesses, the most reliable witnesses, and multiple early witnesses. Transcriptional evidence supports reading 1 since it is the more difficult reading; the variant seems unlikely in a superficial reading of the text but makes very good sense in the context after careful reflection. Scribes would be expected to conform the reading to other references to the "only Son" in John. If they had attempted to impose a higher Christology on the text by revising "only Son" to a clearer reference to Jesus' deity, we would expect the change to be made more than just this single time. Yet no witnesses have the reading μονογενὴς θεός

---

31. Philip W. Comfort, *A Commentary on the Manuscripts and Text of the New Testament* (Grand Rapids: Kregel, 2015), 248.

32. Ehrman, *Orthodox Corruption of Scripture*, 82.

33. In April 2024, the Smithsonian Museum's Freer Gallery of Art gave me the rare opportunity to examine features of the first quire of John in W with a digital microscope in visible, ultraviolet, and near-infrared light. My paleographical study of the sloping pointed majuscule script, chromatic analysis of the parchment, and examination of other important features in the manuscript, such as recovered erasures, all support the tentative conclusion that Sanders's original 4th-century date for this quire is correct.

instead of μονογενὴς υἱός elsewhere. The grammar of reading 1 may be understood in two different ways. If the adjective is substantival, the construction only reaffirms what has already been stated in John's Prologue. If the adjective is attributive, the sense of the construct closely resembles a variety of other constructions used to refer to the uniqueness of God elsewhere in Johannine literature (John 5:44; 17:3; 1 John 5:20). Thus, both external and internal evidence favor reading 1.

Most present-day critical editions of the Greek NT and the most widely used modern English translations agree that the original reading was μονογενὴς θεός. Tregelles's multi-volume critical edition of the Greek NT was the first printed edition to adopt the reading μονογενὴς θεός.[34] This reading was soon adopted by Westcott and Hort and Weiss. The UBS[5], NA[28], and SBLGNT also print reading 1 as the primary text.[35] The UBS[5] gives reading 1 a B rating. This reading emphasizes the deity of Jesus, perhaps with allusion to OT texts affirming the oneness and uniqueness of God.

---

34. See Samuel P. Tregelles, ed., *The Greek New Testament* (London: Samuel Bagster and Sons, 1857), 2:378. Tregelles defended the reading in *Account of the Printed Text of the Greek New Testament*, 234–35. Although the Tyndale House Greek New Testament is based on Tregelles's work and adopts his critical principles, it adopts reading 2. However, the editors plan to adopt reading 1 in the 2nd edition.

35. Michael W. Holmes, ed., *The Greek New Testament: SBL Edition* (Atlanta: Society of Biblical Literature, 2010).

EXAMPLE C

Colossians 1:12

C.1. Preliminary Considerations

In the UBS[5], Col 1:12 contains three variant units. The focus of this exercise will be the first of these, which is the fourth variant unit in the chapter, marked with the superscript 4:

12 εὐχαριστοῦντες τῷ πατρὶ[4] τῷ ἱκανώσαντι[5] ὑμᾶς[6] εἰς τὴν μερίδα τοῦ κλήρου τῶν ἁγίων ἐν τῷ φωτί·

C.1.1 Identify the Variant Readings

The superscript number directs attention to the following note in the text-critical apparatus:

{B} τῷ πατρί 𝔓[61] A C* D Ψ 33 81* 424 1175 1241 1739* 1852 1912 1962 2200* 2464 *Byz* [K L P] it[b, d, mon] vg[ww, st] syr[pal] cop[sa mss, bo] geo Origen Basil Didymus[dub2/3] Theodore[lat] Cyril[4/7]; Ambrosiaster Augustine // ἅμα τῷ πατρί 𝔓[46] B // τῷ θεῷ πατρί ℵ (F G θεῷ τῷ πατρί) it[f, g] vg[cl] syr[p] cop[sa ms], bo[ms] arm Origen[lat]; Speculum // τῷ θεῷ καὶ πατρί C[3] 075 0150 6 81[c] 104 256 263 365 436 459 1319 1573 1739[c] 2127 2200[c] *Lect* it[ar, o] vg[mss] syr[h with *] slav Athanasius Didymus[dub1/3] Cyril[3/7] Theodoret[lem]; Pelagius Varimadum // *omit* 1881

C.1.2 Analyze the Nature of the Differences Between the Variants

The variant unit contains five variants. Three of the variants relate to the identity of the person to whom the thanksgiving is directed. One witness omits the indirect object entirely. Other witnesses vary on whether the thanksgiving is directed to "the Father" or "to God, Father," "to God the Father" or "to the God and Father." Finally, witnesses vary on the inclusion of the adverb ἅμα ("with, at the same time").

C.1.3 Reflect on the Implications for the Text's Meaning

Since "the Father" in readings 1 and 2 is a reference to the heavenly Father, readings 3 and 4 merely explicate what is already implied in the other readings. Thus, those variations do not greatly impact the meaning of the verse. The omission of the indirect object has greater repercussions since this would result in τῷ ἱκανώσαντι functioning substantivally as the indirect object and would leave the identity of the one who qualified the Colossian believers for a portion of the heavenly inheritance unclear. The ἅμα in reading 2 also affects the sense of the text since it implies that the participle εὐχαριστοῦντες occurs concurrently with the other adverbial participles in verses 10–11 that modify the infinitive περιπατῆσαι. The significance of this will be explored further in the treatment of intrinsic evidence.

C.2. External Evidence

C.2.1 CRITERION 1: Prefer readings that can be shown to be early

Table C.1. Manuscripts of the Greek New Testament

Variant	3rd c.	4th c.	5th c.	6th c.	7th c.	8th c.
1. τῷ πατρί			A C*	D		$\mathfrak{P}^{61}$
2. ἅμα τῷ πατρί	$\mathfrak{P}^{46}$	B				
3. τῷ θεῷ πατρί		ℵ				
4. τῷ θεῷ καὶ πατρί						
5. omit						

Table C.2. Early Church Fathers

Variant	3rd c.	4th c.	5th c.	6th c.	7th c.	8th c.
1. τῷ πατρί	Origen	Basil	Theodore[lat] Cyril[4/7] Ambrosiaster Augustine			
2. ἅμα τῷ πατρί						
3. τῷ θεῷ πατρί	Origen[lat]		Speculum			
4. τῷ θεῷ καὶ πατρί		Athanasius	Cyril[3/7] Theodoret[lem] Pelagius Varimadum			
5. omit						

The two earliest manuscripts support reading 2. However, the testimony of Origen implies that either reading 1 or 3 (depending on whether one follows Greek or Latin manuscripts) is of equal antiquity. No Greek manuscripts from the 8th century or earlier support reading 4 and no witnesses of any kind from this period support reading 5 (1881 dates to the 15th c.). Since preference is given to manuscripts of the Greek NT rather than citations in the church fathers (and since the evidence for Origen's reading is conflicted), this criterion best supports reading 2.

ADDITIONAL CONSIDERATION 1: Reevaluate the date assigned to readings found in early witnesses from various regions

Table C.3. Geographical Distribution

Variant	North	Northeast	East	Southeast	Southwest	Northwest
1. τῷ πατρί	Basil	syr[pal]	**Origen** vg[ww, st] Theodore[lat] Ambrosiaster	$\mathfrak{P}^{61}$cop[samss, bo] Cyril[4/7]	Augustine	it[b, d]
2. ἅμα τῷ πατρί			B[1]	$\mathfrak{P}^{46}$		
3. τῷ θεῷ πατρί		syr[P]	ℵ **Origen**[lat] vg[cl]	cop[sams, boms]	Speculum	
4. τῷ θεῷ καὶ πατρί		syr[h with *] Theodoret[lem]	vg[mss] Pelagius	**Athanasius** Cyril[3/7] Varimadum		
5. omit						

Reading one has the widest geographical distribution. Not surprisingly, since reading 2 is supported by only two witnesses, it has the smallest geographical distribution. However, the wide geographical distribution of readings 1, 3, and 4 does not seem sufficiently early to push the presumed date of the reading to the era prior to the ancestors of $\mathfrak{P}^{46}$ and B in the 2nd century.

ADDITIONAL CONSIDERATION 2: Reevaluate the date assigned to readings shared by early witnesses that are not closely related to each other

Although data from the ECM on Paul's letters is not yet available, Zuntz's research showed that $\mathfrak{P}^{46}$ and B are closely related to each other.[2] If this is correct, we cannot demonstrate that the reading in these two manuscripts dates significantly earlier than its earliest extant witness.

Several of the early manuscripts that support reading 1 are not closely related. In the old text-type approach, scholars classified the text of Paul's letters in A as Alexandrian, in C as a mixed text with both Alexandrian and Byzantine readings, and D as Western. Although the text-type approach is problematic, it does reflect earlier scholars' observations that these manuscripts are not closely related, and for now we could resort (despite our reservations) to this old approach for classifying textual relationships until the better data from the ECM is published.

---

1. The provenance of Vaticanus and Sinaiticus cannot be determined with certainty. However, a Caesarean provenance is probable.

2. Zuntz, *Text of the Epistles*, 61–83.

Since the reading appears in several 5th- and 6th-century witnesses that do not appear to be closely related, the reading probably predates these earliest witnesses by several generations of copies. This suggests that the reading dates to the 4th or even the 3rd century. However, this evidence does not suggest that the reading predates the time of Origen or 𝔓⁴⁶. Thus, no adjustment to the dates of the readings suggested earlier is advisable.

Furthermore, the presence of the reading in early witnesses that are not closely related does not *necessarily* imply that the reading is several generations of copies older *if* the reading may have resulted from a common scribal change. As discussed earlier, such shared readings may be the result of "multiple emergence" that produced "coincidental agreement." We must examine the transcriptional evidence before determining if the reading shared by distant relatives is truly significant.

C.2.2 CRITERION 2: Prefer readings in witnesses that are known to be reliable and accurate

Since ECM data is not presently available for Paul's letters, we begin by using the Alands' categories.

Table C.4. Category I and II Witnesses

Variant	Aland Category I	Aland Category II
1. τῷ πατρί	A	𝔓⁶¹ C*
2. ἅμα τῷ πατρί	𝔓⁴⁶ B	
3. τῷ θεῷ πατρί	ℵ	
4. τῷ θεῷ καὶ πατρί		
5. omit		

Günther Zuntz's detailed study of the text of Paul's letters concluded that 𝔓⁴⁶ B and 1739 are the best witnesses to the original text.[3] Though B dates to the 4th century and 1739 to the 10th century, Zuntz recognized that these joined 𝔓⁴⁶ as witnesses for a text dating to AD 200. Notably, two of these three witnesses support reading 2 (1739 supports reading 1). Based on the Alands' categories and especially on Zuntz's evaluation, this criterion best supports reading 2.

C.2.3 CRITERION 3: Prefer readings found in multiple early witnesses

This criterion supports readings 2 and 1 in descending order of preference. Although 𝔓⁴⁶ and B are the only witnesses to reading 2, Zuntz identified several readings "definitely or possibly genuine" for which 𝔓⁴⁶ and B were the only evidence.[4]

---

3. Zuntz, *The Text of the Epistles*, 71–78, 83, 212–13.
4. Zuntz, *The Text of the Epistles*, 61.

Since readings 3, 4, and 5 do not appear in multiple early Greek manuscripts, this criterion does not apply to those readings.

C.2.4 Summarizing the External Evidence

Table C.5. External Evidence

Evaluation of External Evidence for Variant Unit in Col 1:12	
Criterion	*Preferred Reading(s)*
1. Prefer readings that can be shown to be early.	2, 3, 1
a. Reevaluate the date assigned to readings found in early witnesses from various regions.	NA
b. Reevaluate the date assigned to readings shared by early witnesses that are not closely related to each other.	NA
2. Prefer readings in witnesses that are known to be reliable and accurate.	2, 3, 1
3. Prefer readings found in multiple early witnesses.	1, 2, 3, no preference

C.3. Internal Evidence

C.3.1 TRANSCRIPTIONAL EVIDENCE: Prefer the reading *least* likely to have resulted from common scribal changes.

Which reading did NOT likely result from common errors related to sight, hearing, or memory?

Reading 5 is probably the result of an error of sight resulting from parablepsis. As the scribe looked back and forth from the exemplar to his copy, he leapt "from same to same." Although the apparatus treats reading 5 as an omission of τῷ πατρί, it is more likely the result of an omission of πατρὶ τῷ. After copying the τῷ before πατρί, the scribe's eye returned to the τῷ after πατρί and continued by copying ἱκανώσαντι. Since reading 5 appears in only one late (14th c.) witness and can be easily explained as the result of a common scribal error, it is highly unlikely that it is the original reading.

Which reading did NOT likely result from the scribe's effort to correct a perceived error, clarify the meaning, improve the style or grammar, harmonize to a parallel or the context, or conflate variants?

Scribes often expanded references to the persons of the Trinity out of an apparent reverence for the Deity. In general, scribes were more likely to expand these references than to reduce them. Consequently, readings 3 and 4 are likely scribal expansions. Scribes would not likely omit τῷ θεῷ on purpose, and no features of the text support the omission being a common error of sight, hearing, or memory. Some scribes may have added the τῷ θεῷ to clarify that the divine Father rather than a human father was in view. Although human fathers qualify sons and daughters for a share of the inheritance, it is God the Father who qualifies spiritual sons and daughters for a share of the inheritance of the saints in light.

The addition of θεῷ may also be explained as an effort to harmonize to the context. In Col 1:3, a form of the verb εὐχαριστέω is followed by θεῷ (καὶ) πατρί. Similarly, Col 3:17 uses precisely the same form of εὐχαριστέω as Col 1:12 (εὐχαριστοῦντες) followed by τῷ θεῷ (καὶ) πατρί. Readings 3 and 4 conform Col 1:12 to these references to thanksgiving in the surrounding context. This conformity could have been due to an accidental error of memory or an attempt to correct an assumed error in the exemplar based on the expectation that Paul would have been consistent in these references.

Reading 1 may be explained as an attempt to correct reading 2 by an omission of the ἅμα. When ἅμα serves as a preposition with an object in the dative case, it means "together with" and indicates that the subject of the verb and the personal object of the preposition cooperate in the action. A scribe would likely be puzzled by a description of giving thanks "*together with* the Father" since the other references to thanksgiving in the letter indicate that believers are to give thanks "*to* God, the Father." In other words, the scribes recognized that the Father is the one to whom thanksgiving should be addressed, not a fellow participant in the act of thanksgiving. A scribe could easily have regarded reading 2 as a "nonsense reading" that he then sought to correct by omitting the preposition.

Which reading initially seems difficult but makes better sense after further study?

Reading 2 is the most difficult reading for two reasons. First, like reading 1, the reference to God simply as "the Father" initially seems uncharacteristic of Paul's writings since he so frequently specifies the identity of the Father by combining πατήρ with θεός (cf. Rom 1:7; 15:6; 1 Cor 1:3; 8:6; 1 Cor 15:24; 2 Cor 1:3; 2 Cor 11:31; Gal 1:1, 3; Eph 1:2, 3; 5:20; 6:23; Phil 1:2; 2:11; Col 1:2, 3; 3:17; 1 Thess 1:1, 3; 3:11, 13; 2 Thess 1:1, 2; 2:16; 1 Tim 1:2; 2 Tim 1:2; Phlm 3). Although the scribes allowed a few simple references to the Father in Paul's letters to stand without elaboration, Eph 3:14 illustrates the scribal tendency to expand such references. Although all Greek manuscripts of Eph 3:14 from the 5th century or earlier refer simply to "the Father" ($\mathfrak{P}^{46}$ ℵ A B C) and this is definitely the original reading, the early corrector of ℵ, the majuscules from the 6th to the 8th century, and the vast majority of minuscules all add the phrase "of our Lord Jesus Christ." Our discussion of intrinsic evidence will demonstrate that the simple reference to "the Father" is rarer in Paul's writings but still consistent with Paul's style.

The difficulty of reading 2 is compounded by the presence of the ἅμα, which is widely assumed to be a "nonsense reading" since the Father who is the source of all good things (Jas 1:17) does not owe thanksgiving to anyone. Several scholars have referred to the ἅμα as a "palpable error" or obvious error.[5] However, this difficulty exists only if the ἅμα is

---

5. Zuntz, *Text of the Epistles*, 40; Lukas Bormann, *Der Brief des Paulus an die Kolosser*, THKNT 10 (Leipzig: Evangelische Verlagsanstal, 2012), 1.

assumed to function as a preposition. The dative τῷ πατρί that immediately follows the ἅμα naturally gives the impression that the word is functioning as a preposition. Yet, other possibilities exist. The word ἅμα often serves as an adverb marking simultaneous occurrence or denoting association. If marking simultaneous occurrence, the ἅμα could stress that the thanksgiving is to be offered simultaneously with the fruit-bearing, growth in knowledge, and divine empowerment described in 1:10–11 so that all four participles define characteristics of the godly lifestyle of the believer. If denoting association, the ἅμα could stress that the plural participle εὐχαριστοῦντες describes a corporate action rather than the independent action of multiple individuals. Thus, believers should express thanks to the Father together with one another. If τῷ πατρί is regarded as the indirect object of εὐχαριστοῦντες, as in the other readings, rather than as the object of a preposition, the ἅμα makes excellent sense in context. The initial "difficulty" of the reading is readily understood as arising merely from a misinterpretation shared by ancient scribes and several modern interpreters.

Which reading best explains the origin of the other readings?

Reading 5 may have resulted from any of the readings that begin with τῷ if reading 5 is an accidental omission resulting from a shift in focus from one τῷ to another in v. 12 as a result of parablepsis as explained earlier. Reading 4 may have developed from readings 1 or 3. Reading 3 likely developed from reading 1.

Scholars often suggest that reading 2 also developed from reading 1. If so, a scribe simply added the ἅμα to the τῷ πατρί that he found in the exemplar. However, no persuasive explanation for this addition has been offered. Bernhard Weiss suggested that the scribe added the ἅμα under the influence of Col 4:3.[6] This seems very unlikely since the two passages have little in common and it is hard to imagine that a scribe would know this letter so well as to anticipate an unrelated construction that appeared nearly three chapters later as he copied Col 1:12.

The committee responsible for the UBS edition of the Greek NT regarded "the prefixing of ἅμα" in 𝔓[46] and B as "a noteworthy coincidence in error." However, evidence for a tendency of ancient scribes to add ἅμα is completely lacking. A search for all instances of ἅμα in the CNTTS Apparatus (available in Accordance or Logos) shows that copyist errors related to ἅμα usually involved an error of sight in which ΑΛΛΑ or ΜΙΑ was confused for ΑΜΑ. Codex B never adds ἅμα. 𝔓[46] does so only once. However, that single example (Rom 8:4) does not seem to be the scribe's insertion since several Latin manuscripts and the Latin translation of Irenaeus were based on Greek texts that also had the ἅμα. If the Latin translation of Irenaeus accurately preserves his original Greek text, the ἅμα was found in 2nd-century manuscripts that predate 𝔓[46]. Furthermore, since ἅμα in Rom 8:4 seems to have a different sense ("alternatively") rather than any of the senses likely in the variant in Col 1:12, the variant in Rom 8:4 does not explain an impulse to add ἅμα in Col 1:12.

---

6. Bernhard Weiss, *Textkritik der Paulinischen Briefe* (Leipzig: J. C. Hinrichs, 1896), 103.

Since a plausible explanation for the development of reading 1 from reading 2 can be offered, but explanations for the development of reading 2 from reading 1 are weak, reading 2 is the reading that best explains the origin of the other readings. We can illustrate the emergence of the variants with this local stemma:

Figure C.1. Local Stemma of Variants in Col 1:12

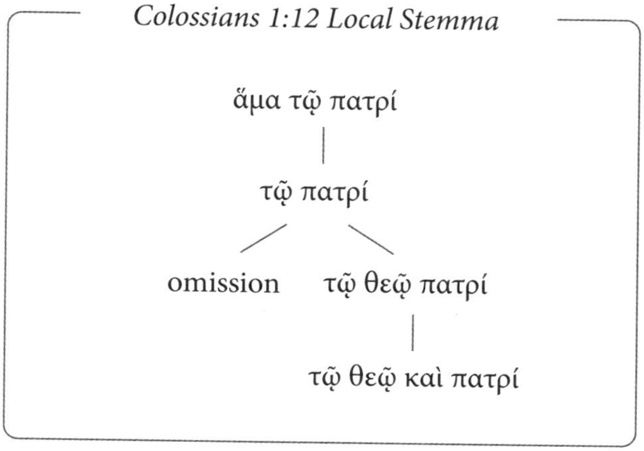

Colossians 1:12 Local Stemma

ἅμα τῷ πατρί

τῷ πατρί

omission   τῷ θεῷ πατρί

τῷ θεῷ καὶ πατρί

C.3.2 INTRINSIC EVIDENCE: Prefer the reading that the author was *most* likely to have written

Which reading is most consistent with the author's grammar, style, and vocabulary?

All of the readings are consistent with Paul's grammar, style, and vocabulary. Although reading 5 has been dismissed on other grounds, even it is consistent with Paul's style since he sometimes refers to thanksgiving without explicitly identifying the one to whom that thanksgiving is offered (1 Cor 1:14?; 10:30; 14:17; Eph 1:16, etc.). Readings 3 and 4 are likewise consistent since, as discussed earlier, Paul often refers to God as "God, the Father" or "the God and Father." Although a simple reference to "the Father" (readings 1 and 2) is less common, Paul uses it four times in his letters (Rom 6:4; 8:15; Eph 2:18; 3:14). In Romans, half of Paul's references to the Father occur without the noun θεός in the immediate context.

Reading 2 is also consistent with Paul's style. If the word ἅμα is used adverbially as suggested earlier, it appears as a postpositive. Interestingly, ἅμα appears as a postpositive adverb in Col 4:3 as well. Although the positioning of the adverb between the participle and the indirect object in Col 1:12 is likely what caused scribes to misinterpret the ἅμα as a preposition, this position is consistent with Paul's style in Colossians. When Paul uses ἅμα as a preposition, it is usually part of a pleonastic construction with the preposition σύν (1 Thess 4:17; 5:10).

Which reading best fits the immediate context?

Reading 2 fits remarkably well with the understanding of the structure and syntax of this text by most English translators and recent commentators. Although the UBS[5] and NA[28] punctuate the Greek text in a way that requires εὐχαριστοῦντες to serve as an independent imperatival participle, this usage is rare in the NT. The SBLGNT and most recent English translations place a minor break at or near the end of v. 11, so that "giving thanks" is the fourth participle in a series of descriptions of the worthy walk introduced in 1:10. The argument here is not that the variant that best supports modern interpretations is most likely the original reading. The argument is that the ἅμα supports the interpreta- tion of the text that most recent scholars affirm based on other features of the text. Thus, reading 2 best fits the immediate context.

Several features suggest that εὐχαριστοῦντες is adverbial. For example, Col 1:12 closely resembles the three preceding participial clauses. In those clauses the participles also have adverbial modifiers, and the first and third have prepositional phrases before the parti- ciples. Furthermore, Colossians emphasizes the importance of thanksgiving by mentioning it in every chapter of the letter (Col 1:12; 2:6; 3:15; 4:2), and this supports the view that Paul regarded thanksgiving as an essential feature of the worthy walk. The adverbial ἅμα should therefore be regarded as Paul's way of clarifying this precise understanding of the text.

Which reading best fits with the author's theology?

All the readings appear to be consistent with Paul's theology.

C.4. Exploring Other Potentially Relevant Evidence

Our earlier analysis of the variants led to the suspicion that readings 3 and 4 resulted from scribes adapting Col 1:12 to conform to the references to the Father in Col 1:3 and 3:17. If this theory is correct, we would expect the texts that had "to the God and Father" in Col 1:12 to have the same reading in 1:3 and 3:17. Similarly, the texts that have "to God, Father" should have this same reading in 1:3 and 3:17. A close look at a sample of manuscripts finds several witnesses that have the same reading in all three texts (e.g., 075 0150 6 104 256 365 436 459 1319 1573 2127 2200).

C.5. Weighing the Evidence

Although reading 2 is supported by only two ancient witnesses ($\mathfrak{P}^{46}$ and B), these are the earliest and best witnesses to the text of Paul's letters. Reading 2 is the reading that best explains the emergence of the other readings, a reading that was easily confused as a nonsense reading by scribes yet makes excellent sense in the context when it is properly understood. Reading 2 fits Paul's style and supports the understanding of the text that most interpreters affirm on other grounds. Reading 2 should be recognized as the probable original reading and assigned a B rating.

APPENDIX I

A GUIDE TO ASSESSING VARIANT READINGS

Preliminary Steps
1. Identify the variant readings.
2. Analyze the nature of their differences.
3. Reflect on the implications for the text's meaning.

Evaluation of External Evidence	
Criterion	*Preferred Reading(s) in descending order*
1. Prefer readings that can be shown to be early.	
a. Reevaluate the date assigned to readings found in early witnesses from various regions.	
b. Reevaluate the date assigned to readings shared by early witnesses that are not closely related to each other.	
2. Prefer readings in witnesses that are known to be reliable and accurate.	
3. Prefer readings found in multiple early witnesses.	

Evaluation of Internal Evidence	
Transcriptional Evidence: *Prefer the reading <u>least</u> likely to have resulted from common scribal changes.*	
Which reading did *not* likely result from common errors related to sight, hearing, or memory?	
Which reading did *not* likely result from the scribe's effort to correct a perceived error, clarify the meaning, improve the style or grammar, harmonize to a parallel or the context, or conflate variants?	

Which reading initially seems difficult but makes better sense after further study?	
Which reading best explains the origin of other readings?	
Intrinsic Evidence: *Prefer the reading that the author was <u>most</u> likely to have written.*	
Which reading is most consistent with the author's grammar, style, and vocabulary?	
Which reading best fits the immediate context?	
Which reading best fits with the author's theology?	
Explore other potentially relevant evidence.	
Weigh the evidence (when different lines of evidence conflict, prefer the evidence that is most persuasive).	

APPENDIX II

EARLY CHURCH FATHERS

List of Greek Church Fathers				
Name in UBS[5] (or NA[28] if not in UBS[5])	Abbreviation in NA[28]	Location(s)	Region(s)[1]	Date of Death
Acacius, of Caesarea	Acac	Caesarea	E	365
Acacius-Melitene		Melitene	NE/R	about 438
Adamantius	Ad	Syria or Asia Minor	NE/N	300/350
Alexander, of Alexandria		Alexandria	SE	328
Ammon, Bishop		Egypt	SE	IV
Ammonas		Egypt	SE	IV
Ammonius-Alexandria		Alexandria	SE	V/VI
Amphilochius		Iconium	N	after 394
Anastasius-Sinaita		Sinai	E	after 700
Andrew, of Caesarea		Caesarea (Cappadocia)	N	VI/VII
Apollinaris, of Laodicea		Laodicea Antioch	NE	about 390
Apostolic Canons		Antioch	NE	IV
Apostolic Constitutions		Antioch	NE	about 380
Arians[acc. to Epiphanius]		see Arius[acc. to Epiphanius]	SE	IV
Arius[acc. to Epiphanius]		Alexandria	SE	336
Arsenius, Anachoreta		Rome Egypt	NW/SE	about 450
Asterius, Sophist		Cappadocia Antioch	N/NE	after 341

1. For a description of the various regions, see p. 59 of the present book.

Asterius-Amasea		Amasea (Pontus)	N	about 410
Athanasius, of Alexandria	Ath	Alexandria	SE	373
Athenagoras	Athen	Athens	N	before 180
Basilidians[acc. to Clement]	BasilCl	Alexandria	SE	II
Basil, the Great	Bas	Caesarea (Cappadocia)	N	379
Basil-Ancyra	BasA	Ancyra (Galatia)	N	about 364
Celsus[acc. to Origen]		Alexandria	SE	about 178
(John) Chrysostom	Chr	Antioch Constantinople	NE/N	407
Clement, of Alexandria	Cl	Alexandria Antioch Jerusalem	SE/NE/E	before 215
Clement[from Theodotus]	Cl[exThd]	Asia Minor	N	before 215
Ps-Clementine Homilies	Cl[hom]		NW?	IV?
2nd Epistle of Clement	2Cl		NW?	before 150
Cyril, of Alexandria	Cyr	Alexandria	SE	444
Cyril-Jerusalem	CyrJ	Jerusalem	E	386
Diatessaron, of Tatian		Syria	NE	II
Didache	Didache	Syria or Palestine	NE?/E?	about 100
Didymus	Did	Alexandria	SE	398
Diodore		Antioch Tarsus	NE/N	before 394
Dionysius, of Alexandria	Dion	Alexandria	SE	264/265
Docetists[acc. to Hippolytus]				II/III
Ephraem Syrus	Ephr	Syria	NE	373
Epiphanius	Epiph	Salamis (Cyprus) Judea Egypt	N/E/SE	403
Eunomians			N	IV/V
Eunomius, of Cyzicus		Cyzicus (Mysia)	N	about 394
Eusebian Canons		see Eusebius, of Caesarea		
Eusebius, of Caesarea	Eus	Caesarea (Palestine)	E	339
Eusebius-Emesa		Emesa (Syria)	NE	about 359
Eustathius, of Antioch		Antioch	NE	before 337
Evagrius, of Pontus		Pontus Jerusalem Nitria (Egypt)	N/E/SE	399
Flavian-Antioch		Antioch	NE	404

Flavian-Constantinople		Constantinople	N	449
Gregory-Nazianzus		Athens Nazianzus Constantinople	N	about 390
Gregory-Nyssa	GrNy	Nyssa	N	about 395
Gregory-Thaumaturgus		Palestine Neocaesarea (Pontus)	E/N	about 270
Hegemonius		Syria	NE	IV
Hegesippus		Syria Greece Rome	NE/N/NW	after 180
Heracleon[acc. to Origen]			NW	II
Heraclides[in Origen]				about 245
Hesychius, of Jerusalem	Hes	Jerusalem	E	after 450
Hippolytus	Hipp	Rome	NW	235
Letter of Hymenaeus		Jerusalem	E	about 268
Hyperechius		Zela	N	IV/V
Irenaeus	Ir	Smyrna Lyon (France)	N/NW	II
Irenaeus, Armenian translation	Ir[arm]		NW	IV/V
Isidore, of Pelusium		Egypt	SE	about 435
John-Damascus		Damascus Sabas (near Jerusalem)	NE/E	before 754
Julius Cassianus[acc. to Clement]	JulCl		NW/SE	about 170
Justin	Ju	Palestine Ephesus Rome	E/N/NW	about 165
Lactantius	Lact	Nicomedia	N	about 330
Macarius/Symeon		Between Mesopotamia and Asia Minor	N	IV/V
Marcellus, of Ancyra		Ancyra (Galatia)	N	about 374
Marcion[acc. to Tertullian/ Origen/Adamantius/ Epiphanius]	Mcion[T/E/A]	Pontus Rome	N/NW	II
Marcus-Eremita	Marc	Ancyra (Galatia) Palestine	N/E	after 430

Marcus, Gnostic[acc. to Irenaeus]	MarIr	Lyon (France)	NW	II
Maximus-Confessor		Constantinople Chrysopolis Alexandria Carthage	N/SE/SW	662
Meletius, of Antioch		Sebaste (Armenia) Antioch	R/NE	381
Methodius	Meth	Olympus Lycia	N	after 250
Naassenes[acc. to Hippolytus]				II/III
Nestorians[acc. to Cyril]		Arabia, Persia, Mesopotamia	R	V
Nestorius		Constantinople	N	after 451
Nilus	Nil	Ancyra (Galatia)	N	about 430
Ophites according to Irenaeus	Ophites[Ir lat]	Alexandria?	SE?	II
Origen	Or	Alexandria Caesarea (most writings)	SE/E	253/254
Origen, *Supplement*	Or[s]			
Orsiesius		Egypt	SE	about 380
Paul-Emesa		Emesa (Syria)	NE	after 432
Perateni[acc. to Hippolytus]			SE	II/III
Peter-Alexandria		Alexandria	SE	311
Philo-Carpasia		Carpasia (Cyprus)	N/E	IV
Polycarp	Polyc	Smyrna	N	156
Polychronius		Verdun (France)	NW	about 430
Porphyry		Sicily Rome	NW	301/304
Proclus		Constantinople	N	446
Prosper	Prosp	Marseille (France)	NW	after 455
Ps-Athanasius			SE	III/IV
Ps-Clement, of Rome			NW	III
Ps-Clementines			NE?	IV
Ps-Dionysius			N	V
Ps-Eustathius			NE?	IV/V
Ps-Gregory-Thaumaturgus			N	
Ps-Hippolytus			NW	
Ps-Ignatius				IV/V

Ps-Justin				IV/V
Ps-Oecumenius				VI
Ps-Peter-Alexandria			SE	
Ptolemy	Ptol		NW	after 180
Ptolemy[Flora acc. to Irenaeus]	Ptol[Ir]			II
Serapion		Thmuis (Egypt)	SE	after 362
Severian		Gabala (Syria)	NE	after 408
Severus, of Antioch		Antioch (Pisidia) Egypt	NE/SE	538
Socrates, of Constantinople	Socr	Constantinople	N	after 439
Theodore, of Mopsuestia		Antioch Mopsuestia	NE/N	428
Theodore-Heraclea		Heraclea (Thrace)	N	355
Theodoret, of Cyrrhus	Thret	Cyrrhus (Syria)	NE	about 466
Theodotus, Gnostic		see Clement[from Theodotus]	SE?/N?	II
Theodotus-Ancyra		Ancyra (Galatia)	N	V
Theophilus, of Antioch		Antioch	NE	after 180
Theophilus-Alexandria	Theoph	Alexandria	SE	412
Timothy-Alexandria		Alexandria	SE	IV/V
Titus-Bostra	Tit	Bostra (Jordan)	NE	before 378
Valentinians[acc. to Irenaeus/Hippolytus]		Rome	SE/NW	II

List of Latin Church Fathers				
Name in UBS[5] (or NA[28] if not in UBS[5])	Abbreviation in NA[28]	Location(s)	Region	Date of Death
Ambrose	Ambr	Milan (Italy)	NW	397
Ambrosiaster	Ambst		NW	after 384
Apringius	Apr	Pace (Portugal)	NW	after 551
Arnobius	Arn	Africa Rome	NW	after 455
Augustine	Aug	Hippo	SW	430
Beatus	Bea	Liébana (Spain)	NW	798
Bede	Beda	Britain	R	735
Caesarius, of Arles		Arles (France)	NW	542

Cassian	Cn	Bethlehem Egypt Constantinople Marseille (France)	E/SE/N/ NW	about 435
Cassiodorus	Cass	Scyllaceum (Italy)	NW	about 580
Chromatius		Aquileia (Italy)	NW	407
Clement of Alexandria, Latin translation	Cl[lat]	see Clement, of Alexandria		
Cyprian	Cyp	Carthage (Tunisia)	SW	258
Facundus		Hermiane (Africa)	SW	after 571
Faustinus			NW	IV
Faustus, of Riez		Lérins (France) Riez (France)	NW	490/500
Faustus-Milevis		Milevum (Algeria) Rome	SW/NW	IV
Ferrandus		Carthage	SW	VI
Firmicus	Firm	Sicily	NW	after 360
Fulgentius	Fulg	Ruspe (Tunisia)	SW	533
Gaudentius		Brescia (Italy)	NW	after 406
Gildas		Britain	R	about 570
Gregory-Elvira		Elvira (Spain)	NW	after 392
Hilary	Hil	Poitiers (France)	NW	367
Irenaeus, Latin translation	Ir[lat]		NW	before 395
Jerome	Hier	Chalcis (Syria) Rome Bethlehem	NE/NW/ E	419/420
Julian-Eclanum		Eclanum (Italy)	NW	about 454
Juvencus		Spain	NW	IV
Leo		Rome	NW	461
Lucifer, of Calaris	Lcf	Calaris (Sardinia)	NW	370/371
Maximinus		Trier (France)	NW	IV/V
Maximus, of Turin		Turin (Italy)	NW	IV/V
Nicetas	Nic	Remesiana (Serbia)	N	after 414
Novatian	Nov	Rome	NW	after 251
Optatus		Milevum (Algeria)	SW	IV
Origen, Latin translation	Or[lat]		SE/E	
Orosius	Oros	Braga (Portugal) Africa	NW/SW	after 418
Pacian		Barcelona (Spain)	NW	before 392

Flavian-Constantinople		Constantinople	N	449
Gregory-Nazianzus		Athens Nazianzus Constantinople	N	about 390
Gregory-Nyssa	GrNy	Nyssa	N	about 395
Gregory-Thaumaturgus		Palestine Neocaesarea (Pontus)	E/N	about 270
Hegemonius		Syria	NE	IV
Hegesippus		Syria Greece Rome	NE/N/NW	after 180
Heracleon[acc. to Origen]			NW	II
Heraclides[in Origen]				about 245
Hesychius, of Jerusalem	Hes	Jerusalem	E	after 450
Hippolytus	Hipp	Rome	NW	235
Letter of Hymenaeus		Jerusalem	E	about 268
Hyperechius		Zela	N	IV/V
Irenaeus	Ir	Smyrna Lyon (France)	N/NW	II
Irenaeus, Armenian translation	Ir[arm]		NW	IV/V
Isidore, of Pelusium		Egypt	SE	about 435
John-Damascus		Damascus Sabas (near Jerusalem)	NE/E	before 754
Julius Cassianus[acc. to Clement]	JulCl		NW/SE	about 170
Justin	Ju	Palestine Ephesus Rome	E/N/NW	about 165
Lactantius	Lact	Nicomedia	N	about 330
Macarius/Symeon		Between Mesopotamia and Asia Minor	N	IV/V
Marcellus, of Ancyra		Ancyra (Galatia)	N	about 374
Marcion[acc. to Tertullian/ Origen/Adamantius/ Epiphanius]	Mcion[T/E/A]	Pontus Rome	N/NW	II
Marcus-Eremita	Marc	Ancyra (Galatia) Palestine	N/E	after 430

Paulinus-Nola		Nola (Italy)	NW	431
Pelagius	Pel	Britain Rome North Africa Palestine	R/NW/ SW/E	after 418
Petilianus		Numidia (Algeria)	SW	IV/V
Phoebadius		Agen (France)	NW	after 392
Primasius	Prim	Hadrumetum (Tunisia)	SW	about 567
Priscillian	Prisc	Avila (Spain)	NW	385
Ps Ambrose	PsAmbr	see Ambrosiaster		
Ps-Cyprian			SW	IV
Ps-Vigilius			SW	V
Quodvultdeus	Qu	Carthage	SW	about 453
Rebaptism (*De Rebaptismate*)			SW	258
Rufinus		Rome Egypt Jerusalem Italy	NW/SE/ E	410
Salvian		Marseille (France)	NW	about 480
Sedulius Scottus		Gaul or Italy	NW	IX
Severus		Aquitaine (France)	NW	V
Speculum	Spec		SW	V
Sulpicius		Aquitaine (France)	NW	about 420
Tertullian	Tert	Carthage Rome	SW/NW	after 220
Tyconius	Tyc	Africa	SW	after 390
Victorinus-Pettau	Vic	Pettau (Slovenia)	N	304
Victorinus-Rome, Marius	MVict	Rome	NW	after 363
Victor-Tunis		Tunisia	SW	after 566
Vigilius	Vig	Thapsus (Tunisia)	SW	after 484
Zeno		Mauritania Verona (Italy)	SW/NW	IV

APPENDIX III

PROBLEMS WITH THE TEXT-TYPE APPROACH

Historically, scholars have referred to groups of closely related texts by various names.[1] Throughout the 20th century, the leading textual critics referred to these groups as text-types.[2] Epp prefers the term "textual clusters."[3] Scholars in the 19th and 20th centuries assigned manuscripts to several different text-types. The four major text-types in this approach are Alexandrian, Western, Caesarean, and Byzantine.

Johann Albrecht Bengel (1662–1742)[4] attempted to make the growing amount of manuscript evidence more manageable by dividing manuscripts into major families. Many scholars recognize Bengel as the "father of modern textual criticism," in part, due to this important contribution to the discipline. Bengel identified two major classifications of manuscripts, the Asiatic and the African. These classifications are roughly equivalent to the Byzantine and Alexandrian text-types in the text-critical scholarship of the 19th and 20th centuries.

Some scholars have preferred readings shared by multiple text-types. Greenlee stated, "A reading which is supported by good representatives of two or more text-types may be preferable to a reading supported by one text-type exclusively."[5] He explained, "If a reading

---

1. Johann Albrecht Bengel, possibly the first textual critic to assign texts to such groups, described the textual groups as companies, families, tribes, and nations (Vincent, *History of the Textual Criticism*, 87. Johann Salomo Semler called them "recensions" (Vincent, *History of the Textual Criticism*, 92). Later textual critics such as Tregelles also used the same term (*Account of the Printed Text of the Greek New Testament*, 84). However, these scholars used the term merely to refer to groups of texts with similar readings. In more recent works, recension refers specifically to a text produced by intentional editorial work.

2. Aland and Aland, *Text of the New Testament*, 55–56; Metzger and Ehrman, *Text of the New Testament*, 276–80.

3. See Eldon J. Epp, "The Significance of the Papyri for Determining the Nature of the New Testament Text in the Second Century: A Dynamic View of Textual Transmission," in *Studies in the Theory and Method*, 283–95; and Epp, "Textual Clusters: Their Past and Future," in Ehrman and Holmes, *Text of the New Testament in Contemporary Research*, 520–41.

4. Lake, "Text of the New Testament," 65.

5. J. Harold Greenlee, *Introduction to New Testament Textual Criticism*, rev. ed. (Grand Rapids: Baker, 1993), 114.

has the support of good witnesses of several text-types it is more probable that the reading antedates the rise of the local texts instead of having originated in one of the local texts."[6] Similarly, Black suggests that text critics should "prefer the reading supported by the greatest number of text-types" since "the greater number of text-types in support of a reading, the greater probability of its originality."[7]

Greenlee recommends tabulating the witnesses for each reading from the various text-types by using a chart like this one:[8]

	Alexandrian	Caesarean	Western	Byzantine
Reading 1				
Reading 2				

However, most reasoned eclectics are more concerned with the number of *earliest* text-types that preserve a reading rather than the number of text-types in general. Thus, they look primarily for the agreement of the best representatives of the two most ancient text-types, the Alexandrian and the Western.[9] Griesbach argued that when these two early text-types agree, the reading is likely original.[10] Later scholars like Zuntz, Metzger, and

---

6. Greenlee, *Introduction to New Testament Textual Criticism*, 114.

7. Black, *New Testament Textual Criticism*, 35, 38–41. Black's approach is influenced by the "reasoned conservatism" approach, put forth in Sturz, *Byzantine Text-Type and New Testament Textual Criticism* (Nashville: Thomas Nelson, 1984).

8. Greenlee, *Introduction to New Testament Textual Criticism*, 119. Greenlee has charts showing the primary witnesses to each text-type for the major corpora of the New Testament on 117–18. Cf. Black, *New Testament Textual Criticism*, 63–65, 69.

9. For the view that there are "only two clear textual streams or trajectories through all of our material from the first four centuries or so of textual transmission, and these two trajectories are what we have long called the Neutral (or Alexandrian/Egyptian) and the Western text-types," see Epp, "The Twentieth-Century Interlude in New Testament Textual Criticism," in *Studies in the Theory and Method*, 93. Fifteen years later, Epp argued that three text-types existed in the early period. He labeled these B, C, and D. See his "Significance of the Papyri," 283–97. These include a cluster agreeing with Codex B, another agreeing with Codex D, and another to which Codex W belongs.

10. Tregelles (*Account of the Printed Text of the Greek New Testament*, 84) states: "The critical authorities were ranged by Griesbach under his three recensions; and each was valued, not so much for its absolute evidence as for contributing its testimony as to what the reading is of the recension to which it belongs. Thus, in forming his text he placed more reliance upon union of recensions in attesting a reading, than upon other external evidences." Griesbach saw the Western and Alexandrian text-types as dating back to the 2nd century. He viewed the Constantinopolitan (Byzantine) text-type as much later. He also saw the Alexandrian text-type as a revision of the earlier Western text that sought to correct the errors that had accumulated in the Western text. See Tregelles, *Account of the Printed Text of the Greek New Testament*, 84–85. Vincent (*History of the Textual Criticism*, 101–2) states: "In deciding on a reading he [Griesbach] relied chiefly on the evidence furnished by union of families. The agreement of the Western and Alexandrian he regarded as particularly important, often decisive." This position was also affirmed by Scrivener (*Plain Introduction to the Criticism of the New Testament*, 2:274–301).

Ehrman also argue that the agreement of these two early text-types constitutes significant evidence for determining the original reading.[11]

Unfortunately, this principle is not as easy to apply as it may first appear. Even the best witnesses of these early text-types do not necessarily belong to that single text-type in all portions. Gordon Fee, for example, argued that the text of John 1:1–8:38 in ℵ belongs to the Western text-type, even though this majuscule is regarded as one of the best Alexandrian witnesses overall.[12] This phenomenon is known as "block mixture." Unfortunately, some studies have assigned manuscripts to a particular text-type or cluster based on the analysis of a relatively small number of test passages, sometimes from a single NT book or chapter. Consequently, cases of block mixture may have been overlooked and the text's true complexion may have been misunderstood.

Furthermore, although the appeal to various text-types is a time-honored approach to textual criticism, several scholars have called for the abandonment of this approach. They have pointed out several serious problems with the standard text-type classifications.[13] First, the theories of text-types seem to have been developed primarily through research in the Gospels, and the categories do not work as well for other sections of the NT like the Catholic Epistles and Revelation.[14] Second, the names of the text-types imply the association of these texts with specific geographical locations, but these associations are misleading. The "Western" texts, for example, come from all over the Mediterranean world and not merely the West. Third, the term "text-type" must have several different meanings simultaneously in the traditional system. Thousands of texts belong to the Byzantine text-type, but only a few to the Alexandrian text-type. Furthermore, the Western texts do not have the homogeneity of readings that characterizes the other types. The Western texts sometimes differ from each other as much as or even more than they differ from texts of other types. Finally, the term "text-type" could incorrectly imply that the texts in these categories are recensions, each produced by intentional revision of the NT text.

Other scholars have voiced disagreement with some recent objections to the text-type approach. In a detailed study, Epp argues that both a B-textual cluster (roughly equivalent to the traditional Alexandrian text) and a D-textual cluster (roughly equivalent to the

---

11. Zuntz, *Text of the Epistles*, 142; Metzger and Ehrman, *Text of the New Testament*, 318. See Metzger, *Textual Commentary*, 1, 12, 14, 18, 20, 21, etc.; Holmes, "Reasoned Eclecticism in New Testament Textual Criticism," in Ehrman and Holmes, *Text of the New Testament in Contemporary Research*, 790.

12. Gordon D. Fee, "Codex Sinaiticus in the Gospel of John: A Contribution to Methodology in Establishing Textual Relationships," in *Studies in the Theory and Method*, 221–43.

13. For criticisms of the text-type approach, see Parker, *Introduction to the New Testament Manuscripts*, 172–74; Klaus Wachtel, "Towards a Redefinition of External Criteria: The Role of Coherence in Assessing the Origin of Variants," in Parker and Houghton, *Textual Variation*, 1154.

14. David Parker has argued that "the theory of text-types . . . is only applicable strictly in the Pauline corpus where careful research [by Zuntz] has shown genealogical affiliation." He argued that the theory does not apply to Acts, the Catholic Epistles, or Revelation. Parker, *Introduction to the New Testament Manuscripts*, 173.

Western text) do exist in Acts.[15] Some scholars still affirm the legitimacy of what Epp has called the B cluster, a D cluster, and a C cluster, which is another early cluster whose readings were a mixture of the other two clusters.[16]

Fortunately, the CBGM fosters an understanding of the relationships between witnesses accurately and precisely based on a comparison of *all* the variants in the *entire* text. The tools developed for the CBGM and made available by the INTF for public use can help determine if the use of the old text-type approach is valid for Acts.

Epp has identified the primary Greek witnesses of the D-text as D, $\mathfrak{P}^{29}$, $\mathfrak{P}^{38}$, and $\mathfrak{P}^{48}$. Other primary witnesses of the D-text are Latin, Syriac, and Coptic manuscripts and the writings of Irenaeus, Tertullian, Cyprian, Augustine, and Ephrem. These witnesses are not included in the INTF database since they are not continuous-text Greek witnesses.[17] The secondary witnesses to the D-text in Acts include three more Greek texts: Codex Laudianus (08) of the 6th century and codices 383 and 614 of the 13th century.[18] Although we cannot check the relationships between the versions that Epp cites as witnesses to the D-text, we will use the "Comparison of Witnesses" tool to see how closely the Greek witnesses to it in Acts are related to each other, to the primary witnesses to the B-text, and to the MT.

From the INTF database page, click "ECM Acts" under "Links." Next, click "Phase 4." We can find helpful data in earlier phases, but Phase 4 contains the most recent data. Click "Comparison of Witnesses." Now enter the two witnesses that you want to compare. We will start with 05 and 08. After entering these manuscripts in the "Witness 1:" and "Witness 2:" boxes, click "Go." Since we are concerned about the level of agreement throughout the entire book of Acts, we will look at the row "All" under "Chapter." The comparison table gives us more information than we need. We will use the data from the columns "NR" (the rank of closest ancestors), "Perc" (the percentage of variant units on which the two witnesses agree), "Eq" (the number of variant units on which the witnesses agree), and "Pass" (the number of variant units extant in both witnesses). In the tables below, these data units are labeled "Rank," "Percentage," "Agreements," and "Units," respectively. "Rank" refers to how closely related one text is to the selected text in comparison with the other texts in the database. "Percentage" refers to the overall percentage of agreement of the two texts in the variant units in Acts. The "Agreements/Units" column shows the precise number of variant units for which the two texts agree out of the total number of variant units that they share. The most important feature of the data to note is the

---

15. Epp, "Text-Critical Witnesses and Methodology for Isolating a Distinctive D-Text," *NovT* 59 (2017): 225–96.

16. See Epp, "Textual Clusters: Their Past and Future," 519–77.

17. For a more detailed explanation for the exclusion of these witnesses from the database, see Gregory S. Paulson, "Improving the CBGM: Recent Interactions," in *The New Testament in Antiquity and Byzantium: Traditional and Digital Approaches to Its Texts and Editing*, ed. H. A. G. Houghton, David C. Parker, Holger Strutwolf, ANTF 52 (Berlin: de Gruyter, 2019), 296–99.

18. Epp, "Textual Clusters: Their Past and Future," 563; Epp, "Text-Critical Witnesses and Methodology," 235, 238.

percentage of agreement.[19] Each row of each table represents the "All" row that results from a comparison of the named manuscript in the title of that table with the witness named in that row.[20] The witnesses are further grouped by the textual cluster to which Epp assigned them.

Agreement of D (05) with Other Important Witnesses				
Text	Witness	Rank	Percentage	Agreements/Units
D-text	E (08)	143	65.522	3358/5125
	383	145	65.418	3352/5124
	614	113	66.4	3403/5125
B-text	ℵ (01)	76	67.024	3437/5128
	B (03)	25	68.339	3514/5142
MT		22	68.742	3411/4962

Agreement of $\mathfrak{P}^{29}$ with Other Important Witnesses				
Text	Witness	Rank	Percentage	Agreements/Units
D-text	E (08)	4	85.714	12/14
	383	4	85.714	12/14
	614	4	85.714	12/14
B-text	ℵ (01)	4	85.714	12/14
	B (03)	4	85.714	12/14
MT		4	85.714	12/14

Agreement of $\mathfrak{P}^{38}$ with Other Important Witnesses				
Text	Witness	Rank	Percentage	Agreements/Units
D-text	D (05)	172	59.677	37/62
	E (08)	105	59.677	37/62
	383	49	62.903	39/62
	614	6	67.742	42/62
B-text	ℵ (01)	1	69.355	43/62
	B (03)	1	69.355	43/62
MT		48	63.793	37/58

19. "Rank" can be misleading since texts that have identical percentages of agreement sometimes have drastically different ranks.

20. Thus, the information in the row for minuscule 383 in the table "Agreement of D (05) with Other Important Witnesses" below was obtained by entering "05" and "383" in the "Witness 1:" and "Witness 2:" boxes and clicking "Go"—and so on for each of the witnesses.

Agreement of 𝔓⁴⁸ with Other Important Witnesses				
Text	Witness	Rank	Percentage	Agreements/Units
D-text	D (05)	-	-	-
	E (08)	6	55.556	25/45
	383	29	53.333	24/45
	614	76	51.111	23/45
B-text	ℵ (01)	1	57.778	26/45
	B (03)	6	55.556	25/45
MT		28	53.488	23/43

Surprisingly, D has greater similarity to the representatives of the B-text than it has to the Greek representatives of the D-text. It also has greater similarity to the MT (which is similar to the Byzantine text) than to the representatives of the D-text. Epp has argued that comparing other manuscripts to D is "inadequate" for determining whether texts belong to the D cluster since D is a mixed text that should not be regarded as a "closely approximate representative of the D-text" despite D's stature as a "primary witness" to the D-text.[21] Even with the admission that D is a mixed text, the data now available raise serious questions about the legitimacy of the traditional textual groupings. The other primary witnesses in the group also lack strong relationships with each other. 𝔓²⁹ has no greater similarity to the witnesses of the D-text than it has to the witnesses of the B-text and of the MT. 𝔓³⁸ and 𝔓⁴⁸ have higher levels of agreement with the representatives of the B-text than with most of the witnesses in the D-text.[22]

An analysis of the readings in the secondary witnesses to the D-text yields similar results.

Agreement of E (08) with Other Important Witnesses				
Text	Witness	Rank	Percentage	Agreements/Units
D-text	D (05)	143	65.522	3358/5125
	383	131	82.365	5614/6816
	614	139	82.94	5664/6829
B-text	ℵ (01)	107	82.926	5668/6835
	B (03)	97	83.776	5737/6848
MT		1	87.511	5753/6574

21. Epp, "Text-Critical Witnesses and Methodology," 228–29.
22. These papyri contain only small portions of the text of Acts (𝔓²⁹ [Acts 26:7–8, 20]; 𝔓³⁸ [Acts 18:27–19:6, 12–16]; 𝔓⁴⁸ [Acts 23:11–17, 25–29]). Such small samples are not necessarily reliable indicators of the textual nature of the entire manuscripts since such large portions of these manuscripts are no longer extant.

Agreement of 383 with Other Important Witnesses				
Text	Witness	Rank	Percentage	Agreements/Units
D-text	D (05)	145	65.418	3352/5124
	E (08)	131	82.365	5614/6816
	614	40	87.685	6444/7349
B-text	ℵ (01)	136	81.186	5968/7351
	B (03)	129	82.507	6075/7363
MT		2	94.643	6696/7075

Agreement of 614 with Other Important Witnesses				
Text	Witness	Rank	Percentage	Agreements/Units
D-text	D (05)	113	66.4	3403/5125
	E (08)	139	82.94	5664/6829
	383	40	87.685	6444/7349
B-text	ℵ (01)	152	80.835	5943/7352
	B (03)	145	82.51	6076/7364
MT		2	90.339	6387/7070

The witnesses allegedly belonging to the D-text do not display the coherence that one finds in the B-text. The text of E agrees more frequently with B than with other witnesses in the D-text. Although 383 and 614 agree more frequently with each other than with representatives of the B-text, they agree with the MT more frequently than they agree with witnesses to the D-text. Thus, the continuous-text Greek witnesses to the D-text lack both the level of agreement with each other and the level of distinct readings from other textual groups that are needed to define a separate textual group.[23]

Klaus Wachtel's recent comparison of the "Western Text" and the Byzantine tradition concluded:

> The quest for the "Western text" has failed. What we have instead are variants in different kinds of texts. If there are agreements between Irenaeus' citations and variants in 05, this does not mean that the "Western text" goes back to the second century, but that these particular variants do. Thus, the notion of a second century "Western text" should be abandoned once and for all.[24]

---

23. The massive dissertation on D by Peter Lorenz has dealt a devastating blow to the old notion that Bezae is the principal Greek witness of the so-called Western tradition. See Lorenz, *History of Codex Bezae's Text*.

24. Klaus Wachtel, "On the Relationship of the 'Western Text' and the Byzantine Tradition of Acts—A Plea Against the Text-Type Concept," in *Acts of the Apostles*, ed. Holger Strutwolf et al., vol.

Since neither the "Western text" nor the Byzantine text seems to have existed in the earliest centuries of transmission, comparisons of the so-called text-types will not assist in efforts to restore the original text of the Greek NT. The comparisons of texts utilized in the CBGM are much more helpful than text-type assignments for determining the relationships between witnesses.

---

3 of *Novum Testamentum Graecum: Editio Critica Maior* (Stuttgart: Deutsche Bibelgesellschaft, 2017): 3.137–48.

APPENDIX IV

THOROUGHGOING ECLECTICISM

Introductions to New Testament textual criticism ordinarily mention a third method known as "thoroughgoing eclecticism."[1] Scholars have used a variety of labels to identify the method such as "rational criticism," "radical criticism,"[2] "rigorous criticism," "new criticism," and "consistent criticism." However, "thoroughgoing eclecticism" is currently the most commonly used term for the approach.[3] In the late 20th and early 21st century, the leading proponent of the method has been J. K. Elliott (1943–2024), who served as Professor of New Testament Textual Criticism at the University of Leeds.[4] Elliott credited F. C. Burkitt, C. H. Turner, B. H. Streeter, Kirsopp Lake, H. J. Cadbury, A. C. Clark, A. E. Housman, and George Kilpatrick[5] as pioneers and practitioners of the approach.[6]

---

1. Metzger and Erhman, for example, treat "Thoroughgoing Eclecticism" along with the "Majority Text" as "Alternative Methods of Textual Criticism" (*Text of the New Testament*, vii, 222–25); cf. Robert F. Hull Jr., *The Story of the New Testament Text: Movers, Materials, Motives, Methods, and Models*, RBS 58 (Atlanta: Society of Biblical Literature, 2010), 144–46.

2. G. D. Kilpatrick described the method as "rigorous" and "impartial" ("Western Text and Original Text in the Gospels and Acts," *JTS* 44 [1943]: 36; "Western Text and Original Text in the Epistles," *JTS* 45 [1944]: 65).

3. J. K. Elliott seems to have popularized the term "thoroughgoing eclecticism" by using it in the titles of his essays and books. However, he seems to have regretted this and later suggested that "the old name 'rational criticism' may be preferable and more realistic than the inflexible-sounding term 'thoroughgoing criticism'" ("Thoroughgoing Eclecticism," 757).

4. Elliott has made significant contributions to the field of New Testament textual criticism. Perhaps the most important of these is his monumental work, *A Bibliography of Greek New Testament Manuscripts*, NovTSup 160, 3rd ed. (Boston: Brill, 2015).

5. Kilpatrick explained and defended his method in *The Principles and Practice of New Testament Textual Criticism*, BETL 96, ed. J. K. Elliott (Leuven: Peeters, 1990). For a helpful summary of Kilpatrick's method, see I. A. Moir, review of *The Principles and Practice of New Testament Textual Criticism*, by G. D. Kilpatrick, *NovT* 34 (1992): 201–7. Kilpatrick introduced Elliott to this method during Elliott's studies at the University of Oxford, where Kilpatrick served as Dean Ireland's Professor of the Exegesis of Holy Scripture. Elliott honored Kilpatrick as a mentor in the discipline of textual criticism "in whose footsteps I proudly walk" (*New Testament Textual Criticism*, 42). For a helpful discussion of Kilpatrick's contributions to New Testament textual criticism, see Peter R. Rodgers, "The New Eclecticism: An Essay in Appreciation of the Work of Professor George D. Kilpatrick," *NovT* 34 (1992): 388–97.

6. Elliott, *New Testament Textual Criticism*, 1; Elliott, "Thoroughgoing Eclecticism," 748.

In his most recent presentation of thoroughgoing eclecticism, Elliott defines the method thusly:

> Thoroughgoing eclecticism is the method that allows internal considerations for a reading's originality to be given priority over documentary considerations. The thoroughgoing eclectic critic feels able to select freely from among the available fund of variants and choose the one that best fits the internal criteria.[7]

The first sentence of this definition does not clearly distinguish thoroughgoing eclecticism from reasoned eclecticism. In cases where the evaluation of external evidence does not strongly favor a specific reading but internal evidence does, the reasoned eclectic critic "allows internal considerations for a reading's originality to be given priority over documentary considerations."[8] Elliott's descriptions of thoroughgoing eclecticism elsewhere show that the method does not merely allow this approach under certain conditions but generally requires it. The second sentence clarifies that thoroughgoing eclecticism considers only internal evidence in most cases and grants significantly greater weight to internal evidence in all cases. The heavy, often exclusive, focus on internal evidence is the hallmark of this approach.

Textual criticism has been described as both a science and an art.[9] Elliott admits that assessments of the merits of different readings in a variant unit based on internal criteria alone are more art than science and thus more highly disputed. Yet he insists that thoroughgoing eclecticism is grounded on "objectively defensible principles and criteria" that "are by no means subjective."[10] Elliott briefly identifies the most important questions to pose in the analysis of internal evidence, based on these objective principles:

> Which reading best accounts for the rise of the other variants? Which reading is the likeliest to have suffered change at the hands of early copyists? Which reading is in keeping with the style and thought of the author and makes best sense in the context? These considerations, rather than a concern about the weight, provenance, and the alleged authority of the manuscripts supporting the variant, are the important ones.[11]

These principles of internal evidence on which thoroughgoing eclectic critics rely are essentially the same as those enumerated in sections 7.1 and 7.2 of this book.

Elliott notes that the differences in the modern editions are the result of the delicate "balancing act" in which reasoned eclectic critics attempt to balance the sometimes contradictory results of the evaluation of external and internal evidence.[12] By contrast,

---

7. Elliott, "Thoroughgoing Eclecticism," 745.
8. Elliott, "Thoroughgoing Eclecticism," 745.
9. For a brief summary, see Quarles and Kellum, *40 Questions about the Text and Canon*, 102–4.
10. Elliott, *New Testament Textual Criticism*, 18–19.
11. Elliott, "Thoroughgoing Eclecticism," 748.
12. Elliott, "Thoroughgoing Eclecticism," 745. This description of reasoned eclecticism is superior to the descriptions in his work elsewhere. In his essay on thoroughgoing eclecticism originally

practitioners of thoroughgoing eclecticism seek to solve textual variation "with an appeal primarily to purely internal considerations."[13] Attentive readers will probably notice a certain tension in Elliott's description of the method. The adverb "primarily" implies that the practitioner will consider external evidence too, but internal evidence will be granted priority. The adverb thwarts descriptions of the method as one that exclusively considers internal evidence. In an early defense of his method, Elliott objects:

> Thoroughgoing eclectic critics are often misrepresented as having little interest in manuscripts, codicology or palaeography. Kilpatrick and I never subscribed to the opinion, still sometimes to be heard, that we treat manuscripts as mere carriers of variant readings. In practice I have been concerned with the age and character of manuscripts as well as their distinctive readings.[14]

On the other hand, Elliott's definition refers to prioritizing "purely" internal considerations. In this context, the adverb "purely" appears to be a synonym for "exclusively" or "only." Thus, in most cases, the thoroughgoing eclectic critic will not consider external evidence to be a significant factor in textual decisions. Elliott expresses skepticism about appealing to the reliability or age of witnesses (or groups of witnesses), the number of supporting witnesses, or the geographical distribution of a reading in textual criticism.[15] However, he admitted that some of these factors cannot be entirely ignored. For example, Elliott argues against preferring the reading in the oldest manuscripts since the number of copies between that manuscript and the original is unknown. He also criticized preferring the reading found in the majority of manuscripts since late manuscripts were more likely to survive than early ones. The decision regarding which reading is likely original is made "largely independently of the manuscript support for the variant."[16] Yet, he acknowledged, "In practice I must now admit that one feels more comfortable with the favoured reading if it is not found only in a solitary late minuscule or in only a versional witness."[17] Still, the thoroughgoing eclectic critic might affirm a reading found in a single earlier manuscript or a few late minuscules. Elliott explained that "if the arguments on style, usage and other

---

published in 2003, Elliott claimed that the majority of textual critics prefer to follow external evidence over intrinsic probability and resort to relying on intrinsic probability only when external evidence is conflicting and ambiguous. Elliott claimed that reasoned eclectics "resort to principles based on internal evidence or intrinsic probability" whenever their "favorite manuscripts" (Vaticanus and Sinaiticus) disagree. He added, "What has been said so far shows how the majority of textual critics grudgingly apply principles of intrinsic probability to text-critical problems only when their preferred external evidence is unhelpful or ambiguous" (*New Testament Textual Criticism*, 41). Even in his 2014 essay, Elliott summarized the Alands' rule 4 as "external criteria should supersede internal" ("Thoroughgoing Eclecticism," 753). However, this distorts the rule, which states: "Internal criteria . . . can never be the sole basis for a critical decision, especially in opposition to external evidence" (Aland and Aland, *Text of the New Testament*, 280).

13. Elliott, "Thoroughgoing Eclecticism," 745.
14. Elliott, *New Testament Textual Criticism*, 1–2.
15. Elliott, "Thoroughgoing Eclecticism," 745–46.
16. Elliott, *New Testament Textual Criticism*, 42.
17. Elliott, *New Testament Textual Criticism*, 44.

internal criteria point to a reading that may be supported by only a few manuscripts then that reading should nonetheless be accepted."[18]

Despite his general rejection of the importance of external evidence, Elliott did not believe that the careful study of individual manuscripts should be ignored. Elliott affirmed the old maxim of Westcott and Hort that emphasized that "knowledge of manuscripts must precede knowledge of readings." However, in his view the most important feature of a manuscript is not its age, related witnesses, presumed reliability, but its "character." The "character" of the manuscript focused on the tendencies of the individual copyist and the scribal changes that commonly occur in the manuscript. He offers these examples:

> We would be unwilling to accept the originality of a reading found in a manuscript whose known proclivities made certain of its readings improbable as the original text of the New Testament author. For example, a manuscript with a proven track record for expanding the divine names with a liturgical formula would be an unreliable witness in favour of a variant giving a longer, as opposed to a shorter, form of a divine name. Similarly, a manuscript whose scribe was regularly erratic in its spelling or another whose scribe exhibited conspicuous carelessness in word order would not be relied on when supporting, perhaps uniquely, an orthographical variant or a reading offering a changed sequence of words, even where in other circumstances such a variant might be seen as theoretically acceptable as the original.[19]

The "character" of the manuscript relates to issues of transcriptional probability ("What changes was the scribe most likely to make?"), which is generally treated as a subcategory of internal evidence. However, Elliott wisely focuses on the scribal tendencies of individual manuscripts. His descriptions of general scribal tendencies are rather modest and include "a recognition that parablepsis can cause the accidental shortening of the text being copied, that scribes were often prone to harmonize parallel texts which seemed to be divergent, and that scribes tended to improve upon perceived breaches of acceptable standards of language."[20]

Robert Hull correctly observed, "Although Kilpatrick and Elliott have been unyielding in the commitment to internal evidence as the basis for establishing the text, they have had few followers."[21] The waning influence of thoroughgoing eclecticism is the result of several perceived weaknesses of the approach. First, Gordon D. Fee argued persuasively

---

18. Elliott, *New Testament Textual Criticism*, 44.

19. Elliott, *New Testament Textual Criticism*, 45.

20. Elliott, *New Testament Textual Criticism*, 43. Due to his emphasis on internal evidence, Elliott more carefully considered scribal tendencies than some of his peers. For example, he anticipated the firm findings of later studies that challenged the preference for the shorter reading (see section 7.1.1 of this book). He disputed the principle "found in many of the textbooks" and argued that "a reading giving the longer text is more likely to be original than a shortened version, and this is based on the argument that scribes often accidentally, but sometimes deliberately, reduced the text that they were copying" (Elliott, *New Testament Textual Criticism*, 43). Elliott offered important qualifications to the principle, noting that the longer reading should not be preferred if the grammar, vocabulary, style, or theology did not suit the context.

21. Hull, *Story of the New Testament Text*, 145.

that the approach "assumes a faulty theory of textual corruption and transmission."[22] Both Kilpatrick and Elliott followed H. J. Vogels's theory that the great majority of significant and meaningful textual variants entered copies prior to AD 200.[23] After that period, the canonical status of the New Testament made scribes hesitant to introduce intentional changes as they copied their exemplars. This resulted in a process of random transmission in which the original reading might appear in nearly any of the later witnesses. Fee countered that "it is both illogical and unhistorical to imply, as both Kilpatrick and Elliott do, that because no MSS have escaped corruption, therefore all MSS are equally corrupt, and no MS(S) may be judged better than others."[24]

Second, although Elliott denied the subjectivity of the principles used to evaluate different readings in thoroughgoing eclecticism, he admitted that reliable applications of the method depended on drawing conclusions about an author's grammar, style, etc. from "firm examples," that is, examples for which no textual variation existed. However, as scholars study and transcribe more and more manuscripts, newly discovered variant readings reduce the number of these "firm examples." Enough variation exists to cast doubt on whether one can restore the original text based solely on considerations of "what the author was most likely to have written." Assessments of the author's grammar and style often depend on which text the scholar selects for his study. Assessments based on the text in the oldest majuscules and assessments based on later Byzantine manuscripts may lead to very different impressions of the author's grammar and style. For example, manuscripts containing Matt 27:53 vary on whether Matthew used the singular verb or plural verb with an impersonal neuter plural subject. Efforts to trace Matthew's normal style related to the number of verbs with impersonal neuter plural subjects are greatly complicated by frequent textual variations throughout the Gospel.[25] Only a few manuscripts (like W [032]) show much consistency, and the consistency is so rare that one must assume it is the result of the scribe's own efforts to impose this consistency on the text of Matthew. Critics could not solve such a textual puzzle on intrinsic and transcriptional evidence alone.

Third, thoroughgoing eclecticism offers no helpful solution for cases in which the two subsets of internal evidence, transcriptional evidence and intrinsic evidence, seem to conflict. Westcott and Hort note that "a vast proportion of variations" have a specific reading that both the author was likely to have written and scribes would generally have preferred over other variants.[26] In these cases, evaluation of internal evidence alone will not enable the critic to establish the original text.

---

22. Gordon D. Fee, "Rigorous or Reasoned Eclecticism—Which?," in *Studies in the Theory and Method of New Testament Textual Criticism*, 124–40, esp. 125. Fee's critique of thoroughgoing eclecticism is one of the most detailed yet published.

23. Elliott, *New Testament Textual Criticism*, 45.

24. Fee, "Rigorous or Reasoned Eclecticism," 127.

25. For a discussion of the specific challenges, see Charles L. Quarles, "Matthew 27:52–53 as a Scribal Interpolation: Testing a Recent Proposal," *BBR* 27 (2017): 224–25.

26. Westcott and Hort, *Introduction to the New Testament*, 29.

Fourth, scholars sometimes reach significantly different conclusions about what the author was most likely to have written because of their own unconscious biases. In practice, scholars may unintentionally argue for the reading that *they* would have written if *they* were the biblical author.[27] Arguments appealing to transcriptional evidence are often unreliable too since these may be based on anecdotal claims about universal scribal tendencies rather than extensive research on the scribal tendencies in individual manuscripts.

Finally, the method seems to dismiss a valuable body of evidence by focusing almost exclusively on transcriptional and internal evidence to the neglect of external evidence. Reasoned eclectic critics rightly emphasize the importance of considering *all* the available evidence, *both external and internal*. If one affirms the reliability of internal evidence (as all thoroughgoing eclectic critics do), at least some aspects of external evidence should be valued as well. As explained in section 6.2 of this book, assessments of the general reliability of manuscripts by scholars practicing reasoned eclecticism are based primarily on textual decisions that can be made by relying solely on internal evidence. Westcott and Hort advocated a three-stage process in textual decisions. In the first stage, the critic should "endeavor to deal with each variation separately, and to decide between its variants immediately, on the evidence presented by the variation itself in its context, aided only by general considerations."[28] In this stage, they aim to locate the original reading based on internal evidence in cases in which that evidence alone leads to highly probable conclusions. These are cases in which the intrinsic evidence and transcriptional evidence strongly cohere. In the second stage, the scholar should "pass from investigating the readings to investigating the documents by means of what we have learned respecting the readings."[29] In other words, manuscripts rarely preserving the established readings are deemed to be less reliable, and manuscripts consistently preserving the established readings are deemed to be more reliable. In the third stage, the critic should return to the previously established readings to see if those earlier decisions were supported by the manuscripts deemed most reliable. Westcott and Hort rightly argued that this process that appeals to the relative reliability of manuscripts will "depend ultimately on judgments upon Internal Evidence of Readings."[30] Thoroughgoing eclectic critics seem to overlook this crucial observation. Their insistence on merely examining internal evidence without any consideration for the general reliability of certain manuscripts is logically inconsistent. When a thoroughgoing eclectic critic objects to concerns about the "weight" and "alleged authority" of certain manuscripts,[31] the critic rejects the results of the application of his own method.

---

27. Westcott and Hort raised concerns about the subjectivity involved in evaluations of intrinsic evidence (see their *Introduction to the New Testament*, 20–22).

28. Westcott and Hort, *Introduction to the New Testament*, 33.

29. Westcott and Hort, *Introduction to the New Testament*, 33.

30. Westcott and Hort, *Introduction to the New Testament*, 34.

31. Elliott uses these terms when describing principles of external evidence in "Thoroughgoing Eclecticism," 748. He elsewhere objects to giving preference to "favourite" manuscripts (*New Testament Textual Criticism*, 41). As early as his dissertation, he critiqued the "cult of the best manuscripts." See J. K. Elliott, "An Examination of the Greek Text of the Epistles to Timothy and Titus" (PhD thesis, University of Oxford, 1967), 8. Cf. Elliott, "Thoroughgoing Eclecticism," 760.

The role that thoroughgoing eclecticism will play in New Testament textual criticism in the 21st century is uncertain.[32] However, the approach will probably not significantly influence textual criticism in the near future unless the method experiences an unexpected resurgence. The passing of Elliott in 2024 has left a great void. No new champion for the approach has yet emerged. The best applications of the approach that Elliott lists all date to the late 20th century.[33] The last of these was published in 1996. Elliott observes that although thoroughgoing eclectics are a small minority within the guild of New Testament textual criticism, many biblical scholars who are not experts in textual criticism often utilize the method in their research. He repeatedly lists New Testament commentators who generally rely on internal evidence when seeking to establish the original text.[34] Yet Elliott admits that "none would likely claim to be a follower of thoroughgoing eclecticism."[35] Commentators primarily discuss internal evidence because their expertise in the grammar, vocabulary, style, and theology of the author—a byproduct of their exegetical research—especially equips them to contribute to these discussions. The legacy of Kilpatrick and Elliott lives on mainly in the work of reasoned eclectics who have a greater appreciation for the role of internal evidence in textual criticism.[36]

---

32. Since this book focuses on NT textual criticism "for the 21st century," it seemed prudent to treat thoroughgoing eclecticism in this brief appendix to avoid giving the impression that the method is likely to play a significant part in future work.

33. Elliott, "Thoroughgoing Eclecticism," 747, 747n9. However, Elliott later points to the work of Heinrich Greeven and Eberhard Güting as contributions from "thoroughgoing critics" (751). See Heinrich Greeven, *Textkritik des Markusevangeliums*, ed. Eberhard Güting (Münster: LIT, 2005).

34. Elliott, *New Testament Textual Criticism*, 42. Elliott repeated this argument in "Thoroughgoing Eclecticism," 751–52.

35. Elliott, "Thoroughgoing Eclecticism," 751.

36. Cf. Hull, *Story of the New Testament Text*, 145.

Glossary

Abschrift (pl. *Abschriften*): a manuscript with an identified and extant exemplar.

anecdotal method: an approach for describing scribal tendencies based on the general impressions of the scholars who examined a variety of manuscripts.

Ausgangstext: the German term referring to the text of the Greek NT from which all existing texts descended. The English term is "initial text."

Byzantine priorist: a textual critic who affirms that the Byzantine text preserved in the majority of the extant manuscripts of the Greek NT is the most important resource for reconstructing the original text of the NT.

canons, Eusebian: the system developed by Eusebius of Caesarea to mark sections of the Gospels (by the use of section numbers) and help readers locate parallel accounts in other Gospels (by the use of canon numbers and tables).

codex (pl. codices): the ancient book form that consisted of pages stacked on each other and bound together at one edge. The codex is the forerunner of the modern book form.

collation (verb: collate): a detailed comparison of a text with another text. When collating, scholars compare the text in an ancient manuscript with the text of another manuscript or critical edition and note all differences.

colophon: a note at the end of a book that often identifies the scribe who copied the text or an owner of a manuscript.

conflation: the act of blending two variant readings.

contamination: the act of a copyist occasionally consulting a manuscript other than the primary exemplar and incorporating some readings from that manuscript into the copy.

dittography: accidentally copying twice what should have been copied only once.

exemplar: the text or manuscript on which a scribe relies to produce a copy.

Egyptian text: a term sometimes used to refer to the text in witnesses belonging to the Alexandrian text-type.

folio: a leaf in a codex. Ancient manuscripts are traditionally numbered by leaves rather than single pages. The front page of the leaf is called the *recto* and the back page of the leaf is called the *verso*.

homoeoarcton: the phenomenon by which words or lines of text begin with an identical letter or series of letters. This may confuse a scribe in the process of directing his attention back and forth from the exemplar to the copy.

homoeoteleuton: the phenomenon by which words or lines of text end with an identical letter or series of letters. This may confuse a scribe in the process of directing his attention back and forth from the exemplar to the copy.

haplography: the act of accidentally skipping a portion of text in the process of copying it.

initial text: the English term for the *Ausgangstext*, the text of the Greek NT from which all existing texts descended.

internal evidence: features of individual readings that help establish the probability (or improbability) that the readings are original. Subcategories of internal evidence are transcriptional evidence and intrinsic evidence.

intrinsic evidence: the tendencies of the author of a text, or the literary context of a passage, that are used to establish the probability (or improbability) that specific readings are original.

itacism: the evolution of Greek pronunciation in which the distinctions in sound between ι, ει, η, οι, and υ were lost, and these vowels and diphthongs were increasingly all pronounced like ι.

Koine text: an alternative term for the Byzantine text.

leaf: one half of a folded sheet consisting of two pages, one on the front (*recto*) and another on the back (*verso*).

lection: an assigned reading for a specific day in the calendar of the early church.

Liste: a shortened reference to the *Kurzgefasste Liste,* the official registry of NT Greek manuscripts maintained by the INTF (Institute for New Testament Textual Research).

Majority Text: the text of the NT compiled by following the readings contained in the majority of manuscripts. This term is sometimes used imprecisely to refer to the Byzantine text.

majuscule: a bilinear script in which most of the characters resemble capital letters, or a parchment manuscript whose text is written in this script.

menologion: a set of assigned lectionary readings beginning on September 1, the first day of the year in the civil calendar of the Byzantine Empire. The readings celebrate the great feast days and honor the apostles, the family of Jesus, and many respected saints.

minuscule: a quadralinear script using smaller letters that are often connected to one another, or a manuscript whose text is written in this script.

multiple emergence: the phenomenon by which multiple scribes deviate from the reading in their exemplars and independently produce an identical reading by coincidence.

***nomen sacrum* (pl. *nomina sacra*)**: abbreviations used by ancient scribes for divine names or titles and several other important terms.

ostracon (pl. ostraca): piece(s) of broken pottery used as writing material.

paleography: the study of ancient writing often with an emphasis on the evolution of ancient scripts to determine the probable date of manuscripts.

palimpsest: a manuscript whose original text was erased to provide writing material for another text.

pandect: a manuscript of the entire Bible contained in a single codex.

parablepsis: the act of a scribe diverting his focus away from the exemplar in the process of copying the text, or a copyist's error caused by looking away from the exemplar.

parchment: animal skin that has been processed, scraped, and sanded to produce writing material.

provenance: (in paleography) the place where a manuscript was copied or an artifact was found.

quire: a section of a codex formed by stacking sheets of writing material, folding the stack in the middle, and then binding the pages at that fold.

reasoned eclecticism: a method of textual criticism that evaluates both the external and internal evidence supporting individual variants in order to restore the text of the Greek New Testament.

scriptio continua: a style of writing that generally lacks spaces between words or sentences and uses little to no punctuation.

scriptorium: a room where scribes copied manuscripts. The term is used especially for the copying rooms in medieval monasteries.

siglum (pl. sigla): a sign or letter used to identify a feature or represent a word(s) in the critical editions of the GreekN T.

singular reading method: an approach to understanding the tendencies of ancient scribes that focuses on the readings that are found only in one extant manuscript.

synaxarion: a set of assigned lectionary readings for the days of the church year beginning on Easter.

text form: see "text-type."

text-type: a group of closely related texts that have a high percentage of shared readings. Scholars of the 19th and 20th centuries assigned texts to three or four such groups to assist them in managing the enormous amount of textual data resulting from the escalation of discoveries of manuscripts of the Greek NT.

thoroughgoing eclecticism: a method of textual criticism that focuses primarily (though not exclusively) on internal evidence.

traditional text: the term used by John Burgon to refer to the text of the NT found in the majority of Greek witnesses.

transcriptional evidence: the tendencies and common errors of ancient scribes that often explain the origin of variant readings.

uncial: a term often used by scholars of previous generations to refer to majuscule script or manuscripts written in this script. Present-day scholars prefer the term "majuscule" and reserve the term "uncial" for Latin script and manuscripts.

variant: one of the different readings found in ancient manuscripts that textual critics must consider in their efforts to restore the original text of the Greek NT.

variant unit: a point in the text of the NT at which ancient manuscripts have different readings.

Vorlage: a German term for the exemplar or parent manuscript of a copy.

μεταχαρακτηρισμός: a term for the transition to and standardization of minuscule script for copying the text of the Greek NT.

παλαιόν: the ancestor of minuscule 1739 that a copyist described as a "very ancient manuscript."

BIBLIOGRAPHY

Aland, Barbara, Kurt Aland, Gerd Mink, Holger Strutwolf, and Klaus Wachtel, eds. *Catholic Letters*. Vol. 4 of *Novum Testamentum Graece: Editio Critica Maior*. Stuttgart: Deutsche Bibelgesellschaft, 2013.

Aland, Barbara. "Kriterien zur Beurteilung kleinerer Payrusfragmente des Neuen Testaments." Pages 1–14 in *New Testament Textual Criticism and Exegesis: Festschrift J. Delobel*. Edited by Adelbert Denaux. BETL 161. Leuven: Peeters, 2002.

Aland, Kurt, and Barbara Aland. *The Text of the New Testament: An Introduction to the Critical Editions and to the Theory and Practice of Modern Textual Criticism*. Translated by Erroll F. Rhodes. 2nd ed. Grand Rapids: Eerdmans, 1989.

Aland, Kurt, Michael Welte, Beate Köster, and Klaus Junack. *Kurzgefasste Liste der griechischen Handschriften des Neues Testaments*. 2nd ed. Berlin: de Gruyter, 1994. Repr., Berlin: de Gruyter, 2011.

Aland, Kurt. *Kurzgefasste Liste der griechischen Handschriften des Neues Testaments*. Berlin: de Gruyter, 1963.

Allen, T. W. *Notes on Abbreviations in Greek Manuscripts*. Oxford: Clarendon, 1889.

Anderson, Amy S. "Family 1 in Mark: Preliminary Results." Pages 119–62 in *Early Readers, Scholars, and Editors of the New Testament: Papers from the Eighth Birmingham Colloquium on the Textual Criticism of the New Testament*. Edited by H. A. G. Houghton. TS 3.11. Piscataway, NJ: Gorgias, 2014.

———. *The Textual Tradition of the Gospels: Family 1 in Matthew*. NTTS 32. Boston: Brill, 2004.

Anderson, Amy S., and Wendy Widder. *Textual Criticism of the Bible*. Rev. ed. Lexham Methods Series. Bellingham, WA: Lexham, 2018.

Askeland, Christian. *John's Gospel: The Coptic Translations of Its Greek Text*. Boston: de Gruyter, 2012.

Bengel, Johann Albrecht. *New Testament Word Studies*. Translated by Charlton T. Lewis and Marvin R. Vincent. 2 vols. Grand Rapids: Kregel, 1971.

Bentley, Richard. *Remarks upon a Late Discourse in Free Thinking: In a Letter to F. H., D. D.* 8th ed. Cambridge: W. Thurlbourn, 1743.

Birdsall, J. N. "The Text of the Gospels in Photius." *JTS* 7 (1956): 42–55; 7 (1956): 190–98; 9 (1958): 278–91.

Black, David Alan. *New Testament Textual Criticism: A Concise Guide*. Grand Rapids: Baker, 1994.

Bormann, Lukas. *Der Brief des Paulus an die Kolosser*. THKNT 10. Leipzig: Evangelische Verlagsanstal, 2012.

Brennecke, H. C. "Lucian von Antiochien." *TRE* 21 (1991): 474–79.

Brisbane, Arthur. "Speakers Give Sound Advice." *Syracuse Post Standard.* March 28, 1911.

British Library. "Codex Alexandrinus." https://searcharchives.bl.uk/primo_library/libweb/action/dlDisplay.do?docId=IAMS040-002353500&vid=IAMS_VU2&indx=1&dym=false&dscnt=1&onCampus=false&group=ALL&institution=BL&ct=search&vl(freeText0)=040-00 2353500&submit=search.

———. "Codex Alexandrinus." https://www.bl.uk/collection-items/codex-alexandrinus.

Bülow-Jacobsen, Adam. "Writing Materials in the Ancient World." Pages 3–29 in *The Oxford Handbook of Papyrology.* Edited by Roger S. Bagnall. Oxford: Oxford University Press, 2009.

Burgon, John, and Edward Miller. *The Traditional Text of the Holy Gospels Vindicated and Established.* London: George Bell and Sons, 1896.

Burgon, John. *The Revision Revised.* London: John Murray, 1883.

Burnett, Megan Leigh. *Codex Washingtonianus: An Analysis of the Textual Affiliations of the Freer Gospels Manuscript.* TS 3.27. Piscataway, NJ: Gorgias, 2022.

Cameron, Averil, and Stuart G. Hall. *Eusebius: Life of Constantine.* Oxford: Clarendon, 1999.

Carlson, Stephen C. *The Text of Galatians and Its History.* WUNT 2.385. Tübingen: Mohr Siebeck, 2015.

Carson, D. A. *The King James Debate: A Plea for Realism.* Grand Rapids: Baker Academic, 1978.

Center for Research of Biblical Manuscripts and Inscriptions. "CRBMI Searchable Ligature Tool." https://airtable.com/appgrNuo12M56MZkN/shrjBIO9cbWMIZGFO/tbl3GfXLCvhcXclbN.

Chrysostomides, Julian, Charalambos Dendrinos, Basilis Gatos, Pat E. Easterling, Philip Taylor, Konstantinos Palaiologos, Brian McLaughlin, and Christopher Wright, eds. *A Lexicon of Abbreviations and Ligatures in Greek Minuscule Hands: ca. 8th Century to ca. 1600.* Camberley: Porphyrogenitus, forthcoming.

Clivaz, Claire. "SNSF MARK16." Digital Humanities +. 7 March 2020. https://claireclivaz.hypotheses.org/990.

Codex Sinaiticus Project. "About the Project." https://codexsinaiticus.org/en/project/

———. https://codexsinaiticus.org/en/.

Colwell, Ernest Cadman. *Studies in Methodology in Textual Criticism of the New Testament.* NTTS 9. Grand Rapids: Eerdmans, 1969.

Comfort, Philip W. *A Commentary on the Manuscripts and Text of the New Testament.* Grand Rapids: Kregel, 2015.

———. *Encountering the Manuscripts: An Introduction to New Testament Paleography & Textual Criticism.* Nashville: Broadman & Holman, 2005.

Dain, Alphonse. *Les manuscrits.* Paris: Belles-Lettres, 1949.

Danker, Frederick W., Walter Bauer, William F. Arndt, and F. Wilbur Gingrich. *Greek-English Lexicon of the New Testament and Other Early Christian Literature.* 3rd ed. Chicago: University of Chicago Press, 2000.

Davies, W. D., and Dale Allison. *Matthew 8–18*. Vol. 2. *The Gospel according to St. Matthew.* ICC. London: T&T Clark, 1991.

Dickey, Eleanor. "A Re-examination of New Testament Papyrus P99 (Vetus Latina AN glo Paul)." *NTS* 65 (2019): 103–21.

Donaldson, Amy M. "Explicit References to New Testament Variant Readings among Greek and Latin Church Fathers." 2 vols. PhD diss., Graduate School of the University of Notre Dame, 2009.

Ehrman, Bart D. *Misquoting Jesus: The Story behind Who Changed the Bible and Why.* New York: HarperCollins, 2005.

———. *The Orthodox Corruption of Scripture: The Effect of Early Christological Controversies on the Text of the New Testament.* New York: Oxford University Press, 1996.

———. *Studies in the Textual Criticism of the New Testament.* NTTS 33. Boston: Brill, 2006.

Elliott, J. K. *A Bibliography of Greek New Testament Manuscripts.* 3rd ed. NovTSup 160. Boston: Brill, 2015.

———. *Essays and Studies in New Testament Textual Criticism.* EFN 3. Cordoba: Ediciones el Almendro, 1992.

———. "An Examination of the Greek Text of the Epistles to Timothy and Titus." PhD thesis, University of Oxford, 1967.

———. "The Last Twelve Verses of Mark: Original or Not?" Pages 80–102 in *Perspectives on the Ending of Mark: Four Views.* Edited by David Alan Black. Nashville: B&H Academic, 2008.

———. *New Testament Textual Criticism: The Application of Thoroughgoing Principles; Essays on Manuscripts and Textual Variation.* NovTSup 137. Leiden: Brill, 2010.

———. "Thoroughgoing Eclecticism in New Testament Textual Criticism." Pages 745–70 in *The Text of the New Testament in Contemporary Research: Essays on the Status Quaestionis.* Edited by Bart D. Ehrman and Michael W. Holmes. 2nd ed. NTTSD 42. Leiden: Brill, 2013.

Epp, Eldon Jay. "The Eclectic Method in New Testament Textual Criticism: Solution or Symptom?" *HTR* 69 (1976): 211–57.

———. "The Papyrus Manuscripts of the New Testament." Pages 1–40 in *The Text of the New Testament in Contemporary Research: Essays on the Status Quaestionis.* Edited by Bart D. Ehrman and Michael W. Holmes. 2nd ed. NTTSD 42. Boston: Brill, 2013.

———. "The Significance of the Papyri for Determining the Nature of the New Testament Text in the Second Century: A Dynamic View of Textual Transmission." Pages 274–98 in *Studies in the Theory and Method of New Testament Textual Criticism.* Edited by Eldon Jay Epp and Gordon D. Fee. SD 45. Grand Rapids: Eerdmans, 1993.

———. "Text-Critical Witnesses and Methodology for Isolating a Distinctive D-Text." *NovT* 59 (2017): 225–96.

———. "Textual Clusters: Their Past and Future." Pages 519–78 in *The Text of the New Testament in Contemporary Research: Essays on the Status Quaestionis.* Edited by Bart D. Ehrman and Michael W. Holmes. 2nd ed. NTTSD 42. Boston: Brill, 2013.

————. "Traditional 'Canons' of New Testament Textual Criticism: Their Value, Validity, and Viability—or Lack Thereof." Pages 79–128 in *The Textual History of the Greek New Testament: Changing Views in Contemporary Research*. Edited by Klaus Wachtel and Michael W. Holmes, TCS 8. Atlanta: Society of Biblical Literature, 2011.

————. "The Twentieth-Century Interlude in New Testament Textual Criticism." Pages 83–108 in *Studies in the Theory and Method of New Testament Textual Criticism*. Edited by Eldon Jay Epp and Gordon D. Fee. SD 45. Grand Rapids: Eerdmans, 1993.

Erasmus, Desiderius. *Controversies*. Edited by Guy Bedouelle. Vol. 83 of *Collected Works of Erasmus*. Toronto: University of Toronto, 1998.

Evans, Craig A. "How Long Were Late Antique Books in Use? Possible Implications for New Testament Textual Criticism." *BBR* 25 (2015): 23–37.

Farnes, Alan Taylor. *Simply Come Copying: Direct Copies as Test Cases in the Quest for Scribal Habits*. WUNT 2.481. Tübingen: Mohr Siebeck, 2019.

Faulmann, Carl. *Das Buch der Schrift, enthaltend die Schriften und Alphabete aller Zeiten und aller Völker des gesammten Erdkreises; Zusammengestellt und erläutert*. Wein: K. K. Hof- und Staatsdruckerei, 1878.

Fee, Gordon D. "Codex Sinaiticus in the Gospel of John: A Contribution to Methodology in Establishing Textual Relationships." Pages 221–98 in *Studies in the Theory and Method of New Testament Textual Criticism*. Edited by Eldon Jay Epp and Gordon D. Fee. SD 45. Grand Rapids: Eerdmans, 1993.

————. "Rigorous or Reasoned Eclecticism—Which?" Pages 124–40 in *Studies in the Theory and Method of New Testament Textual Criticism*. Edited by Eldon Jay Epp and Gordon D. Fee. SD 45. Grand Rapids: Eerdmans, 1993.

————. "The Text of John and Mark in the Writings of Chrysostom." *NTS* 26 (1980): 525–47.

————. "The Use of the Greek Fathers for New Testament Textual Criticism." Revised by Roderic L. Mullen. Pages 351–74 in *The Text of the New Testament in Contemporary Research: Essays on the Status Quaestionis*. Edited by Bart D. Ehrman and Michael W. Holmes. 2nd ed. NTTSD 42. Boston: Brill, 2013.

————. "The Use of Greek Patristic Citations in New Testament Textual Criticism: The State of the Question" Pages 344–59 in *Studies in the Theory and Method of New Testament Textual Criticism*. Edited by Eldon Jay Epp and Gordon D. Fee. SD 45. Grand Rapids: Eerdmans, 1993.

Fennema, D. A. "John 1.18: 'God the Only Son.'" *NTS* 31 (1985): 124–35.

Gamble, Harry Y. *Books and Readers in the Early Church: A History of Early Christian Texts*. New Haven: Yale University Press, 1995.

————. "Codex Sinaiticus in Its Fourth Century Setting." Pages 3–18 in *Codex Sinaiticus: New Perspectives on the Ancient Biblical Manuscript*. Edited by Scot McKendrick, David Parker, Amy Myshrall, and Cillian O'Hogan. Peabody, MA: Hendrickson, 2015.

Gascou, Jean. "The Papyrology of the Near East." Pages 473–94 in *The Oxford Handbook of Papyrology*. Edited by Roger S. Bagnall. Oxford: Oxford University Press, 2009.

Greenlee, J. Harold. *Introduction to New Testament Textual Criticism*. Grand Rapids: Eerdmans, 1964.

———. *Introduction to New Testament Textual Criticism*. Rev. ed. Grand Rapids: Baker, 2012.

Griesbach, Johann Jakob. *Novum Testamentum Grace: Textum ad fidem codicum versionum et partum*. 2nd ed. 2 vols. London: Elmsly, 1796–1806.

Greeven, Heinrich. *Textkritik des Markusevangeliums*. Edited by Eberhard Güting. Münster: LIT, 2005.

Gundry, Robert H. *Matthew: A Commentary on His Handbook for a Mixed Church under Persecution*. 2nd ed. Grand Rapids: Eerdmans, 1994.

Head, Peter M. "Observations on Early Papyri of the Synoptic Gospels, Especially on the 'Scribal Habits.'" *Bib* 71 (1990): 240–47.

Hernández, Juan, Jr. *Scribal Habits and Theological Influences in the Apocalypse: The Singular Readings of Sinaiticus, Alexandrinus, and Ephraemi*. WUNT 2.218. Tübingen: Mohr Siebeck, 2006.

Hixson, Elijah. "Does It Matter If Our New Testament Manuscripts Are Early?" Paper presented at the Annual Meeting of the Evangelical Theological Society. Denver, CO, 16 November 2022.

———. *Scribal Habits in Sixth-Century Greek Purple Codices*. NTTSD 61. Leiden: Brill, 2019.

———. "When a Marginal Note Becomes the Text." *Evangelical Textual Criticism* (blog). October 19, 2022. http://evangelicaltextualcriticism.blogspot.com.

Hobbs, Edward. "Prologue: An Introduction to Methods of Textual Criticism." Pages 1–27 in *The Critical Study of Sacred Texts*. Edited by Wendy D. O'Flaherty. Berkeley Religious Studies Series 2. Berkeley: Graduate Theological Union, 1979.

Hodges, Zane C., and Arthur Farstad. *The Greek New Testament according to the Majority Text*. Nashville: Thomas Nelson, 1982.

Holmes, Michael W. "From 'Original Text' to 'Initial Text': The Traditional Goal of New Testament Textual Criticism in Contemporary Discussion." Pages 637–88 in *The Text of the New Testament in Contemporary Research: Essays on the Status Quaestionis*. Edited by Bart D. Ehrman and Michael W. Holmes. 2nd ed. NTTSD 42. Boston: Brill, 2013.

———, ed. *The Greek New Testament: SBL Edition*. Atlanta: Society of Biblical Literature, 2010.

———. Review of *The Byzantine Text-Type and New Testament Textual Criticism*, by Harry A. Sturz. *TrinJ* 6 (1985): 225–28.

———. "Working with an Open Textual Tradition: Challenges in Theory and Practice." Pages 65–78 in *The Textual History of the Greek New Testament: Changing Views in Contemporary Research*. Edited by Klaus Wachtel and Michael W. Holmes. TCS 8. Atlanta: Society of Biblical Literature, 2011.

Hort, F. J. A. *Two Dissertations*. Cambridge: Macmillan, 1876.

Houghton, H. A. G. "Unfinished Business: The Ending of Mark in Two Catena Manuscripts." *NTS* 69 (2023): 35–42.

———. "The Use of the Latin Fathers for New Testament Textual Criticism." Pages 375–406 in *The Text of the New Testament in Contemporary Research: Essays on the Status Quaestionis*. Edited by Bart D. Ehrman and Michael W. Holmes. 2nd ed. NTTSD 42. Boston: Brill, 2013.

Hull, Robert F., Jr. *The Story of the New Testament Text: Movers, Materials, Motives, Methods, and Models*. RBS 58. Atlanta: Society of Biblical Literature, 2010.

Hurtado, Larry W. *The Earliest Christian Artifacts: Manuscripts and Christian Origins*. Grand Rapids: Eerdmans, 2006.

———. "Introduction." Pages 1–16 in *The Freer Biblical Manuscripts: Fresh Studies of an American Treasure Trove*. Edited by Larry W. Hurtado. Atlanta: Society of Biblical Literature, 2006.

———. Review of *The Byzantine Text-Type and New Testament Textual Criticism*, by Harry A. Sturz. *CBQ* 48 (1986): 149–50.

Institute for New Testament Textual Research. "Index." http://egora.uni-muenster.de/intf/index_en.shtml.

———. New Testament Virtual Manuscript Room. "Liste." https://ntvmr.uni-muenster.de/liste.

Jackson, Donald. "Some Books Carried by Lewis and Clark." *Bulletin of the Missouri Historical Society* 16 (1959): 3–13.

Jones, Brice C. *New Testament Texts of Greek Amulets from Late Antiquity*. LNTS 554. New York: Bloomsbury T&T Clark, 2016.

Jongkind, Dirk. *Scribal Habits of Codex Sinaiticus*. TS 3.5. Piscataway, NJ: Gorgias, 2007.

Kilpatrick, G. D. *The Principles and Practice of New Testament Textual Criticism*. BETL 96. Edited by J. K. Elliott. Leuven: Peeters, 1990.

———. "Western Text and Original Text in the Epistles." *JTS* 45 [1944]: 60–65

———. "Western Text and Original Text in the Gospels and Acts." *JTS* 44 (1943): 24–36

Krans, Jan, et al., eds. *The Amsterdam Database of New Testament Conjectural Emendation*. https://ntvmr.uni-muenster.de/nt-conjectures.

Lafleur, Didier. *La Famille 13 dans l'évangile de Marc*. NTTSD 41. Leiden: Brill, 2013.

Lake, Helen, and Kirsopp Lake. *Codex Sinaiticus Petropolitanus: New Testament, the Epistle of Barnabas and the Shepherd of Hermas*. Oxford: Clarendon, 1911.

Lake, Kirsopp, and Silva New. *Six Collations of New Testament Manuscripts*. HTS 17. Cambridge: Harvard University Press, 1932.

Lake, Kirsopp. *The Text of the New Testament*. 6th ed. Oxford Church Text Books. London: Billing and Sons, 1959.

Levy, B. A. "Role of Articulation in Auditory and Visual Short-Term Memory." *Journal of Verbal Learning and Verbal Behavior* 10 (1971): 123–32.

Locke, J., and F. Fehr. "Subvocalization of Heard or Seen Words Prior to Spoken or Written Recall." *American Journal of Psychology* 8 (1972): 63–68.

Lorenz, Peter E. *A History of Codex Bezae's Text in the Gospel of Mark*. ANTF 53. Berlin: de Gruyter, 2022.

Lowndes, John. *A Modern Greek and English Lexikon*. London: Black, Young, and Young, 1837.

Maas, Paul. *Textual Criticism*. Translated by Barbara Flower. Oxford: Clarendon, 1958.

Malik, Peter. *P.Beatty III (𝔓47): The Codex, Its Scribe, and Its Text*. NTTSD 52. Leiden: Brill, 2017.

Mastricht, Gerhard von. *Η ΚΑΙΝΗ ΔΙΑΘΗΚΗ, Novum Testamentum*. Amsterdam: H. Wetstein, 1711.

McReynolds, Paul. "John 1:18 in Textual Variation and Translation." Pages 105–18 in *New Testament Textual Criticism: Its Significance for Exegesis; Essays in Honour of Bruce M. Metzger*. Edited by Eldon J. Epp and Gordon D. Fee. Oxford: Clarendon, 1981.

Metzger, Bruce M. "Explicit References in the Works of Origen to Variant Readings in New Testament Manuscripts." Pages 78–95 in *Biblical and Patristic Studies in Memory of Robert Pierce Casey*. Edited by J. N. Birdsall and R. W. Thomson. Freiburg: Herder, 1963.

———. *Manuscripts of the Greek Bible: An Introduction to Palaeography*. New York: Oxford University Press, 1981.

———. *A Textual Commentary on the Greek New Testament*. 2nd ed. Stuttgart: Deutsche Bibelgesellschaft, 1994.

———. "When Did Scribes Begin to Use Writing Desks?" Pages 123–37 in *Historical and Literary Studies: Pagan, Jewish, and Christian*. NTTS 8 Grand Rapids: Eerdmans, 1968.

Metzger, Bruce M., and Bart D. Ehrman. *The Text of the New Testament: Its Transmission, Corruption, and Restoration*. 4th ed. New York: Oxford University Press, 2005.

Miller, J. David. "The Long and Short of *lectio brevior potior*." BT (2006): 11–16.

Milne, H. J., and T. C. Skeat. *Scribes and Correctors of the Codex Sinaiticus*. London: British Museum, 1938.

Min, Kyoung Shik. *Die früheste Überlieferung des Matthäusevangeliums (bis zum 3./4. Jh.): Edition und Untersuchung*. ANTF 34. New York: de Gruyter, 2005.

Mink, Gerd. "Contamination, Coherence, and Coincidence in Textual Transmission: The Coherence-Based Genealogical Method (CBGM) as a Complement and Corrective to Existing Approaches." Pages 141–216 in *The Textual History of the Greek New Testament: Changing Views in Contemporary Research*. Edited by Klaus Wachtel and Michael W. Holmes. TCS 8. Atlanta: Society of Biblical Literature, 2011.

Myshrall, A. C. "An Introduction to Lectionary 299." Pages 169–268 in *Codex Zacynthius: Catena, Palimpsest, Lectionary*. Edited by H. A. G. Houghton and D. C. Parker. TS 3.21. Piscataway, NJ: Gorgias, 2020.

National Library of France. "Codex Ephraemi." https://gallica.bnf.fr/ark:/12148/bt-v1b8470433r/f1.item.r=.langEN.zoom.

New Orleans Baptist Theological Seminary. "General Overview of the CNTTS." http://www.nobts.edu/cntts/general-overview.html.

Nolland, John. *The Gospel of Matthew*. NIGTC. Grand Rapids: Eerdmans, 2005.

———. *Luke 1–9:20*. WBC 35A. Dallas: Word, 1989.

Nongbri, Brent. "The Date of Codex Sinaiticus." *JTS* 73 (2022): 516–34.

———. *God's Library: The Archaeology of the Earliest Christian Manuscripts*. New Haven: Yale University Press, 2018.

Origen. *The Commentary of Origen on the Gospel of St Matthew*. Translated by Ronald Heine. 2 vols. Oxford Early Christian Texts. Oxford: Oxford University Press, 2018.

Osburn, Carroll. "The Greek Lectionaries of the New Testament." Pages 93–115 in *The Text of the New Testament in Contemporary Research: Essays on the Status Quaestionis*. Edited by Bart D. Ehrman and Michael W. Holmes. 2nd ed. NTTSD 42. Boston: Brill, 2013.

Pack, F. "Origen's Evaluation of Textual Variants in the Greek Bible." *ResQ* 4 (1960): 139–46.

Pardee, Cambry G. *Scribal Harmonization in the Synoptic Gospels*. NTTSD 60. Leiden: Brill, 2019.

Parker, David C. *Codex Bezae: An Early Christian Manuscript and Its Text*. Cambridge: Cambridge University Press, 1992.

———. *Codex Sinaiticus: The Story of the World's Oldest Bible*. Peabody, MA: Hendrickson, 2010.

———. *An Introduction to the New Testament Manuscripts and Their Texts*. Cambridge: Cambridge University Press, 2008.

———. "The Majuscule Manuscripts of the New Testament." Pages 41–68 in *The Text of the New Testament in Contemporary Research: Essays on the Status Quaestionis*. Edited by Bart D. Ehrman and Michael W. Holmes. 2nd ed. NTTSD 42. Boston: Brill, 2013.

———. "Scribal Tendencies and the Mechanics of Book Production." Pages 173–84 in *Textual Variation: Theological and Social Tendencies? Papers from the Fifth Birmingham Colloquium on the Textual Criticism of the New Testament*. Edited by H. A. G. Houghton and David C. Parker. TS 3.6. Piscataway, NJ: Gorgias, 2008.

———. *Textual Scholarship and the Making of the New Testament*. Oxford: Oxford University Press, 2012.

Paulson, Gregory S. "Improving the CBGM: Recent Interactions." Pages 295–308 in *The New Testament in Antiquity and Byzantium: Traditional and Digital Approaches to Its Texts and Editing*. Edited by H. A. G. Houghton, David C. Parker, and Holger Strutwolf. ANTF 52. Berlin: de Gruyter, 2019.

———. "An Investigation of the Byzantine Text of the Johannine Epistles." *RevExp* 114 (2017): 580–89.

———. "A Proposal for a Critical Edition of the Greek New Testament Lectionary." Pages 121–50 in *Liturgy and the Living Text of the New Testament: Papers from the Tenth Birmingham Colloquium on the Textual Criticism of the New Testament*. Edited by H. A. G. Houghton. TS 3.16. Piscataway, NJ: Gorgias, 2018.

Pendrick, Gerard. "Μονογενης." *NTS* 41 (1995): 587–600.

Perrin, Jac D. *Family 13 in St. John's Gospel: A Computer Assisted Phylogenetic Analysis*. NTTSD 58. Leiden: Brill, 2019.

Pisano, Stephen. "The Vaticanus graecus 1209: A Witness to the Text of the New Testament." Pages 77–97 in *Le manuscrit B de La Bible (Vaticanus graecus 1209): Introduction Au Fac-Similé: Actes Du Colloque Du GenèVe*. Edited by Patrick Andrist. Histoire du texte biblique 7. Lausanne: Éditions du Zèbre, 2009.

Pope, Alexander. "An Essay on Criticism." Pages 17–39 in *The Major Works*. Edited by Pat Rogers. Oxford: Oxford University Press, 2006.

Porter, Stanley E., and Andrew W. Pitts. *Fundamentals of New Testament Textual Criticism*. Grand Rapids: Eerdmans, 2015.

Quarles, Charles L. "Matthew 16.2b–3: New Considerations for a Difficult Textual Question." *NTS* 66 (2020): 228–48.

———. "Matthew 27:52–53 as a Scribal Interpolation: Testing a Recent Proposal." *BBR* 27 (2017): 224–25.

———. *Matthew*. Exegetical Guide to the Greek New Testament. Nashville: B&H Academic, 2017.

———. "The Usefulness of Pre-genealogical Coherence for Detecting Multiple Emergence and Coincidental Agreement: Matthew 16:2b–3 as a Test Case." *NTS* 67 (2021): 424–46.

Quarles, Charles L., and L. Scott Kellum, *40 Questions about the Text and Canon of the New Testament*. Grand Rapids: Kregel Academic, 2023.

Robinson, James M. *The Story of the Bodmer Papyri: From the First Monastery's Library in Upper Egypt to Geneva and Dublin*. Eugene, OR: Cascade Books, 2011.

Robinson, Maurice A., and William G. Pierpont. *The New Testament in the Original Greek: Byzantine Textform 2005*. Southborough, MA: Chilton Book Publishing, 2005.

———. *The New Testament in the Original Greek: Byzantine Textform 2018*. Nuremberg: VTR Publications, 2018.

Robinson, Maurice A., William G. Pierpont, and William McBrayer, eds. *The New Testament in the Original Greek: According to the Byzantine/Majority Textform*. Atlanta, GA: Original Word, 1991.

Robinson, Maurice A. "The Case for Byzantine Priority." *TC* 6 (2001).

Rodgers, Peter R. "The New Eclecticism: An Essay in Appreciation of the Work of Professor George D. Kilpatrick." *NovT* 34 (1992): 388–97.

Royse, James R. *Scribal Habits in Early Greek New Testament Papyri*. NTTS 36. Leiden: Brill, 2008.

Sanders, Henry A. *Facsimile of the Washington Manuscript of the Four Gospels in the Freer Collection*. Ann Arbor: University of Michigan, 1912.

———. *The New Testament Manuscripts in the Freer Collection*. New York: Macmillan, 1912.

Scrivener, F. H. A. *A Plain Introduction to the Criticism of the New Testament: For Use of Biblical Studies*. Edited by Edward Miller. 4th ed. 2 vols. London, 1894.

Sider, David. "The Special Case of Herculaneum." Pages 303–19 in *The Oxford Handbook of Papyrology*. Edited by Roger S. Bagnall. Oxford: Oxford University Press, 2009.

Skeat, T. C. "The Codex Sinaiticus, the Codex Vaticanus and Constantine." *JTS* 50 (1999): 583–625.

Smith, W. Andrew. *A Study of the Gospels in Codex Alexandrinus: Codicology, Palaeography, and Scribal Hands*. NTTSD 48. Boston: Brill, 2014.

Soden, Hermann Freiherr von. *Die Schriften des Neues Testaments in ihrer ältesten erreichbaren Textgestalt hergestellt auf Grund ihrer Textgeschichte*. I. Teil, *Untersuchungen*. Berlin: A. Glaue, 1902–1913.; II. Teil, *Text mit Apparat*. Göttingen: Vandenhoeck & Ruprecht, 1913.

Sophocles, E. A., J. H. Thayer, and H. Drisler. *Greek Lexicon of the Roman and Byzantine Periods (from B.C. 146 to A.D. 1100)*. New York: C. Scribner's Sons, 1900.

Strutwolf, Holger, Georg Gäbel, Annette Hüffmeier, Gerd Mink, and Klaus Wachtel, eds. *Acts of the Apostles.* Vol. 3 of *Novum Testamentum Graecum: Editio Critica Maior.* Stuttgart: Deutsche Bibelgesellschaft, 2017.

Strutwolf, Holger. "Original Text and Textual History." Pages 23–42 in *The Textual History of the Greek New Testament: Changing Views in Contemporary Research.* Edited by Klaus Wachtel and Michael W. Holmes. TCS 8. Atlanta: Society of Biblical Literature, 2011.

Sturz, Harry A. *The Byzantine Text-Type and New Testament Textual Criticism.* Nashville: Thomas Nelson, 1984.

Swiss National Science Foundation. "Mark16." https://mark16.sib.swiss.

The Center for the Study of New Testament Manuscripts. https://www.csntm.org.

Thesaurus Linguae Graecae. https://stephanus.tlg.uci.edu/index.php.

Tregelles, Samuel P. *An Account of the Printed Text of the Greek New Testament: With Remarks on Its Revision upon Critical Principles.* London: Samuel Bagster & Sons, 1854. Repr., London: Forgotten Books, 2017.

———, ed. *The Greek New Testament.* London: Samuel Bagster and Sons, 1857.

———. *Matthew and Mark.* Vol. 1 of *The Greek New Testament.* London: Samuel Baxter and Sons, 1857.

University of Cambridge Digital Library. "Codex Bezae." https://cudl.lib.cam.ac.uk/view/MS-NN-00002-00041/1.

———. "Codex Zacynthius." https://cudl.lib.cam.ac.uk/collections/codexzacynthius/1.

University of Münster. "Mark Phase 3.5." http://ntg.uni-muenster.de/mark/ph35.

Vaganay, Léon, and Christian-Bernard Amphoux. *An Introduction to New Testament Textual Criticism.* Translated by Jenny Heimerdinger. 2nd ed. Cambridge: Cambridge University Press, 1991.

Vatican Library. "Manuscript - Vat.gr.1209." https://digi.vatlib.it/view/MSS_Vat.gr.1209.

Vincent, Marvin R. *A History of the Textual Criticism of the New Testament.* London: Macmillan, 1899.

Wachtel, Klaus. "The Corrected New Testament Text of Codex Sinaiticus." Pages 97–106 in *Codex Sinaiticus: New Perspectives on the Ancient Biblical Manuscript.* Edited by Scot McKendrick, D. C. Parker, Amy Myshrall, and Cillian O'Hogan. Peabody, MA: Hendrickson, 2015.

———. "On the Relationship of the 'Western Text' and the Byzantine Tradition of Acts—A Plea Against the Text-Type Concept." Pages 127–49 in *Acts of the Apostles.* Edited by Holger Strutwolf, George Gäbel, Annette Hüffmeier, Gerd Mink, and Klaus Wachtel. Vol. 3 of *Novum Testamentum Graecum: Editio Critica Maior.* Stuttgart: Deutsche Bibelgesellschaft, 2017.

———. "Short Guide to the CGBM-Mark (Phase 3.5)." Revised by Greg Paulson. https://ntg.uni-muenster.de/pdfs/Short_Guide_CBGM_Mark_KW.pdf.

———. "Towards a Redefinition of External Criteria: The Role of Coherence in Assessing the Origin of Variants." Pages 109–27 in *Textual Variation: Theological and Social Tendencies? Papers from the Fifth Birmingham Colloquium on the Textual Criticism of the*

New Testament. Edited by H. A. G. Houghton and David C. Parker. TS 3.5. Piscataway, NJ: Gorgias, 2008.

Wallace, Daniel B. *Greek Grammar beyond the Basics: An Exegetical Syntax of the New Testament.* Grand Rapids: Zondervan, 1996.

———. "The Majority Text Theory: History, Methods, and Critique." Pages 711–44 in *The Text of the New Testament in Contemporary Research: Essays on the Status Quaestionis.* Edited by Bart D. Ehrman and Michael W. Holmes. 2nd ed. NTTSD 42. Boston: Brill, 2013.

Wallace, William. "An Index of Greek Ligatures and Contractions." *JHS* 43 (1923): 183–93.

Wasserman, Tommy, and Peter J. Gurry. *A New Approach to Textual Criticism: An Introduction to the Coherence-Based Genealogical Method.* Atlanta: Society of Biblical Literature, 2017.

Wasserman, Tommy. "Criteria for Evaluating Readings in New Testament Textual Criticism." Pages 579–613 in *The Text of the New Testament in Contemporary Research: Essays on the Status Quaestionis.* Edited by Bart D. Ehrman and Michael W. Holmes. 2nd ed. NTTSD 42. Boston: Brill, 2013.

Weiss, Bernhard. *Textkritik der Paulinischen Briefe.* Leipzig: J. C. Hinrichs, 1896.

Welsby, Alison Sarah. *A Textual Study of Family 1 in the Gospel of John.* ANTF 45. New York: de Gruyter, 2013.

Wendel, C. "Die ΤΑΠΕΙΝΟΤΗΣ des griechischen Schreibermönches." *Byzantinische Zeitschrift* 43 (1950): 259–66.

Westcott, B. F., and F. J. A. Hort. *Introduction to the New Testament in the Original Greek with Notes on Selected Readings.* New York: Harper and Brothers, 1882. Repr., Peabody, MA: Hendrickson, 1988.

Zuntz, Günther. *The Text of the Epistles: A Disquisition upon the Corpus Paulinum.* London: Oxford University Press, 1953. Repr., Eugene, OR: Wipf & Stock, 2007.

Index of Biblical References

Old Testament

Genesis
1:27 LXX   89
17:15–16   94

Exodus
34:6   124

Deuteronomy
4:35   125
4:39   125
17:6   69
19:15   69

Judges
11:34 LXX   124n26

1 Kings
8:60   125

Psalms
21:21 LXX   125n30
24:16 LXX   124n26
34:17 LXX   125n30

Isaiah
45:5   125
45:6   125
45:14   125
45:18   125
45:21   125
46:9   125
49:18   99

Jeremiah
31:33   95

Ezekiel
36:27   95

Daniel
3:29   125

Deuterocanon

Tobit
3:15 LXX   124n26
6:11 LXX   124n26
8:17 LXX   124n26

Wisdom of Solomon
7:22 LXX   125n30

Old Testament Pseudepigrapha

Psalms of Solomon
18:4 LXX   124n26

New Testament

Matthew
1:1–25:6   14
2:1   82
2:3   79n34, 82
2:16   64, 82n46
4:18   86
4:23   90–92
4:25   79n34
5:4   80
5:10   87n62
5:19–20   81
5:22   82
6:9–13   87
7:21   80
8:5   86
8:26   82

8:35   92
9:13   111
10:17   92
12:5   111
12:9   92
12:38–39   109–11
12:39   109
13:47   80
13:54   92
14:22   86
15:1   79n34
15:14   111
16:1–4   109
16:2b   108
16:2b–3   103, 104–5, 104n3, 105n5, 108, 110–11
16:4   112
16:6   112
18:8   84
18:15   47–48, 53–54, 61, 65–67, 70, 83, 87
18:16   69
19:4   88
20:28   104n4
22:18   85
22:20   85
22:34   92
23:16   111
23:19   111
23:24   111
23:26   111
23:37   79n34
25:43   11n17
26:2–3   11n17
27:53   159

Mark
1:7–9   9
1:16–18   9

1:23   92
1:39   90–92
2:1–26   9
4:36–40   9
5:15–26   9
5:38–43   9
6:1–3   9
6:16–25   9
6:36–50   9
7:2   86
7:3–15   9
7:25–37   9
8:1   9
8:10–26   9
8:12–13   112
8:34–38   9
9:1–9   9
9:18–31   9
11:27–33   9
12:1   9
12:5–8   9
12:13–19   9
12:24–28   9
16:8   6, 31
16:9–11   31n42

Luke

1:5   90
4:15   92
4:31   90–91
4:44   90–93
5:1   90–91
6:17   90
7:17   90
7:31   86, 86n54
10:27   81
11:2   87n62
11:2–4   87
12:54–56   104–5, 109
17:3   54, 87
21:38   19
23:5   90
23:45   69

John

1:1   124
1:1–18   124
1:1–5:11   16, 114, 119
1:1–8:38   149
1:2   124
1:6   124

1:12–13   124
1:14   122, 124, 125
1:18   38, 101, 113, 113n1, 114,
   116, 122, 124–25, 124n28, 125,
   125n30
1:28   68n58
3:16   122–24
3:18   122–24
5:44   125, 127
6:50–8:52   14
7:30   88
7:53–8:11   19, 26n14
8:20   88
8:26   84
10:30   125
17:3   125, 127

Acts

1:1   67n56
2:9   90
6:8   89
10:37   90
11:1   90
11:29   90
15:1   90
18:27–19:6   152n12
19:12–16   152n12
20:28   89
23:11–17   152n12
23:25–29   152n12
26:7–8   152n12
26:20   152n12

Romans

1:1   97n81
1:7   133
2:16   99
3:6   99
4:12   81
4:19   94
4:20   94
4:22   97n81
4:24–25   94
5:2   97n81
6:4   135
7:20   97n81
8:4   134
8:15   135
8:34   97n81
9:4   95–96
11:27   95

11:31   97n81
14:3   99
14:4   99
14:5   97n81
14:10   98
14:12   98–99
14:19   83
15:6   133

1 Corinthians

1:3   133
1:14   135
5:13   99
8:6   133
10:30   135
11:25   95
14:17   135
15:24   133

2 Corinthians

1:3   133
3:3   95
3:6   95
4:13–12:6   14
5:10   98–99
5:12   98
8:5   86
11:31   133
13:1   69

Galatians

1:1   133
1:3   133
3:15   95
4:24   95
5:15   20

Ephesians

1:1   20
1:2   133
1:3   133
1:16   135
2:12   95
2:18   135
3:14   133, 135
5:20   133
6:23   133

Philippians

1:2   133
2:11   133

Colossians
1:2   133
1:3   133, 136
1:10   136
1:10–11   129, 134
1:11   136
1:12   101, 128, 133–36
2:6   136
3:15   136
3:17   133, 136
4:2   136
4:3   134–35

1 Thessalonians
1:1   133
1:3   133
2:13–14   81
3:11   133
3:13   133
4:17   135
5:10   135

2 Thessalonians
1:1   133
1:2   133

1:5   99
2:16   133

1 Timothy
1:2   133
3:13–4:8   9n9
3:16   80
5:19   69

2 Timothy
1:2   133
4:1   99

Philemon
3   133

Hebrews
1:3   4
9:14   14
10:28   69
10:38   82

James
1:10–12   10, 29
1:11   29
1:12   93

1:15–16   29
1:15–18   10
1:17   29, 133
1:18   93
2:5   93
2:11   93
2:13   20
2:19–26   10
3:1–9   10
3:13–18   10
4:1–4   10
4:8   93
4:9–17   10
4:10   93
5:1   10

1 John
4:9   122–24
5:20   125, 127

3 John
11–15   15n53